HOWLING *in* MESOPOTAMIA

An Iraqi-American Memoir

HAIDER ALA HAMOUDI

BEAUFORT BOOKS
NEW YORK

DISCLAIMER
The names of the vast majority of people living in Iraq who appear in this memoir have been changed to protect their identities.

Library of Congress Cataloging-in-Publication Data

Hamoudi, Haider Ala.
Howling in Mesopotamia : an Iraqi-American memoir / Haider Ala Hamoudi.
p. cm.
ISBN 978-0-8253-0548-1 (alk. paper)
1. Hamoudi, Haider Ala. 2. Arab Americans--Iraq--Biography. 3. Postwar reconstruction--Iraq. 4. Iraq--Description and travel. 5. Iraq--History--2003- I. Title.

DS79.66.H36A3 2008
956.7044'31—dc22
[B]
2007052205

Published in the United States by Beaufort Books
www.beaufortbooks.com
Distributed by Midpoint Trade Books
www.midpointtrade.com

10 9 8 7 6 5 4 3 2 1

Printed in the United States of America

To my grandmother Wajeeha Al Chalabi,
whose generosity and love allowed me to write this book.
Rest in God's Paradise.

Contents

Spring 2004: Failure

PART II • MARRIAGE, ELECTION, AND BEYOND

Summer 2004: Hope and Despair

Introduction

ON JULY 14, 2003, the forty-fifth anniversary of Iraq's independence
from Great Britain, I left Kuwait on a C-130 transport plane bound for
Baghdad, the city of my ancestors and a place I had not been, and to
which I could not travel, for the previous thirteen years. Two nations could
legitimately claim me as their native son. The first was the United States,
where I was born and raised, whose influence was, obviously, very real and
direct. The second was Iraq. Iraq occupied something of a hallowed place
in my childhood home, a rose-colored enigma, almost the childlike recon-
stitution of fragments of a barely understood dream, but it was the land
where my parents were born, and therefore the source, at least to my own
mind, of much of what I held dear, among them faith and family. But
these two countries—America, where I lived by day, and my own images
of Iraq, about which I dreamed every night—had long been at war, or at
least uneasy détente, and travel between them was impossible, until
Saddam Hussein fell. Less than one hundred days after that event, which
was so momentous for me and for both my countries, I returned.

I wrote this memoir as an Iraqi and an American, to convey to Americans, as an American, what the lives of ordinary Iraqis are like, by living
as closely as possible to Iraqis themselves, as an Iraqi, with neither an
American force nor a protected zone between me and the people of Iraq.
During the two years I spent in Iraq, I came to know Iraqis of every religious persuasion and ethnicity: brave men, women, and children with

whom I lived and worked and shared experiences both joyful and tragic. They are simple, ordinary people whose lives deserve more attention than they have been given. If, as all too often happened, their lives were tragically cut short, their deaths also earned them more than the anonymous recognition of casualty figures in newspaper headlines. These were human beings in all their wonderful and multifaceted complexity, and it is on their shoulders that the catastrophe of Iraq will continue to weigh mightily for decades to come.

My task of recording my adventures has not been easy to accomplish. When I try to sort out the chaotic and turbulent mix of emotions within me during that first eighty-three-minute plane ride to Baghdad, I suppose I would say that I was terrified about the prospect of getting killed, elated about seeing Iraq once more, worried about how I would fare in a nation so damaged by decades of totalitarian rule, excited about the personal and professional opportunities that awaited me, concerned about my ability to settle into and become part of a society so different from the one in which I grew up, anxious that I was not going to be able to enter into any conversation with any relative that did not involve when and who I was going to marry, overjoyed at the prospect of eating proper Iraqi food regularly once again, nervous about regaining weight I had worked so hard to lose, worried about whether or not my stomach could withstand any microbes that might be in the food, concerned about the state of health care, and so on. No one thought could dominate my mind for very long—there were too many contending for primacy, some important and some of only minor and tangential concern. Despite the confusion and incoherence, however, I was going to Baghdad to stay, or so I believed.

My plans after landing were as uncertain as my emotional state. I had no idea what I wanted to do other than serve the country in some way. I am an attorney and a graduate from one of America's premier law schools, and served as a federal judicial clerk in New York before working for one of the largest law firms in New York as an associate. This, combined with my Iraqi ethnicity, my Arabic language skills, and my Shi'i religious heritage qualified me more than almost anyone, I believed, to contribute to the rebuilding of Iraq's devastated legal culture.

My ultimate goals were many and varied. Having been a commercial lawyer for the better part of a decade, I wanted to make money. Naively, I imagined investors pumping large streams of capital into this oil-rich and undeveloped land, and I knew well their first rule when making investments in such areas—get a lawyer. Teamed with a competent Iraqi partner, I thought I would be among the best qualified to handle such work. I could bridge the legal cultures, translate the issues of foreign investors in a way that an Iraqi attorney would understand them, and bring the solution to clients in a way they could grasp.

Material impulses aside, my greatest desire was to participate in the development of a brave new legal world in Iraq—one that depended on the rule of law and not the idiosyncratic and at times utterly irrational whims of a mad dictator. The idea of assisting in the drafting of laws, and better yet a permanent constitution, was very appealing to me. And to have a hand in guiding the country toward a prosperous, stable, and bright future, away from its dark and bloody past, was something I had longed dreamed of, but never considered possible until the day I saw Saddam's statue fall in Firdous Square. Only then did I think that anything might be possible, and so I went, and learned firsthand that not everything is possible, and you can't do everything you set your mind to, no matter what schoolteachers and football coaches might say.

PART I

Dream and Disillusionment

Summer 2003: A Time of Hope

CHAPTER 1

Arrival

AIRPLANES LANDING IN BAGHDAD do not descend gradually. This would put them dangerously close to the ground as they approach the airport, close enough by the time they reach the hotspot of Falluja, just west of Baghdad, to be within the reach of a well-aimed rocket propelled grenade. As a result, the plane reaches the airport runway without descending at all, and then initiates a rapid spiral descent toward the airstrip, which seems to resemble free-fall. A landing that under normal circumstances takes just over twenty minutes is completed in less than four. Throughout our descent, I looked at the soldiers around me. They stared back, at first blankly and then with increasing distrust. Maybe they were worried I would become sick, but their expressions and the weapons they carried were quite a persuasive deterrent. I sat quietly and soon enough we landed in the American-occupied Baghdad Airport.

Other than runways, and a terminal somewhere in the distance used by humanitarian personnel, the airport was scarcely recognizable from my visit thirteen years before. Bunkers, sandbags, mounted automatic weapons, bulletproof vests, tents, tanks, and armored convoys were everywhere; it looked nothing like Baghdad to me, but more like I imagined Saigon to be at the height of the Vietnam War (leaving aside the obvious fact that we were in a desert, not the tropics). The sight of so much armor was deeply disturbing to me, and my expression must have betrayed my feelings, for a friendly Texas-based employee of Kellogg, Brown & Root

(KBR) struck up a conversation immediately about the appearance of the airport. KBR is a subsidiary of oil giant Halliburton and a premier contractor for the United States military in Iraq.

"Y'all not used to this sorta thing in your country, living in America and all," he said.

I turned around to face the direction he was looking, expecting to see several Iraqis behind me discussing weaponry. It didn't occur to me that he hadn't thought of me as an American and that "my country" would not be the United States. This was, for me, an unusual experience as an adult. After some hesitation, I agreed with his initial assessment.

"Yup," he continued, "I hear the Iraqis are a peaceful people except for the terrorists. Must be tough to see all them guns in Iraq then."

He was entirely mistaken. I was disturbed, this much was true, but it had nothing to do with the fact that I was an Iraqi. I grew up the child of two doctors in a suburb of Columbus, Ohio. I had lived the last ten years of my life as an attorney in New York, Indonesia, and Hong Kong. I had only rarely heard the term "y'all" directed toward me, and I was not used to seeing guns anywhere except on the belts of police officers. Here, I could count at least twenty-five types of weapons in every conceivable direction that, by mistake or design, could obliterate me, and everyone around me, in an instant. His indifference to this plethora of weaponry puzzled me, but I did not ask about it. I was not particularly sociable upon landing because I was still nauseated from our descent.

After I recovered, I asked a group of American soldiers from Long Island when they thought the airport would open to civilian traffic.

"Tomorrow," replied one of them.

I looked around again, trying to see where a civilian airplane would land in this encampment, where passengers would disembark, how they would get their luggage, who would pick them up, how their papers could be processed, and so forth. "Tomorrow?" I asked. "How?"

"Don't know, but tomorrow."

"And when do you guys leave?"

Silence. I tried to look into their faces, but I could not see anything. They were wearing sunglasses, looking in various directions but not at me. They were not interested in pursuing this line of questioning. As a result, I diverted the conversation to a friendlier topic, notably sports. This turned out to be a bad idea. They were from Florida and insisted that the Ohio State Buckeyes did not deserve to win the 2001 National Championship. Being from Ohio, I found this unacceptable—far more so than the proposed opening date of the airport—and so I took issue. They insisted that as an Iraqi I knew nothing. I told them they knew less. Then a sergeant came over and ordered the soldiers to board the convoy, and the conversation ended, just before I thought they were ready to designate me an enemy combatant.

I did not stay at the airport long; KBR ran a convoy leaving for the Republican Palace shortly after our arrival, and the military expected me to be on it. My plan was to go to the palace and then leave as soon as possible so I would get to my grandmother's house before dark. I would be staying with my grandmother for some time, after which I had planned to purchase my own home. Once I had my own base, I thought I could start a law firm that would assist in reconstruction and earn handsome returns.

Given the recent news about attacks on American troops near the airport, the trip to the Republican Palace turned out to be the most terrifying I have ever taken. There were only a few civilians on the bus, and we were placed in aisle seats in the middle of the bus. Soldiers surrounded us. U.S. military snipers drew guns on either side, ready to fire at any moment. A mounted AK-47 on a jeep led us, and another trailed us, and all were clad in bulletproof vests and helmets. The fact that I was not going to be staying in the Republican Palace but leaving to walk the very streets that inspired such fear in the most fearsome army in the world terrified me further.

Sensing my discomfort, one of the soldiers turned to me to strike up a friendly conversation.

"Yo, Iraqi Buckeye. Got a question."

Long *I* on the Iraqi. I hate that. I looked at him suspiciously.

"That little fruit thing on a palm tree, what is that thing?" he asked.

"Harris, you never heard of a damn coconut?" another said.

"Ain't no coconut on the tree. There's hundreds of 'em up there," Harris replied.

"Those are baby coconuts," the other soldier said.

"Actually," I added, "they are called dates, and they are a staple of the Iraqi diet."

"They must really like 'em, right? I mean they got tons of palm trees here," a somewhat more thoughtful soldier chimed in.

"It's like potatoes to an American, they eat them all the time," I said.

"I got a different question, how do I tell some asshole to fuck off in Iraqi?" someone else asked.

"Excuse me?" I asked, somewhat surprised.

"Fuck off, how do I say fuck off in Arabic?"

"It does not translate very well. Try 'teer,' that gets your point across." "Teer" means fly or get lost, but it is quite rude in the Iraqi context and anything worse was bound to create trouble between them and whoever they might be speaking with.

A chorus of "teers" among the soldiers followed.

"Yo, Iraqi Buckeye, most Iraqis like us out there, you think? They on our side or not?"

The question surprised and embarrassed me. The fact of the matter is that I really did not know. I certainly knew how I felt, having had numerous relatives murdered by the previous regime and dozens of other relatives sent into exile. To me, America was at fault, but only for waiting too long to act. But the bombs fell nowhere near me; the risks of an occupation gone awry, or civil war, would not affect me as they would someone inside the country, and so it was not my opinion that was important. I did not know how Iraqis living within the country felt. Conversations about politics over the telephone were impossible during Saddam Hussein's time. I had spoken to an uncle, an aunt, and several cousins after the American invasion, but it was only in an attempt to ascertain their well-being. We did not speak about politics, only the dangers of bombing, and, in my uncle's case, about *his* concern for *my* well-being because I had been in Hong Kong during the SARS epidemic. The fact that I was moving to a country where I knew so little about what people were thinking about so fundamental a topic was unsettling.

I did not have time to reflect on my ignorance of how Iraqis within Iraq felt for very long because we reached the Republican Palace soon after the question had been asked. KBR and the American military seemed to have transformed the palace into Topeka, Kansas, set amidst what appeared to be the backdrop of a gaudily designed theatrical adaptation of *A Thousand*

and One Nights. American soldiers were everywhere, tracking the ubiquitous Baghdad dirt onto Saddam's marble floors with their thick black boots. Exactly what they were doing while moving around within the palace grounds was not easy to determine, but most seemed eager to get somewhere. Personnel from KBR moved among them, distinguishable from the soldiers largely by their age and dress, but not by social class or general demeanor. These were all the children of the heartland, not a well-traveled journalist or an East Coast sophisticate among them. Their lunches were served at 11:30, not the Iraqi time of 1:30. None of Baghdad's food—none of its kabobs and Arab salads, stews and fish grilled Iraqi style over an open fire, lamb and fresh dates—could be found at mealtime. It was a strictly tuna fish, hot dog, and potato chip affair. I saw some Iraqis, but not many, and the ones I saw were meal servers, toilet cleaners, and, on occasion, translators. No Iraqis were permitted to eat in the main dining room or make use of Saddam's lavish swimming pool. Unfortunately, this had to be the place of my first meal while I waited for permission to leave from someone in the Byzantine organization that had taken up residence here. I could only hope that one of the people scurrying around was handling my permission papers.

Among the men of KBR and the military men, I noticed a motley crew of carpetbaggers of one sort or another searching for whatever work they might get. One such carpetbagger was on the plane with me from Kuwait. He spoke to every armed twenty-three-year-old and every overweight middle-aged country boy he could find, promising to staff their jobs with foreign developing-world workers who had experience at the tasks needed, whatever they might be, rather than Iraqis, who just didn't know how to do the job, whatever it was. I asked about his work experience. Apparently he had done little work of this sort until arriving in Iraq.

The palace itself is astonishingly large, the American soldiers play touch football in the central hall without difficulty. There are marble floors, arched ceilings, domed roofs, gold faucets, elaborate swimming pools, seemingly infinite hallways with back offices of one sort or another, and along many of the walls, some of the sayings of the former president. All of this is designed without the slightest bit of taste or discretion. I considered it ironic that an Arab nationalist ruler who endlessly preached

Arab independence and unity was so willing to subject his own heritage to such a silly stereotype.

In any event, it was fairly clear that the palace's current inhabitants gave this matter little thought. This in fact provided a small level of comfort to me. There was a time only a few months before when Saddam's sayings, senseless as they were, had to be venerated and memorized. Now the Americans had humbled Ozymandias, and the sayings remained on the walls without a single soul caring to read them.

Gaining permission to leave the Republican Palace was not easy. After some waiting, I finally asked one of the soldiers from the convoy for help. He took me to an office where I found another soldier.

"I think we lost your authorization. Where are you seeking clearance to go again?" he asked. I think he was an officer.

Hayy al. . . ." I tried to respond before he cut me off.

"Where?" he asked, confused by my use of Arabic to describe a location in Baghdad.

I pointed to a map on the wall just behind him. "Oh, Red Zone," he replied. Apparently all of Baghdad not subsumed by Topeka was now Red Zone.

"And what's your security clearance?" he asked.

"None, I'm not affiliated with you. I just want to leave so that I can go into the city and live." I was growing increasingly irritated.

"If you are not affiliated with us, you have no right to be in the Green Zone," he responded curtly.

"Fine, throw me out, preferably near a taxi."

"You wanna die or something? Know what it's like out there?"

"Yes I do, can I go?" Actually, I had no idea what it was like in the "Red Zone," but I couldn't stay here any longer. I knew that much.

Discussions, muttering, and further questioning about my sanity ensued. Then I was sent out, and after a short dip in the swimming pool, I finally received an answer.

"Okay, we'll escort you to your location in an armored vehicle," the officer muttered, once he found me.

I did not consider this offer for very long—both the thought that by being in a vehicle of this sort I would immediately become a target for the insurgents subjecting the U.S. to constant attack, and the ridiculous image of a tank going up and down streets in my grandmother's neighborhood as I tried to remember exactly which house was hers, backing up in driveways and turning about right and left in a turret searching for the proper direction, convinced me that this was not a very good idea.

Besides, I was in the superior bargaining position; they had no place to put me and hardly wanted to deal with me for much longer. So less than an hour and considerable pleading later, I found myself on the Red Zone side of the American encampment, wished well, and left by my American compatriots to survive on my own. From there, with suitcase and laptop in hand, I hailed a taxi. I was terrified about what any witnesses to this strange event might be thinking, or, worse, planning. If ever I needed an honest taxi driver, it was now. Fortunately, I got one, at nearly 2 p.m. in the midst of unbearable heat.

My grandmother's house was not easy to find, and the directions I had were not helpful. While Baghdad is neatly divided into districts, places, sections, and house numbers, these are all universally ignored by the residents, who prefer to direct someone by telling them to go left at the Jedy restaurant, right at the house with the big arch, left at the big street after that, then another left at Hajj Abi Abbas's laundry shop, and it would be the seventh house on that street. This technique did not seem to work, and so the taxi driver and I had to ask residents in the neighborhood which way to go. Unfortunately, none of them seemed to know my grandmother, though they were kind enough to apologize about this and to bring us cold water to quench our thirst. Not surprisingly, a few invited us to a late lunch, which we, as all Iraqis must under such circumstances, politely declined. With every such offer, my heart warmed a little. This was Baghdad as I remembered it, and these were its warm, hospitable people. War and decades of sanctions and neglect had decimated the city, but its soul was alive if weakened, its heartbeat palpable if fluttering. I had never been so happy to leave the American heartland.

After more than an hour with an increasingly frustrated taxi driver, we prevailed upon a resident to allow us to call my grandmother's house (telephones worked in her district and several other districts of Baghdad, news reports notwithstanding). My grandmother's house guard answered and agreed to meet us at a certain location. When he arrived, I paid the taxi driver five dollars for his many troubles and got into the guard's car. Later I was told this was an exorbitant sum and two dollars would have been more than enough.

My grandmother's guard had been family help for a number of years and he was an honorable man, refusing as so many guards did to leave the house during the bombings and the war, instead staying to protect it because nobody else was there to do it. His mother was still my grand-mother's housekeeper. The inclination of many guards to run at the first sight of trouble has made me wonder whether most are worth the invest-ment. One could safely assume that when everything is calm and nothing suspicious is afoot, a house guard is not helpful, I thought. Still, I did not question the wisdom of the residents on this matter, at the time.

My grandmother was not in Iraq when I arrived in Baghdad. She had left prior to the invasion to live abroad in the various homes of her many children while hostilities raged. By the time I arrived, she was just begin-ning to plan her return. My uncle Isam, however, had remained and lived with his wife three doors down from her home. He was a surgeon and the only one of my uncles and aunts on my mother's side to have remained in Baghdad. His son Ali and Ali's wife Alia' lived with them on the second floor of the house, along with their newborn daughter, Rania. I remem-bered Ali well. He had earned me the wrath of my parents and grand-mother nearly two decades earlier in that same house when I helped him pick all of the oranges from my grandmother's two trees while the oranges were still green. Not coming from a climate where oranges grew, Ali had patiently explained to me that they wouldn't become orange until they were picked. Regretfully, I believed him. I destroyed my grandmother's entire crop that year.

Ali and his father visited me almost immediately after I arrived. Ali had changed. I would have never guessed this generous and sincere yet introverted young man to have been the same person who once stalked the neighborhood's fruit trees. From our first embrace and warm exchange of kisses, as was Arab custom, to his offer to let me sleep in his extra room until I had an opportunity to make my grandmother's house more habitable, to his bringing me six loaves of bread when he heard I was hungry, it was perfectly obvious that I had made a friend for life with a cousin I had not seen for years and who I had never been fond of as a child.

My uncle Isam, by contrast, was the same as I remembered him thirteen years previous. He was always friendly to me, and we always got along, but there was a reticence that accompanied Isam, a kind of privacy he insisted on keeping. No doubt in some ways this was a personality trait from his childhood, but the fear inspired by decades of totalitarian dictatorship also played a role. During my previous visit, my uncle had sternly warned me not to speak ill of the regime in the car because Saddam had bugged the street lamps. Now, whenever he discussed the previous regime, I watched his eyes scan the room, his muscles go tense, and his jaw set as the denunciations of Saddam and his family spewed out.

Isam and Ali could see I was exhausted from my journey and left me to rest less than an hour after they had arrived to welcome me. I spent the rest of the afternoon and evening speaking with Ra'ad, the guard, and the housekeeper, Sa'diya, both of whom seemed less concerned with my state of exhaustion. I asked them about the war, and they proceeded to tell me stories concerning all that had transpired.

My grandmother's house is situated between the center of Baghdad and the airport, and thus served as a kind of no man's land for several days between the Americans, who controlled the airport, and the Iraqi Army, which controlled the city. There appeared to be relatively little fighting from the descriptions of Ra'ad and Sa'diya. American tanks would patrol through the area, Ra'ad told me, but nobody would be outdoors and soon enough the tanks continued on their way to the city itself. They claimed that once, a man with a thick Palestinian accent stood on a neighbor's rooftop and proclaimed a *jihad,* indicating that the infidel tanks of the Americans were coming and that it was an Islamic obligation to resist.

"So what did you do?" I asked. I was not sure whether such a claim carried resonance in Iraq or whether Iraqis were more interested in seeing the United States depose Saddam than conducting a *jihad.* I heard an answer that was much less ideological and, in retrospect, more natural than the one I envisioned.

Ra'ad responded, "We told him to get the hell down, because if he didn't somebody from somewhere was going to start shooting something, and we'd be in the middle of it. We'd rather stay alive than deal with this nonsense between George Bush and Saddam Hussein."

CHAPTER 2

Baghdad

EXCEPT FOR THE AIRPORT, Baghdad had not changed during my thirteen-year absence. Absurd as that may sound given the recent wars, it is a devastating fact when literally true. I expected to see the effect of bombing everywhere—destroyed homes, businesses, bridges, power plants, telephones, and the like. But this was not the case. The bridges stood, homes were intact, and the same businesses functioned. The destruction of a few significant facilities was the only evidence that America had soundly defeated this country in war twice in the past thirteen years, and that the country had fought a nine-year war to a standoff immediately before that.

Yet nothing had changed. There was not a single new car on the street, not a traffic light had been repaired, not a home remodeled, not a tennis court refurbished, and not a park maintained. There was nothing to mark the past thirteen years but a horrible erosion of a city and its soul. This depressed me more than destruction would have. War is a matter to which one grows accustomed despite its awful, destructive nature. This was neglect of the most malignant kind, a regime leaving its people to fend for themselves while granting itself the finest luxuries. I knew what they had done to those they did not favor, but I did not know what they had done to Baghdad, the capital of the country they ruled. Only the Mongols, at least according to the legends, have betrayed her worse.

I often took taxis around town in the early days, not so much because an air-conditioned car and driver was beyond my means, but because I liked to feel the heartbeat of the city, talk to its residents, and hear their opinions on various matters. On the drives from my grandmother's house to the central area of Karrada, often lasting more than an hour, I had the opportunity to speak at length to one native Iraqi, the cab driver. Most often the conversation centered on complaints concerning the roads. The drive to Karrada should not take more than twenty minutes, but the Americans had shut off a large central part of the city, which held the Republican Palace, the Convention Center, the Rashid Hotel, and other national landmarks, and designated it the Green Zone. This forced the rest of us to take circuitous routes that were not designed to handle the traffic resulting from the forced detour.

Some roadblocks seemed entirely without purpose. Abi Nuwas Street, a Baghdad thoroughfare running alongside the Tigris River, was closed near the Palestine Hotel. This cut off all riverside traffic at that point, forcing it into the middle of the busiest part of the city where the resultant traffic jam delayed everyone for nearly half an hour. The path was maddening, and seemingly unnecessary, given that the Palestine Hotel was a considerable distance from Abi Nuwas Street, far enough away that a car bomb on the street would do nothing to the hotel.

On one taxi ride, an American officer was being interviewed on the radio about some of the Baghdad inconveniences. The interview was conducted in Arabic, with simultaneous translation for the officer's benefit.

The interviewer asked, "Sir, are you concerned with the fact that the traffic in Baghdad is entirely impossible to negotiate, and that part of the problem is your armed forces and your authorities that prevent access to several square kilometers in the heart of the city?"

"I understand the difficulties of Iraqis, I do understand that," he replied. "Saddam didn't build enough power plants, so they have no electricity, and Saddam didn't care about infrastructure, so they suffered. And Saddam kept his people poor, so they had no cars, but now cars are coming across the borders by the hundreds each day, and that means traffic."

"Sir, the closed roads have an effect too, don't they?"

"Well, sure they do. But we have to balance the interest of Iraqis not wanting to sit in traffic jams—and believe me they can be frustrating, anyone in one of our own cities could tell you that—with the lives of my soldiers. And if there is one thing I will never compromise on, it is protecting the lives of my soldiers whenever I can."

"That man's mother is a whore," Abdullah, the cab driver, intervened. "Bring this chaos to America and give them our heat and take away their air conditioners and how do you think they'll do? They'll start killing each other in the streets, worse than us. I read an article about some place in Texas where everyone has guns and they shoot each other for fun. What would they do in this hell fire?"

Incendiary rhetoric aside, I understood Abdullah's frustrations well. What seemed like an inconvenience could drive a man to madness if endured long enough. The number of Iraqis I have seen threatening violence on the jammed roads is frightening. On one ride, an amiable enough taxi driver, Haider, who was talking politely about the types of foods available in various supermarkets, saw a car cut in front of him. He responded by passing the car, slowing to a halt in front of it, getting out of his car, ripping off his belt, and hitting the other driver with fearsome violence. Cooler heads less terrified than mine separated the two, and in a short while later he resumed driving me, and talking about food.

The incident shocked me, but in fact it should not have. We had been sitting in the heat for twenty minutes on a jammed road near the Jadriyah Bridge, one of the few open bridges over the Tigris. He looked like he had not slept well. I figured he probably could not afford the type of generator that could run an air conditioner (about $2,000), and it is nearly impossible to sleep in 115-degree heat without air conditioning. He had filled his car with gas that morning, which in itself is a three to four hour ordeal. As Abdullah had pointed out, any one of these occurrences would drive many Americans to violence, let alone a people accustomed to witnessing appalling levels of barbarity over the past three decades.

Taxi drivers, like most Iraqis, always seemed to be complaining about something. If it was not the Americans, the power cuts, gas lines, and the traffic, it was the brutality of the previous regime. Sometimes both were complained about in the same sentence. But when cornered and forced to decide, very few indeed preferred prewar Iraq, at least immediately following the invasion.

I often had lunch at the homes of relatives throughout Baghdad, but a favorite place of mine was the home of my aunt Zahra who lived relatively close to my grandmother, just west of her and only five miles from the airport. On one such occasion, other relatives had been invited and my aunt had ordered fish from a nearby vendor. Iraqis are very fond of fish that is raised in tanks on the banks of the river Tigris. When ordered, the fish is then split from the spine, butterflied, cleaned, and cooked during a long smoking process away from an open fire. It is, without question, my favorite Iraqi dish and one I have never seen properly prepared outside of Iraq. I once tried to ask someone at a seafood market in my neighborhood in Manhattan to split a fish along the spine, hoping then to broil it in a manner that might approach the Iraqi method. He looked at me as if I were insane. Since then, I have given up trying to eat this particular type of fish outside of Baghdad.

When I arrived at my aunt's house for her famed lunch, my cousin Amin had gone to fill his car with gas at eleven in the morning. Because of the lines, he did not return until four that afternoon, after we had nearly consumed the entire fish. He was naturally angry and upset, and his complaints about the lines for gas in such an oil rich country, as well as his complaints about the appalling administrative capacity of the Americans, received a sympathetic ear. It was not until he mentioned that in Saddam's time gas lines were not like this that my aunt retorted, only by politely agreeing and helpfully adding that in Saddam's time the only bad thing that could happen to a man was to watch his child being dragged away by security forces, knowing he would never return. Perspectives like this explain in large part why the entire country had not erupted in revolt despite all the troubles.

I stayed with my cousin Ali while we refurbished a room upstairs in my grandmother's house that I could call my home for as long as I wished. I intended to reside there temporarily, and so I only purchased those items I considered absolutely necessary—a generator powerful enough to accommodate air conditioning, a large desk for writing, a television and satellite dish, and a light that functioned by battery well as electricity.

Satellite dishes had been banned in Iraq during Saddam's rule, and their proliferation was probably one of the most hopeful signs for change, as Iraqis became exposed to ideas from all over the world. I noticed that the younger generation even watched the Israeli channels, particularly when they were replaying American sitcoms. Sa'diya is from a generation that would object if she knew that I was watching an Israeli station. However, Iraqis have been so far removed from any links to Israel that they have no idea what Hebrew sounds like or looks like, so I just told her it is actually a Czech channel, and to this she had no objection. As for the younger generation, it seems that they've had enough of grand Arab causes. Ali tends to think about as much about Israel as he does about Scotland, which is to say not very much at all. He is more interested in the quality of the television program than whoever happens to be broadcasting it.

Having said that, Iraqis were addicted to hearing the news immediately after the fall of the regime. Both Ali and my uncle Isam spent their time watching Arab satellite news channels as if they were highly-regarded films. I had never known anyone who could watch four to six consecutive hours of news programming every single day, but they seemed to enjoy it immensely. The reason was that they were not used to receiving any sort of reliable news. Iraqi news had for decades been more or less a tedious summary of the comings and goings of Saddam Hussein. Saddam went to the girls' school and people cheered; Saddam went to the factory and people cheered; Saddam went to the palace and people cheered, without end. Now they could learn about the starvation in Somalia if they wished, and this seemed to create endless amounts of excitement, and at times, anger, particularly at the pan-Arabist bias of channels like Al-Jazeera. One such moderated panel, which took place a few weeks after I arrived, went like this:

"And we return to our discussion today, with our distinguished guests, on the subject of the Iraqi resistance. We were talking about the resistance and the civilian casualties it caused." The moderator then asks for the views of a Palestinian commentator.

"The noble Iraqi resistance, the shining cause in our blighted Arab world that will lead us over the shackles of imperialism and Zionism and colonialism and teach those who exploit us that Allah is more powerful than His enemies. This mighty resistance . . ."

At this point, Abu Ahmed, a neighbor of ours I had just met, inter-venes. "Dog son of a dog! Your resistance kills women and children! Who is this resistance killing? Ten Iraqis for every American. Idiot. Never did a country deserve occupation by Jews more than you bastards. And where was your resistance when Saddam was around? When he was killing us Shi'a? I am changing the channel!" Abu Ahmed announces. He then clicks to Fox News.

Abu Ahmed was a proud Shi'i, at times more sectarian than he should have been for his own good. He was mildly distrustful of the Americans but ultimately grateful to them for creating the first opportunity for Shi'a rule in Iraq since its creation by the British after the First World War. Talk of a noble resistance tends to anger him.

We listened to the Fox News Channel for about ten minutes.

Then, much more quietly, Abu Ahmed said, "I wish I knew English. I think the Americans and this O'Reilly fellow on this channel sometimes make much more sense than the Al-Jazeera people ever did, but I cannot understand what they are saying."

CHAPTER 3

Najaf

I WAS IN BAGHDAD less than a week when I planned my first trip to the Shi'i holy city of Najaf, about one hundred miles to Baghdad's south. This is where the mausoleum of Shi'ism's founder is located and the place where Iraqi Shi'is bury their dead. I had not seen Najaf for over a decade and, given its importance to the Shi'i imagination, I did not want to delay the trip for very long. The first and most important task that I wanted to undertake in Najaf was to visit the family tombs and pay respects to the many interred there after my last visit, but I also wanted to visit the burial sites of some of Shi'ism's most revered figures, in Najaf and nearby Kerbala.

I hired a driver whose name was Abbas to take me. Abbas was a large, jovial fellow, at least 250 pounds and fond of jokes of the most vulgar and sexist variety. Yet he was also deeply religious, as indicated by the posters of various Shi'i revered figures laid out carefully in the back seat of his car. Every five minutes or so he would tell a joke, and then apologize to the posters (or, more accurately, to the images they represented) for his vulgarity, taking his eyes off of the road in the process. When I asked him if perhaps he should avoid the jokes and thus the need to make subsequent apologies, he indicated that he was not some sort of crazy fundamentalist. When I asked him if perhaps then he should put the posters away so they couldn't see the sin, he informed me these were posters and they couldn't see anything. I chose not to test his logic any further. We soon arrived in Najaf.

It took some effort to find my family tomb. It seems that Najafis are no more sensible in giving directions than the people of Baghdad. My relatives told me it was just in front of a particular monument. After finding the monument and realizing that there must be several hundred tombs that could fairly be described as "just in front" of it, I went back to the gravedigger's office and insisted he take me in person. He sent his aide, who turned out to be a sweaty, unpleasant, and angry man who said he now understood why Americans, among whom he included me, had such a difficult time finding Saddam (this was during Saddam's period in hiding) they can't even find dead people. In the end, he helped us locate the tomb, and I descended.

I am a Shi'i and a Muslim. My parents raised me bilingually in English and Arabic and taught me to memorize large portions of the Koran as a child, yet the first words that came to me when I entered the family tombs on that day were from a gay beat poet on an acid trip: I have seen the best minds of my generation destroyed by madness.

My paternal grandmother gave birth to fourteen children. Of those, four remain alive and in Iraq. The others were killed, fled, or exiled to neighboring countries. Of the four, the Ba'ath tortured one in prison. Another was forced to watch most of her children escape the country and leave her in fear of their lives, except for her youngest child, Hasan, who at twelve was considered too young to make such a dangerous journey. So he stayed, and two years later Saddam's security forces abducted him. His corpse was returned to his mother seven years later and buried, ultimately, in his family tomb in Najaf.

We are not alone. Many Shi'is tell similar stories. Najaf is the world's largest cemetery, the birthplace of Shi'ism and its holiest city, and the burial ground of the Shi'is. It stands as a testimony to both the endurance of a vibrant and living faith and the pain its people have suffered over centuries. In our often-told legends, we have been the victims of nearly every dynasty, every ruler, and every regime that has tread upon this land. The Umayyads killed our earliest leaders—the Imams, or infallible disciples of the Prophet Muhammad—the Abbasids killed all but one of the rest, and the Ottomans taxed us excessively. And then came the state of Iraq and eighty years of discrimination and oppression. And our dead are buried in Najaf, in the cemetery known as the Valley of Peace, laid in rows and rows so wide, so long, and so deep (many, including most of my family, are buried several stories beneath the earth), that the mind struggles to comprehend its vastness.

To descend into tombs in Najaf is a sobering experience. A ladder brought me down into the cool darkness while a man above chanted the Koran, hoping that he would be favored with a tip when I rose into the light once again. Elsewhere the wailing and moaning of women throwing themselves against the tombs of the newly departed could be heard, along with the horn of the odd car navigating its way through the cemetery, the occasional braying of a donkey, and children playing hide and seek in this territory ideally suited for the game. And along the barely lit wall was where my family lay buried, each placed feet first into a space in the wall, which is then filled in with earth and a name painted in front, on the clay. Some women, some men, some children, some holes filled in more than two centuries ago and some as yet unfilled, for those that will follow.

What was most striking, however, were the premature dates of death of the males buried in nearly all Najaf family tombs in the last twenty-five years. Other than my grandfather and an uncle, whose death in his early sixties was at least partially attributable to the repeated interrogations to which the previous regime subjected him, all of the males in my father's family who died in Iraq in the past thirty years never reached the age of fifty. Poets, scholars, merchants, engineers, and doctors of an entire generation destroyed by madness.

I remained below for some time, long enough that even the Koran chanter had given up any hopes for a tip and moved on to more promising territory. I began to imagine what life would have been like had these murders never happened, but it was too painful to contemplate. No dream ever affects me more than the one I frequently have in which our entire family, maternal and paternal, the living and the dead, gather together on the banks of the Euphrates for a picnic. Nothing happens in the dream outside of the picnic and a game of baseball, an ironic choice of game given that nobody in my family would know how to play it. But it is a dream, and eventually I awake, and I remember the reality. I can handle it when I am in Ohio, New York, Hong Kong, or wherever else my travels have taken me, but to even think about such things in the tombs of Najaf was more than I could bear.

So, mostly I sat and thought. When finally I had gathered my thoughts, I recited one of the common prayers of the Prophet Muhammad that my father taught me as a child, in which Muhammad asks God to enter the silent tombs and grant peace to the dead, to feed the hungry, to clothe the naked, to give water to the thirsty, to enrich the poor, and to lift from the hearts of the people of the world all the concerns that weigh upon them. It must have been the first time I had recited this prayer in a decade, and I could imagine nothing more appropriate. It was the religion I had been taught as a child, a warm faith in a just and merciful Creator who cares about His believers more deeply than a mother for her infant child, who answers the pleas of those who seek His aid, and lifts their cares from their hearts. A man can forget many things in his life, particularly when he is given the opportunities to travel far and wide as I have, but inevitably something happens, and he realizes that while changed, there are roots that provide the greatest, indeed the only, source of stability.

When I emerged from the cool darkness of the depths below into the searing heat above, my driver and I set off toward the Imam Ali mosque. We drove by tomb after tomb on our way, with no end in sight and nothing interrupting the miles of dead. On one wall alongside a tomb we drove by, there was written, in large spray-painted script: *A thousand blessings upon your house, O Bush, you sent the comrades* [colloquial term for Ba'athists] *to lie with the cows.*

I asked Abbas if he would like to visit his family tombs while we were in Najaf. He said it was no longer possible. In the 1991 uprising, some of the rebels, their advance halted by the Ba'ath, fled into the tombs on the outskirts of Najaf, seeking refuge from Saddam's approaching tanks. Saddam overran the tombs, interring the living inside, then paved over them and removed any markers from them. Hundreds of years of personal history for thousands of people, instantly obliterated by madness.

An American tank was parked on the left as we left the tombs. Two soldiers sat on the roof, their legs idly dangling. Abbas pointed to them and said gravely that the tank was on former burial ground. That did not upset him, he told me, when I offered to make the futile gesture of asking them to move. The Americans did not recognize their error and were in his eyes blameless. What did upset him was that the tank could have been there in

1991, when the U.S. army was less than three hundred miles away, and the uprising was at its peak. If it had come then, he said, the soldiers would have known not to put the tank at that spot because the tombs would still be there. But it did not come, and this he said he could never forget, or forgive. It was another forty-five minutes before Abbas told another joke.

Eventually we reached the Imam Ali mosque. It is impossible to describe what it means to a Shi'i to enter the Imam Ali mosque in Najaf, the place where Shi'ism's leader, the Prophet Muhammad's son-in-law, lies buried. It is harder still to describe what it means to enter the tomb of Imam Hussein, Shi'ism's principal martyr, the Prophet Muhammad's grandson, located only an hour away in Kerbala. To a Westerner, no doubt the scene is disturbing, with frenzied crowds screaming the name of the Imams as they circumambulate the tomb and seek to grasp its edges, women clothed in black beating their breasts, annoyed guards trying to make sure the crowds keep moving, elderly men recounting the martyrdom of Imam Ali or of Imam Hussein in a sweet singsong voice as many raise their voices in cries of blessings upon Muhammad and the family of Muhammad.

Those from nonwestern cultures more accustomed to such emotional displays are probably not so much disturbed as confused, as emotional urgency of this sort is not unusual in many cultures upon the recent death of a loved one, but is unheard of for people dead over 1400 years. As a Shi'i, I can only say that the wild display of emotion is not exclusively in favor of men long dead, but has to do with a very real and very current anguish and frustration. It is, more than anything else, the lament of a wronged people, crying out fervently against the injustices, real or perceived, against them. It would not be hard, I believe, for most Shi'is to forgive and forget the wrongs perpetrated against their Imams if they did not believe that these same wrongs were being perpetrated against them today.

But even this brief and most inadequate of descriptions requires context. According to the Shi'a, upon the death of the Prophet Muhammad, the Islamic community ignored the specific directive of the Prophet to leave the Muslim community in the hands of Muhammad's son-in-law, Ali. We Shi'a were the exceptions, the partisans (or Shi'a in Arabic) of Ali. Ali later became caliph, or leader, of the entire Muslim community, but only briefly because other members of the Islamic community never stopped warring against him. Upon his death, those at war with Ali, the Umayyads, seized control of the caliphate.

It was the second Umayyad caliph, Yazid, who initiated a chain of events that would culminate in the day that defines Shi'ism. Upon hearing that Hussein, Ali's son and Muhammad's grandson, was coming to Iraq to see if he could gather popular support for his own claim to the caliphate, Yazid sent an army of thousands to intercept him and demand an oath of loyalty from him. Hussein, with a band of less than one hundred friends and relatives, refused to give such an oath, and Yazid's army killed him along with all the other men in his company. This happened on the tenth of Muharram, the day known as Ashura, on the banks of the Euphrates, in fields now named Kerbala.

We Shi'a will often say that every day is Ashura and every land is Kerbala. This day, above all else, rises in our consciousness to define who we are. The stories told about the tragedy of Kerbala are endless. They are the stories of a people whose first leader was denied his due and had a son wrongfully murdered. They are also the stories of a people who, though the clear majority of Iraq's population, were never given until now the opportunity to hold any degree of power within the country, who live in considerable poverty relative to Iraq's other populations, and who suffered particularly acutely under the previous regime. If asked why Iraqi Shi'a are so fervent in their devotion to Imam Hussein, it is because we see no distinction between Yazid who killed Hussein and Saddam who killed our clerics and families. Our legends tell of one long succession of wrongs committed against us, and the frenzied devotion to the Imams our sole source of emotional respite from what we view as centuries of pain and oppression. We are unabashedly obsessed with this stylized history of oppression and our self-reinforced culture of victimization; our mistreatment by so many is for us a point of pride and not shame.

We paid our respects to the Imams in accordance with Shi'i tradition. As a child, when visiting the burial place of Imam Ali, I would grasp the tomb for as long as I could, until the surging crowd or a guard who took notice of me forced me on. I believed that somehow as I touched that tomb, the Imam was touching me, inspiring me, and urging me on to greater things. It was with Imam Ali that I always thought I had the greatest connection because my name, an archaic Arabic name for lion, was one of the names given to Imam Ali. Even now, as an adult, I would not leave Najaf until I had pushed forward and after twenty minutes of effort grasped the tomb, if only briefly.

The Hunting Club

ONE WARM SUMMER EVENING, my second cousin Leila and her husband Zaid, both of whom live only blocks from my grandmother's house, invited me to The Hunting Club, one of Baghdad's premier country clubs. Though the general manager is quick to point out that no senior party members were members of the club, it had been long known as the favorite recreation spot for Saddam's two children, Uday and Qusay, as well as other members of the Ba'ath elite. Their failure to gain membership did not in any way prevent their using the club and its facilities at will. It is of little surprise to anyone within Iraq that Saddam's sons, who were both quite wealthy by virtue of having stolen billions from the national treasury, refused to pay the modest membership fees. This type of arrogance is quite demonstrative, in fact, of the general attitude of the Hussein children toward national self-possession. The two of them could never conceive of having to pay money to do anything they pleased within the country that belonged exclusively to them; the idea was as offensive to them as asking a person to pay an entry fee to use their own bed, speak to their own children, or make love to their own spouse. To the Hussein sons, Iraq was a possession, and it existed for their exploitation.

Friday nights at the Hunting Club were popular. Most members preferred to sit in the large, airy garden, which held hundreds, have coffee or a meal, and, much to my surprise, play bingo. Many of my relatives were keen on this particular activity at the club. I can recall the first time I was asked to participate.

"Haider, why don't you play?" Leila asked.

"No, I'd really rather not play," I replied. What I was thinking was, *You must be kidding. Is this a church basement? Am I a seventy-five-year-old woman?*

Zaid, her husband, interjected, "Haider, don't be shy in front of us. We are family. Here's a card for the next turn." He thrust a bingo card at me.

I swiftly countered, "No no no, here, take it back. I really don't want to, but thank you so much for the offer. I'd rather talk with you because I have not seen you in so long."

Just then, to quiet the slowly growing noise in the garden, a voice came over the public announcement system. "Would the audience please keep quiet so we can play bingo!"

A sudden hush followed, and I took advantage of the interruption to resume a conversation and avoid the bingo game.

The garden was quite lovely, much as one would expect a country club to be in Baghdad. Groups of visitors sat clumped together in loosely organized tables, which tended to be reorganized rapidly as people fluttered from one table to the next to extend greetings to their many acquaintances.

Young women, those in their late teens and early twenties, felt freer to dress as they pleased within the relatively safe confines of the club. The tight jeans and exposed midriffs common on New York City streets were seen at the club, though the jeans weren't quite so low nor the shirts so high. Also common, in a way that was fairly rare thirteen years previous, were women wearing scarves and veils to cover their hair. Amidst this motley assortment of people, smells of cardamom-flavored Turkish coffee and thick, sweet apple-flavored tobacco wafted through the garden. The toss of an odd pair of dice or the movement of pieces of a backgammon set could be heard faintly.

Conversation at the Hunting Club mainly concerned one of two topics. First, there was the club itself and why its facilities were so much better than its long-standing competitor, the grand Alwiyah Club, Baghdad's first country club, which had been established by the British during the monarchy and had been viewed historically as the best. The other topic of conversation was the dishonor to which the club was subjected by Uday and Qusay.

I can provide little detail about the first of these topics of conversation, as the subject was altogether too dry to retain my interest. This was hardly the case for the prominent families, including my own, that made up most of the club's membership. They seemed to feel that their social status depended largely on that of the club, and never tired of promoting it.

The second topic of conversation was considerably more interesting, though the reported crimes of Uday and Qusay at the club were of a considerably more benign nature than others they had committed. Uday was a monster; he was reputed to have kidnapped teenage girls in various Iraqi villages, and then proceeded to rape and kill them. Yet this was barely discussed. Instead, I would overhear something like the following conversation:

"Did you know that Uday once made a married woman sit next to him the whole time while her husband had to stay at his table by himself? Can you believe that? Just four months ago, I saw it with my own eyes."

I wasn't sure of this account. It could well be true, but I had begun to understand Iraqi hyperbole. *Saw it with my own eyes* meant *I am fairly certain this happened. I heard* meant *I don't have a damn idea whether this is true but I'll throw it out because I'd like it to be.*

Another story came from my second cousin Leila concerning Qusay, who was reputedly crueler than his brother and who stole one billion dollars in cash reserves from an Iraqi bank just before the arrival of the U.S. forces. "One time Qusay told someone to buzz off a table because he needed it," she said. "And the family had to go home. 'Buzz off,' can you believe that?"

"That's all he knows how to say," added a friend. "Qusay can't even speak proper Arabic. Village schoolteachers can talk better than he can."

"He ate with his fingers you know. Qusay did." the friend's husband said.

"I thought it was Uday," said Leila.

"Both of them actually," the wife clarified.

To some extent, I had heard this before. Many Iraqis enjoyed ridiculing the Ba'ath elite for their poor education and lack of refinement. One of the aspects of Iraq I find most pleasing is its emphasis on the importance of education. Everyone, irrespective of their own educational status, tends to value it in others.

The Hunting Club stories, however, revealed a deeper class-based fault within Iraqi society that is largely not discussed in media circles. In a society torn by divisions over religion, tribe, and ethnicity, class is not the premier distinction most Iraqis make with respect to one another, but it does exist. Families that are prominent and well-known tend to stay prominent and well-known. Individuals from families who are not prominent can graduate as a doctor from a top medical school or as a professor well respected in his field, but the opportunities for social advancement are considerably more limited. There is almost no chance for that graduate to join the Hunting Club, for example. Similarly, if I were to think of marrying woman from the slum of Sadr city, even one with a medical degree and a professorship, it would become a scandal.

In some ways, this conception of class exemplifies the contempt for Saddam and his family among the Hunting Club patrons. To them, there were few greater indignities than being ruled by peasants from Tikrit, Saddam's hometown.

I left the Hunting Club slightly more uneasy than I had been. Class was a distinction I never favored, and it bore me no pleasure to witness its strong presence. However, it would be a mistake to overstate the class-related problems in Iraq. The neighbor across the street from me was a taxi driver, two doors down there was a surgeon, and in between an obvious millionaire. They were all from very different social classes, yet they greeted each other in the morning, gave each other rides to work, visited each other's homes in the evening, and attended the other's weddings and funerals; this was not the *ancien regime* of Louis XIV. Still, I could not help but think of the patent injustice that prevents the son of the taxi driver, headed to Baghdad medical school this year, from being able to marry the daughter of the surgeon, who may well become a medical school student herself, solely because of the circumstances of their birth.

CHAPTER 5

The Question

A DAY NEVER PASSED in Iraq that I was not faced with one question from Iraqis and Americans alike—whether I considered myself an Iraqi or an American. This was a common question of my oldest uncle, Nawfal, who ran his own business and who I would visit once a week for lunch to discuss the economic situation in Iraq. The question always struck me as absurd and entirely unbefitting this modern global era of multicultural families, dual citizenships, foreign residency, and immigration. The tendency to compartmentalize, to reduce, and to simplify seemed universal, but while it was easy and therefore appealing to the intellectually incurious, it was, for those of us raised as I was, utterly incongruous to the nature of our existence and upbringing. You might as well ask me if I am my mother's child or my father's.

Nevertheless, antithetical as it was to my own nature to even consider such a question, I had been given cause to reflect on it by my uncle Nawfal, among others. Iraqis tend to view the matter of my identity genetically, at least on a presumptive level. The child of an Iraqi father is an Iraqi, and though it adds to the presumption if the child's mother is Iraqi, it is not necessary.

To Abu Ahmed, for example, who comments on this matter quite a bit in our neighborhood, I am clearly an Iraqi born in the United States because both my mother and father are Iraqi. If my behavior was excessively American, my language skills poor, my respect for my family and elders not high enough, I might be considered Americanized, or even American. For proud people like my uncle Nawfal, or Abu Ahmed, this is not a good thing. It is akin to Esau selling his birthright for a mess of pottage.

On the other hand, a child of two Syrians born in Iraq is not an Iraqi, and Abu Ahmed routinely in my presence indicates that such "foreigners" do not care for the country as we Iraqis do and should go home. His willingness to say this to me strikes me as odd, for if the Iraqi-born Syrian is foreign, then, I assumed, I would be even more foreign given that I have not lived in Iraq. The opposite, however, is true for Abu Ahmed, simply on the basis of genetics.

This also helps to explain my parents' persistent attempts in the U.S. to arrange "serendipitous" meetings for me with women whose sole connection to Iraq is that their parents were born there. These women speak no Arabic and there is nothing in their bearing, behavior, temperament, or cultural outlook that distinguishes them from any American. The question of why such women would be particularly well suited for parents looking to preserve their culture in their children would confound anyone not familiar with the genetic basis of Iraqi identity.

Americans, on the other hand, for good and valid reasons, tend to regard such genetic determinism as arbitrary and inherently unjust. However, Americans do question my cultural identity quite often, albeit on different bases. On my first ride into Baghdad, a fellow civilian passenger, Ryan, said something to me that I regarded at the time as innocuous, and still do, though it is fairly representative of how Americans in Iraq regard me. He patted me on my back and said, "Welcome home." Home. A country I never lived in, but that he regarded without ever speaking with me at length as my home. Ryan meant no ill will. In fact, he was only wishing the best for me, and most importantly, he was in some respect right. Still, the step from his well-intentioned assumption that Iraq was my home to the suggestions of others that people like me should be sent back to "wherever we came from" is not a great one.

Similar experiences followed during my time in Iraq. Most memorably, a U.S. adviser asked me once to try to institute a program respecting the education of women, which I did not find workable for cultural reasons. I did not object to the program as such, only to that aspect of its implementation that required the women to travel alone to Baghdad from outlying provinces. I knew that few families would send their daughters unsupervised to study on their own. I offered alternatives that would involve the women having greater options in their own regions. She said she could understand my respect for the culture, but that the culture was sexist and wrong in this instance even if I disagreed. She indicated that she was going to make this program work, so that Iraqis would learn the ways of modernity.

The entire experience offended me. The adviser had made an assumption regarding my views on the culture, which was erroneous, and she was determined despite her own ignorance of the culture to press ahead with her unworkable plan, on the theory that eighteen-year-old women in Iraq would start to engage in culturally unacceptable practices because she told them it was a good idea. The adviser would not listen to any alternative scaled down plan because it came from someone who was to some extent an Iraqi.

On other occasions in Iraq, twenty-six-year-old graduates of third-tier law schools have lectured me about how corporations are organized in America, guards at checkpoints have told me that my entry badge did not entitle me to entry into areas that my colleagues frequent with identical badges, and soldiers have asked me when searching my car to pronounce my name in its native tongue. Yet none of this would have happened if I had stayed in the United States. If I did not know Arabic. If I was in New York dating a woman named Judy Jones and didn't know Muhammad from Abraham. Then, culturally, I would be a real American and the questions would never arise.

Because of my ties to Iraq, Americans here don't know how to classify me, so they ask the same question as the Iraqis. *Do you consider yourself an American or an Iraqi?* And I have no answer for them. I speak fluent English, yet insist on speaking Arabic at any occasion where I can. I love American football, yet find indoor soccer ludicrous and a perfect metaphor for what is wrong with America vis-à-vis the world; we can't just play a game like everyone else, we have to change it. My heart leapt when America won the gold medal in hockey in 1980, and leapt again when the Iraqis won the Asia Cup finals in soccer.

This muddle can be dangerous and runs counter to Pat Morita's advice to the Karate Kid to stay on one side of the road or the other, so as not to be run over. On a personal level, it can also be dislocating, confusing, and, particularly in Baghdad, disheartening. But it is also enlightening and enervating and, most important, it is reality, in all of its subtle, multifaceted, and delightful complexity. So I suppose the only response I ever have to this narrow and reductive question to which I am continuously subject, whether from Abu Ahmed or Ryan, is to take refuge, as Salman Rushdie's Moor did, in the words of Popeye the Sailor Man: Am I an American or an Iraqi? I yam what I yam and that's what I yam.

CHAPTER 6

Iraqi Politics

MONARCHY IS RELAXATION. I chuckled when I saw this piece of graffiti in a prominent location on a central Baghdad thoroughfare. From the Arabic above, it was clear that it meant to read *Monarchy is Stability*. And yet try as I might, I could not find anyone with sufficient English skills other than a distant cousin to appreciate the humor in the slogan. In trying to explain the difference between relaxation and stability, to Ra'ad more than anyone, because we passed the sign so often together, all that had been funny about the slogan began to seep away. I tried several times to bring Ra'ad's skeptical mind around to the fact that nobody promotes a political party by promoting the virtues of rest, even in Iraq. He never could understand why not and as a non-English speaker insisted that perhaps there was nuance to the word relaxation that I was missing. Eventually, I gave up.

This particular piece of graffiti aside, political slogans covered Baghdad's streets. A flood of political parties and related political ideas had established themselves in Baghdad virtually overnight, a welcome sight indeed after decades of totalitarian one-party rule. The dominant parties were Kurd- or Shi'i-based led by prominent exiles, and they had been in existence since at least the end of the Gulf War, and in some cases even earlier. Understandably, Iraqis tended to view such parties with some degree of suspicion; why exiles who had left Iraq so long ago felt competent to play any political role in the country confused me, too, at times, particularly when their families quite often lived in the relative shelter of the West. It was not unreasonable for Iraqis to expect that someone who wished to lead them would call Iraq his home and live in Iraq itself rather than have an office and bed in Iraq and a home and family elsewhere.

As a result, the parties' level of organization and influence in the country was somewhat limited. The exiles had no domestic political base, though at least some seemed to be working to correct this. Others seemed quite happy to remain unpopular, confident that the complete lack of any sort of domestic political organization on the ground combined with Iraq's long established proclivity toward nepotism, cronyism, and corruption would allow them to continue to rule the country in some sort of oligarchic fashion well into the future. Signs were unclear at that time as to whether or not this expectation would prove to be well-founded.

In any event, the exiles' dislocation from ordinary Iraqi citizenry left the Ba'ath party, though underground, as the most potent and organized force in Iraqi politics. The power of the Ba'ath in Iraq could not be underestimated; the Iraq Bar Association had held elections in July to replace the Saddam-installed board of directors, dominated by party apparatchiks, with a freely elected board. Nine of the eleven-member board elected turned out to be former party apparatchiks. The head of the bar was not a party member, the massive unpopularity of the party had made that particular achievement impossible, but in electing the ten deputies, nobody could match the organizational capacities of the only organized force in Iraq in thirty-five years, the Ba'ath.

Much of the graffiti that covered nearly every wall in Baghdad was the product of the exile parties. *A Free Iraq for a Free People; No America, No Saddam; Yes, Yes to Islam;* and *The Rule of Law Is the Responsibility of the Iraqi People* are representative examples.

But between the carefully crafted statements of the parties were crudely scrawled slogans, often written in slang rather than proper classical Arabic, and almost surely not composed by the politically minded but by the more common folk that comprised the bulk of the Iraqi population, longing for stability and prosperity but unsure of how to get it. The high-minded ideas of a free Iraq for a free people were not expressed by them. More commonly seen were scrawls like *Where is our gasoline?, Yes, Yes to the*

Islamic schools, and *Saddam is a pimp and his sons are the offspring of a whore.* These feelings were more primal, the needs more basic, the point more simple than the well-padded exiles seemed to comprehend. An ambitious young and budding domestic politician might have been wise to scribble on a wall, *It's the economy, stupid.*

Other than the exile parties and the Ba'ath, the main forms of civic organization (as opposed to individual graffiti scrawls) were the mosque and the tribe. Islamism was probably the most dynamic political force within the country, invigorated not so much by Khomeini-like revolutionary fervor, but more by the comfort religion engendered, as it employed a message and a medium in which nearly all in this deeply skeptical country fervently believed. Among colonials and colonized alike, there were too many liars and cheats, too much chaos and disorder, too many promises broken and deadlines not kept to believe in much of anything that a current politician, American or Iraqi, had to say. Relief existed in Holy Books and Holy Prophets, divinely inspired and sinless, springing from an idealized past where there was no lying, no cheating, and Good always triumphed over Evil. The scholars may not have been Prophets, but in these turbulent times, they were the closest thing for most, and that would have to do.

As for the tribes, I had a hard time understanding the origin and development of their newfound importance. Though Iraqis who had never left the country seemed to believe that tribal affiliation was always an important symbol of identity, and tribal loyalty a fundamental part of Iraqi existence, this was patently untrue among the educated classes in the diaspora. My parents had no idea to which tribe I belonged, none of my Iraqi exile friends seemed to be aware of their tribal links either, and the notion that a tribe would be a relevant factor in determining one's place in society would draw peals of laughter in the diaspora, even among those who would consider family, religious sect, and ethnic identity to be fundamentally important. Growing up, it seemed to me that tribes existed, the uneducated and peasantry paid heed, and nobody else cared.

This seemed to have changed rather dramatically during the reign of Saddam Hussein, at least among the Arabs. Upon my return to Iraq, Iraqis of all educational and social levels asked what my tribal affiliation was, and I received shocked looks when I told those asking that I had no idea. Embarrassed by my ignorance, I immediately did some research (which mostly involved asking my aunt Zahra) and discovered that my tribe was the Rabia, at which point I began to tell people this when they asked. Unfortunately, this came at some cost. One common response was barely concealed hostility and contempt.

Thus, on one cab ride the driver, upon learning my tribe, proclaimed, "So you are Rabia, huh? Whatever, I can't take you in the taxi today. I have other things to do."

"But we just negotiated a price," I protested, suspecting that perhaps the Rabia was to his tribe as the Montagues had been to the Capulets.

"Yeah, but I forgot about my sick aunt. Sorry about it, really, go in the safety of God. Bye."

More common, however, was the opposite reaction.

"You are Rabia! All praise is due to Allah, Lord of the Worlds. My brother, my cousin, my countryman, my friend."

"Uh huh," I replied, "and that's no lettuce on the Shawarma, but extra mayonnaise."

"You must come to my house to meet my family, I am Rabia and the son of a Rabia and my wife is Rabia and my mother is too. We are at the service of all Rabia in all of Iraq, and anywhere they may be found, my dear brother, my long lost brother who I adore as much as my own family."

"Sure, great. And can I get fries with that too?"

This whole matter seemed ridiculous to those of us in the diaspora who considered such affiliations irrelevant, and Iraqis interested in the subject had advanced many reasons for it. Essentially, however, whatever reasons they gave they related to two primary developments: the encouragement by the Ba'ath party of tribal affiliation (because loyal tribal followers were easy to control by controlling the tribal elders) and the desire of Iraq's citizens to develop and maintain relationships among each other when nearly every other social or civic organization had either been subsumed by the party or destroyed entirely.

The inability of the exile parties to establish roots, the force of the mosque, the increased relevance of the tribes, and the continuing formidable organizational capacities of the Ba'ath all pointed toward the danger of premature elections. Genuine democrats would find it almost impossible to succeed in this hostile environment. More development, more time, and more resources would be necessary before the country would have any hope of democracy. Freedom was inspiring, but the overall situation remained quite dangerous. Care had to be taken to nurture the seeds, or evil could yet again poison the land.

CHAPTER 7

Assassination

I WAS AT MY uncle Nawfal's house enjoying a summer lunch when the wails came. A woman clad in a head-to-toe black chador (known in Iraq as the *abbaya*) came to my uncle's home, banging fiercely on the outer door and demanding to be let in, asking urgently about the safety of relatives. We had no idea what she was screaming about, and so we turned on the television to hear in shock what had brought this about. In Shi'sm's holiest shrine, on Islam's holy day, a much-revered Shi'i scholar, Ayatollah Muhammad Baqir Al-Hakim, was blown to bits along with eighty of his followers. A more incendiary and provocative action against Iraq's majority Shi'is could scarcely be imagined. I suppose it was not quite equivalent to the Pope being killed in St. Peter's Cathedral, but it was close.

Knowing I had no relatives in Najaf that day, I only listened, stunned by the news they were reporting and uncertain what I was supposed to think or where I was going to go. Female cousins and aunts began screaming and beating their chests and their foreheads. There was a frantic rush to the television set to hear the reports, and the streets were filled with frantic, passionate mourning and shouts of revenge among the young. Iraq, I felt, was going to come apart.

Hakim had spent more than two decades in Iran avoiding Saddam's savage repression of the Shi'is, only to be killed now that Iraq was supposedly free. He was the son of one of Iraq's most revered Ayatollahs,

Muhsen Al-Hakim, himself the target of oppression by a previous regime. All of the elder Hakim's male children (and there were over a dozen) but one were now dead, all killed or at least allegedly killed by the Ba'ath. The shock for us Shi'is could not have been greater.

The point, at least for me, was not so much Hakim himself, who had his own questionable history. Through the end of the 1980s, he appeared to have been a hard-line reactionary very much in the Ayatollah Khomeini mold, though to his credit this image had softened and been moderated considerably in the past several years, in particular after the American occupation began. It was this period, when he urged moderation and restraint from his followers and delivered a peaceful and stable southern Iraq to the American occupation, that will be remembered as his finest hour, even to his earlier detractors, much like Giuliani's days following September 11 will be remembered as his finest. And for this he had earned the eternal wrath of the terrorists that stalk the Islamic world.

I could hear the fury in the full-throated cries of the Shi'i believers within hours. The chant that arose in the streets was clear in its message, threatening in its import, and terrifying in its potential: *Today is the day of the Ja'afaria (*another common term for Shi'is), *there will be no silence, there will be no acquiescence.*" As the night wore on, I became even more scared. I returned home and was sitting in my room with Ra'ad and Sa'diya, watching the news, as voices gathered outside. I looked out and saw the Shi'is in our neighborhood on the streets, dressed in black, some carrying weapons, some visibly red-eyed, every one ferociously stern-faced.

"Falluja, the dogs and pigs of Falluja did this. They'll do anything to bring back Saddam. Did you see them carrying his picture the other day? Always the same with them. The news said that it was the Fallujans," said Abu Ahmed, our neighbor, who was intimately involved in the conversation just outside our home on the street.

"No, Palestinians," another replied. "They benefited from Saddam. He paid $25,000 to each one who blew himself up, and our martyrs in the wars he started get nothing."

This was a common Iraqi complaint, that Saddam did not properly compensate the families of the Iraqi dead from the wars with Iran and the United States, giving the money instead to Palestinian suicide bombers.

The term "martyr" carries little significance in the context of war; it means only a soldier killed in action.

"Sunnis Sunnis Sunnis. Palestinians, Fallujans, it's all the same. Didn't their dog leaders kill Imam Hussein? And now they kill another religious cleric and you are surprised. They want us back in our place below them. And we won't go. We outnumber them. For every one they kill, we'll kill ten. Then let's see what happens," chimed in Abdul Ameer.

Abdul Ameer was always extremely friendly to me, though I tended to avoid him. His anger, frustration, and rage could explode at any moment during any discussion. Less than a week earlier he had been unable to secure a job as a guard at the offices of a large political party and had spent the afternoon rather loudly denouncing that party and threatening their leaders, at least in private conversations. I feared what he might be capable of, so I intended to stay indoors so long as he was on the street.

"It's not all Sunnis, it's the extremist ones, those Wahhabis funded from Saudi Arabia," said my cousin Ali, whose wife, Alia', is Sunni. "But this is bad, very, very bad. Why doesn't Hakim have better bodyguards anyway?"

"Stop defending them, Ali," said Abu Ahmed. "Hakim is the martyr, and they are the murderers. We're not talking about your wife's family anyway. They're good people. It's the other Sunnis we mean."

The conversation was interrupted as a single Sunni scholar, known for his particularly strident anti-Shi'i views, appeared down the street. I never saw him, but I heard them yell his name, and I heard him scream as he ran toward a fence and relative safety. He made it, but I always wondered what might have happened if he didn't. What would they do? What would I have done if they had done something awful? Would I have intervened? Would I have remained hidden in my room, a cowardly witness to barbarism? I'd like to believe I would have saved the man's life, but I don't know. More than anything else, I knew I didn't want to be in such a situation. I hadn't come to Iraq for this.

But then a day later the waters receded. I could not offer a reason; it could have been the unconditional, immediate, and rapid denunciation of the deed by nearly every single responsible Sunni organization and mosque in Iraq as well as every Sunni with whom I spoke (as compared to the mealy mouthed, delayed, and halfhearted statements issued by the

Iraqi Governing Council and the Coalition Provisional Authority). It could have been that cooler heads have a way of prevailing with the passage of a little time, even just one night, or it could have been that the American army was alert and prepared to ensure that communities did not mix hostilely the next day. Whatever the cause, nothing happened. A few people from the heavily Shi'i district of Kadhamiya attempted to cross the Tigris into the heavily Sunni district of 'Adhamiya (the proximity of these two communities, separated only by a river, has been a source of friction many times in years past), but apparently never made it across, or not in sufficient numbers for anyone to notice or care. Other than that, I heard of no incidents of friction. So the moment passed, thankfully, and my deepest fears went unrealized. But the tinder was dry, and some continued to search for a fuse.

CHAPTER 8

Truth and Rumors
in Baghdad

IN LIGHT OF THE lies told by official media sources over the past thirty-five years in Iraq, it should come as no surprise that Iraqis have been ingrained with a healthy skepticism concerning the accuracy of sources of information that are usually taken to be reliable in other parts of the world. Nevertheless, it was alternately startling, amusing, and faintly disturbing, and sometimes all three at once, to observe the method by which Iraqis evaluated the credulity of anything told to them.

Without exception, Iraqis displayed extreme skepticism over the truth of reports by any government or military source. I did not need to grow up in a land where every battleground defeat was proclaimed a glorious victory to consider this skepticism wise; four months of post-Saddam Iraq were enough to justify it. Since the beginning of the war, I had heard from official government sources, mostly American, that Saddam was dead, Saddam was on the run, Basra was taken, Basra was not taken but Umm Qasr was taken, Umm Qasr was not taken because of pockets of resistance, Chemical Ali was confirmed dead following DNA testing, Chemical Ali was captured, and many other astonishing inconsistencies. These had become so common, in fact, that rather than wonder why Iraqis never believed official American sources on matters of importance, I was often left wondering what lead those official American sources to think they should be believed.

Iraqis also rarely trusted any breaking story on television. Shi'is and

Kurds, for example, did not trust Al-Jazeera because it was run by pan-Arab and anti-Shi'i (or anti-Kurd, depending on the neighborhood) fanatics eager to see Iraq fail. Iraqis generally would not trust CNN because to them it was a mouthpiece for President Bush. BBC was a mouthpiece for Prime Minister Blair, the man commonly known in Iraq as "Bush's slipper," and Jews ran Fox News. (Indeed, to Iraqis, Jews run all media outlets, but the Jews, Iraquis would say, it seems take more interest in the day-to-day operations of Fox News, hence its particular unreliability.) If a report, such as the Najaf bombing, appeared on all media outlets, then it was almost instantly accepted (after all, the Jews, President Bush, pan-Arab fanatics, and Bush's slipper could not all be wrong), though discrepancies between them led viewers to discount entirely any area of discrepancy rather than accept one version over the other.

The problem was that not all news stories were reported on all networks, leaving an Iraqi without reliable information in many areas. The peculiar manner in which Iraqis fill this void, namely reliance on speculation and rumor of the most implausible sort, can be startling. Thus, to the ordinary Iraqi, the story on CNN about a soldier who helped rebuild a school in Kirkuk was clearly untrue because it was a news report, but a street rumor that the sunglasses of U.S. soldiers were designed to see through women's clothing was widely accepted, even to some degree among the educated who really should have known better. I have a female acquaintance who is a medical doctor and who refuses to leave her automobile if any soldiers donning sunglasses are in sight, and she is by no means alone among the hospital staff.

I was amused by how such rumors manifested themselves in the reactions of Iraqis. For example, "good girls" disappeared at the sight of any soldier wearing sunglasses, while "bad girls" would saunter by him slowly. I was not, however, inclined to engage in discussions with Iraqis over the patent absurdity of such rumors because, when I did, it proved to be a hopeless endeavor.

One day I spotted a tanned, crew-cut sergeant in a bulletproof vest and helmet, carrying an automatic weapon. He was wearing sunglasses.

"Sergeant," I said, "I am an American. May I borrow your sunglasses, just to show these kids here that you can't use them to see through clothing?"

"Sure, whatever." He handed me the sunglasses.

I approached the kids. "Now look, can you see anything?" I asked.

"Turn them on! Turn them on," they shouted in unison, as one and then the other grabbed them, tried to look through them, and found nothing of interest but the world they already knew in a darker hue.

"There is no 'on,' this is what they do, they protect against the sun!" I explained.

"Come on, people aren't ice cream, they don't need protection from the sun. Nobody likes to see dark objects, turn them on so we can see what we want!"

Just then some older men in the neighborhood stopped by. "Kids, stop that now! You," one pointed to me, "aren't you ashamed teaching our kids how to stare at naked women like Americans do?"

"They can't stare at women, sir, the sunglasses don't do that," I countered.

"Yes they can, my neighbor did it and said he saw naked women with his own eyes," the oldest gentleman replied.

"Sir, please try them and you will believe me," I said, holding the sunglasses out to him. A crowd had gathered.

"I take refuge in Allah from the wiles of Satan!" he responded, scandalized by the suggestion.

Finally the sergeant, not understanding a word of this conversation but watching his sunglasses go from one person to another for several minutes, interjected, "Sir, I need my sunglasses back. I cannot tolerate their being passed around like this, go get your own sunglasses."

"Yes, yes, go get some, and then show us how to turn them on!" one of the kids shouted mischievously as another elderly man raised his hand in the kid's direction, threatening punishment if he should persist in suggesting such lewdness.

CHAPTER 9

The Death of Two Dogs

WHEN I RETURNED HOME on the evening of September 5, 2003, my first thought was that Baghdad had erupted in some sort of inchoate and late-formed rebellion. Overall, it had been a good day until the gunfire began. I had just begun to perform legal work again, for rather small sums and for clients who were more often than not friends and family eager to open companies in Iraq and begin doing business. I had signed my first two clients that day, for the princely sum of $1,500, and had received a telephone call from Fareed, a friend who was advising a member of the Iraq Governing Council (GC), a group of twenty-five Iraqis that the United States had picked to advise its own arm, the Coalition Provisional Authority, in governing the nation. Fareed asked me if I might be interested in providing consulting services for the GC. Though we did not discuss specifics, I finally felt, nearly six weeks after having entered Iraq, that I was making some progress toward my professional goals. I was going to represent clients and make policy.

It was as I was heading home from my last meeting with one of my new clients that the AK-47s began shooting in all directions around me. I had grown accustomed to intermittent and staccato-like bursts of gunfire on occasion, when Iraq won a soccer game or a wedding was taking place, for example. However, these bursts were being discharged in rapid succession by large numbers of people, something I had never witnessed before. In every district I drove through, neighbors were running from one house to the next. I could hear the uniquely Arab female ululations from the deepest parts of curtained homes, from which only sound can emanate. I saw children playing in raw sewage, as children love water and fire hydrants had long ceased to function in Baghdad. Feelings of shock that I was now going to be caught in a war, and disbelief that I had so misjudged the population's feelings toward the occupation, crept into my mind.

But soon another picture emerged, not one born of the pessimism and fear that so often gripped me in this country but one bred of a uniquely American hope. In my tumultuous existence in this country, hope and despair were intimate if uncomfortable bedfellows; one was never far from the other.

Thus in the middle of what I thought to be the start of a bloody rebellion, I saw the bright smile of a young girl. She was skipping rope while three boys danced in circles around her. Upon seeing our car, she smiled directly at me.

The smell of fetid sewage in the streets was overpowering, the clothes the children wore were clearly inadequate, and their instruments of play primitive and worn, but that smile was the most beautiful sight I had seen in weeks. Perhaps this was because of the solace provided in the midst of what had been a terrifying situation or perhaps because it was in the faces of Iraq's children that I often found her deepest hopes revealed. Whatever the cause, it provided me an opportunity to reconsider what was really happening.

This was no uprising. Surely nobody was in the mood for another violent conflict, and certainly if one had appeared, no child would be smiling. The girl may have been only six or seven, maybe a little younger, but she was an Iraqi, born and bred to war, having witnessed it firsthand in a way that very few Americans outside of the military, including me, could claim. Here, even young girls know that war is no laughing matter.

Other signs I should have noticed before began to appear. Nobody had run into their homes to protect themselves from gunfire—in fact, they were running in the opposite direction. The guns were aimed upwards, and not in any hostile fashion. Sufficiently comfortable after about a quarter of an hour that I was not in danger, I asked a man on the street what had happened. Uday and Qusay, the terrifying sons of Saddam Hussein, were dead, he told me.

Initially, few believed they were dead, but when the bodies were shown on television, hope had replaced despair and skepticism, and little girls smiled on the streets. There was among many an enormous feeling of relief that Saddam's obvious successors had been removed and a sense of satisfaction that Saddam, still in hiding, had no doubt seen and heard about the fate of his murderous sons. The occasion was not reservedly happy, however, as most of the revelers told me they regretted that the children had not suffered more in their deaths.

Uday and Qusay were not like the children of other Arab world monarchs and dictators who make use of their privileged positions to study abroad, sow wild oats as wealthy playboys in the "decadent" West where opportunities for debauchery are more plentiful, and then return to their native lands to marry, have children, and more often than not, rule their country. Saddam's children instead followed more the model of the mafiosi, and received during their youth on-the-job training from their father on the fundamentals of sadistic, bloodthirsty rule. Uday was known to abduct, rape, and kill village women he fancied. He also owned lions that were fed political prisoners, thrown alive to them. Qusay, by most accounts, was worse in terms of his capacity for cruelty and the sheer numbers of deaths for which he was responsible.

Given the crimes of the two children, I was anything but distressed at hearing of their deaths. I went to Ali's house and celebrated with him, mostly by sitting in his living room with his wife and child, listening to loud Arabic music as we viewed over and over the videotapes of the corpses on television. The sight was macabre, in some ways gruesome. It certainly felt odd to be so happy at the news of human death, to rejoice while images of death dominated the living room, but too much had happened to Iraq in the past two decades to be troubled seriously by the death of these two particular men. If Iraqis were to believe that any single human death (even that of Saddam's children, even that of Saddam) was infinitely precious and to be mourned when lost, they would have been driven mad decades ago by the deaths of hundreds of thousands of others, entirely innocent.

After we watched the corpses on the television for well over an hour, Ali tried to convince Alia' to shoot his gun into the air with the others. It was fairly clear that Abu Ahmed was doing so, given the sounds of the blasts close by and the shouts we heard from his home. Alia' staunchly refused, and even refused to let Ali take their young daughter outside to shoot his gun with him. The mere thought of the bullets frightened her, something I was not accustomed to seeing among Iraqis, all of whom had weapons of every conceivable variety.

I took my leave of Ali and Alia' when their argument over firing guns into the air began to edge toward a moment of genuine spousal discord, and ran to my grandmother's home as the deafening pops and bursts of bullets continued to tear at the night sky. Suddenly, I heard a shot that I felt would rip my eardrums, followed immediately by what sounded like a wasp buzz past. I froze.

"What was that?" I shouted, nearly at the top of my lungs.

"Oh sorry, sorry, Haider!" I didn't see you. Anyway, I was shooting up at the tree. It would never hit you, don't worry, you are my friend!" I heard Abu Ahmed reply.

"Abu Ahmed, I heard it buzz past, that means it was really close," I replied, trying to remain calm amidst what had started to me to appear increasingly like insanity.

"Oh no, those bullets are loud. You can hear the whoosh anytime, trust me. I was in the Army, I know."

"Great, Abu Ahmed, can you do one thing for me? Can you please just not shoot for the thirty seconds it takes me to get home from here?"

"Oh sure, sure," he replied. "Anyway, I was just celebrating. Did you hear the news? About Uday and Qusay?"

"Umm, yes, Abu Ahmed, I did," I said.

"I'm just happy the bastard father got to watch his own children die first, that was God's Plan, make him suffer, then God will turn to him. Your time is coming, Mr. President!" he shouted, as he fired three more rounds in the air. "You killed my family, now you get yours, you pimp!" Then he paused, and fired another. "What am I doing, what kind of neighbor am I. Haider, come in, take some tea!"

"Abu Ahmed, it's almost midnight and people are shooting everywhere. I really have to get home, but another night, for sure."

"Haider, I cannot let you go without tea! You are my neighbor and friend and brother!"

"I promise another night. You provide me food so often, your generosity is heartwarming, but I promise, soon, I will see you for tea."

"Soon, Haider!"

And with that, I returned home to sleep.

CHAPTER 10

A Walk on Saadoon Street

IN HONOR OF MY mother's birthday, I decided to take a walk that I had intended to take for some time but had not yet had the opportunity. The walk was to begin at Liberation Square, proceed along Saadoon Street to Firdous Square and end at the Alwiyah Club on Firdous Square, where my parents were married.

The rule of the Ba'ath effectively began in Liberation Square in 1969. The Ba'ath hung about a dozen Iraqi Jews in the square and on the Republican Bridge adjoining it and left them there for several days. They had been accused of treason and espionage on behalf of Israel. This incident signified a new level of savagery, even for a country whose history was replete with appalling violence of all kinds. A coup had ended the monarchy in 1958, for example, and the leaders of it ordered that wild horses drag the king and close government associates along the ground until they were dead. In the case of the 1969 hangings, however, the violence was so public and the victims so far removed from the workings of government, that it foretold an ominous future. And that ominous future had become stark reality in Iraq in less than a decade.

Running from Liberation Square toward Firdous Square was Saadoon Street, historically considered Baghdad's Fifth Avenue. I was fortunate never to have seen Saadoon in its prime; many of those I know who have were moved to tears when they saw it after Saddam fell. To describe it as devastated was more than an understatement. There was not a single new business anywhere along it—the buildings were old and worn, walls were crumbling, wires were exposed and hanging, rusting metal frames appeared where once there was concrete, electricity was rare, and tiny mobile generators with wires protruding from every end were everywhere so that I had to engage in a fair amount of jumping and ducking to move forward. Dirt, grime, and dust blanketed the street.

Having made my way along Saadoon Street fairly quickly, I decided to watch a film at the once famous Babylon Cinema, located midway down the street. The cinema was in poor shape, with its tattered seats, torn screen, no climate control, and poor projection. I sat in the cleanest seat I could find, bought a can of Pepsi, and waited for the film to begin. I had no idea what the film was going to be, there was no description anywhere, but my expectations were rather low, given the state of the cinema and given that there was not a single woman, child, or elderly man in the entire theater. Whatever the movie was, it was obviously only of interest to younger males.

The films at the Babylon brought Hollywood's propensity for gratuitous and mindless sex and violence to a new extreme. They were not in fact films at all, but rather a random pastiche of several different B-level kung fu movies and soft pornography spliced together to ensure end-to-end nonstop action and sex without a plot or consistent characters to provide any level of coherence. The movie was not subtitled or dubbed; it didn't need to be. To experience this, in the main cinema of the main street of the capital of a nation that once hosted poets, singers, architects, and painters who were the envy of the Arab world, was terribly difficult.

I left the cinema in low spirits over the sad condition of the Iraqi arts and committed myself to seeing one of Baghdad's many art galleries in the future in order to perhaps experience another, brighter side to the Iraqi arts scene. I then proceeded further along Saadoon Street toward Firdous Square, which I knew would lift my spirits.

Firdous Square was where the horror of the Saddam regime ended, on April 9, 2003. Saddam's famous statue, seen toppled endlessly on television, sat in the middle of this square and surrounding it were Baghdad's most famous landmarks, the Sheraton Hotel (not managed by the Sheraton for decades), the Palestine Hotel (still referred to as the Meridien, though the Merdien management likewise had departed decades ago), and the Alwiyah Club.

The Alwiyah, unsurprisingly, was closed to nonmembers and my pleas to the guards to allow me entrance to the place where my parents had wed were met by polite declines and explanations relating to security concerns. I had never heard stories or known much about my parents' wedding other than it was in the Alwiyah, and I was determined to see it.

"Is there anything you can do to help me out?" I asked.

"You are my brother and my beloved, and if it were up to me, a thousand greetings upon you and your family, and you are welcome. But our manager is always getting complaints from the Americans, and the Americans insist that only members can come in. I'm really sorry. Next time, sweetheart, you just come with a friend that is a member and I'll kiss both your cheeks and let you in without so much as a search."

Such elaborate and terribly flowery rhetoric seems to come naturally to most Iraqis, though I had a harder time with it. I tried to imagine an American security guard saying something like this at an airport, and it caused me to smile.

After these gentle refusals, I left the door of the Alwiyah Club and stood with my back to it, facing Firdous Square. I circled around to the front of the square, where the gargantuan statue of Saddam once stood. It seemed oddly empty, almost barren. In place of the statue there were some pillars and a sculpture behind them, of something that I could not make out—both were tiny relative to the former statue. I did not know what to think of this, the square seemed to be incomplete, as if it were waiting for something grand to take the place of the dreaded statue.

By the time I left Firdous Square, darkness was approaching. I hurried home, distressed in some respects, but also largely content. Saadoon Street may have been a trash pit, Baghdad may have been so dangerous that a well-dressed man could not enter the country club where his parents were wed, and the arts scene may have been dreadfully battered, but one thing had changed. A twenty foot high statue of the dictator, Saddam Hussein, had been removed and hope, in whatever form, had replaced it.

CHAPTER 11

Gasoline

SEVERAL WEEKS AFTER its auspicious beginning my law business was more or less stalled. I had picked up one additional client, again for a modest fee. I spent most of my time visiting Governing Council members and Iraqi ministers as well as their American counterparts at the Coalition Provisional Authority—to pass along greetings and let them know where I was and what I was doing, in hopes that one of my many visits and inter- actions would eventually bear fruit. Nobody was doing business in Iraq at the time in any serious capacity, so I assumed that it was a matter of time, and until the situation stabilized, my time was best spent letting others know what I was doing, and hoping a few along the way might need assis- tance with respect to developing law and policy in commercial and finan- cial matters.

To that end, I had an appointment at the CPA Convention Center at two in the afternoon in the late summer of 2003, in order to discuss my work and whether or not there were opportunities we could discuss mutu- ally. I considered this to be vitally important because if there was any work to do with multinational companies, then the Americans at the CPA would be the first to hear about it. So as to be sure that I would be on time to this critical meeting, I arranged with Ra'ad, our house guard and my part- time driver by this point, to pick me up at 1:15 p.m. at the Internet center where I would be working. The distance from the Internet center, which lay on the banks of the Tigris, to the Convention Center, also not far from the river but on the other side of it, was probably less than ten miles. The shortest road should have taken less than fifteen minutes. Unfortunately, the Coalition Provisional Authority had closed the shortest road, which was across the suspension bridge on the Tigris, because it was deemed sufficiently near their headquarters at the Republican Palace to be a security threat if open to the public.

As a result, two other routes were available: the first, a detour of about six miles upstream to the Jadriyah Bridge and then six miles back, turning the eight mile journey into a twenty mile one. The second option was to proceed along Abi Nuwas Street along the river downstream for several kilometers, then make our way into the middle of the city and over to another bridge, which when crossed placed us quite close to the Convention Center. This route was without question shorter, but it required us to enter the city at its busiest intersection. In earlier times, we could have remained on the riverbank on the relatively traffic-free Abi Nuwas Street, but as I mentioned before, the Americans had closed the road near the center of the city because it ran close to the Palestine Hotel, and this had caused endless traffic difficulties. As a result, our options were not great. In the end, we chose the second route, and prepared for a forty-five minute, twelve mile ride.

Our travel then proceeded relatively smoothly. We expected the snarling traffic that occurred as we left Abi Nuwas and turned in to the heart of the city. The honking of horns, the cursing of the Americans and their closed roads, the anger that had taken root among a frustrated and deprived population, the shouting and threats from one car to another as all sought to make their way forward—all of this had become part of Baghdad life. Yet we snaked our way forward, on schedule.

Then, entering into the heart of the city on Saadoon Street the traffic stopped. Horns honked, people left their cars to see what the matter was, but more than a quarter of an hour passed, and other than American tanks about two hundred yards ahead, I could see nothing. Someone claimed that an American tank was bulldozing a shop owner's place of business, another said the Americans were arresting youths selling gasoline on the black market, and a third claimed that the Americans had found Izzat Ibrahim al-Douri, one of the highest ranking members of the previous regime, still at large and were walking him along Saadoon Street to take him into custody. This latter claim seemed unlikely, both because the U.S. military, which had lately shown a tendency toward assuming the worst of any Iraqis they came across, was not likely to be parading a high Ba'ath official in public for fear of sparking a sympathetic uprising, and partly because a high Ba'ath official was not likely to be shopping on Baghdad's busiest street on a weekday where he could be caught. More than the almost certain falsity of this final claim, however, I was sure of nothing.

I decided to leave my automobile and make my way forward on foot, in order to determine what was happening. As I came quite close to the American tanks, I noticed a strong smell of car gasoline, and a great deal of water running over my feet, almost to my ankles. Then, as I snaked through swarms of people and could see what was happening, it became obvious that what lay under my feet was not water at all, but gasoline. I became witness to a sight I am not likely to forget as a near perfect metaphor for the incompetent colonial exercise in which the United States was engaged. The American soldiers were taking action against black market sellers of gasoline by attempting to destroy the fully loaded containers that held it.

The enforcement of the laws against black market sales of gasoline had modest levels of support. The black marketers were considered rapacious, exploitative, and heartless folk, quite happy to earn an excessive amount off the misery of needy taxi drivers who simply did not have ten hours to stand in line for gasoline. While most (or at least the more educated) would acknowledge that a black market was inevitable in a world of very cheap gasoline and ten-hour gas lines, none had kind words for the black-market sellers themselves.

Still there were various ways in which the American military could enforce the law, and it opted for some unique combination of the ineffective, dangerous, and foolish. They stopped traffic on Baghdad's busiest street, placed all of the containers holding the gasoline in the middle of the street, and started to run tanks over them. Gasoline was running in thick rivers in various directions and down sewers, traffic was at a standstill, and the black-market sellers of gasoline stood aside, seemingly bemused.

Surrounding this surreal scene were about four to five nineteen-year-old soldiers "guarding the perimeter," aiming their weapons at any car and driver daring to honk a horn, and apparently unaware that what they were doing was not halting the advance of any hostile force. Meanwhile, their fellow soldiers were creating a hazard of such proportions that it would dwarf anything a terrorist could manage on his or her own. Any clever, suicidal-minded member of the so-called resistance could have killed dozens with the light of a single match.

I arrived at my appointment exactly one hour and fifteen minutes late, or two hours after I had begun the ten-mile ride. I immediately set about to explain what happened to the three American officials who were there. Two worked with the CPA office that supervised the Ministry of Trade, and one worked with the CPA office that dealt with the Minister of Finance.

"Sorry, U.S. soldiers on the street were running over gasoline containers, and there were thick rivers of gasoline everywhere," I offered.

"No need to apologize, delays happen all the time," one of the CPA officers replied, smiling. "Take your time, we'll get started in two minutes."

"Thanks, but what I am wondering is whether this whole idea of destroying loaded gasoline containers with tanks in this way is good policy or not?" I asked.

"Well, we're here to rebuild the country *and* fight the terrorists, but we focus on the rebuilding side and let the military focus on the terrorist side."

"Let's talk now about this law firm idea you have," said another of the officials, this one more portly and slightly more abrupt in his manner.

I protested. "Sorry to harp on this, but it's hard to think of private enterprise or work when I am wading through streams of gasoline. I mean, who is telling these soldiers to do this?"

The portly one became annoyed. "Look, we can't tell the military how to do its job, they know how to fight terrorists. We know how to build countries. We are experts at that. Two of us have experience in the former Soviet Union."

I didn't push the matter. Instead, we started discussing the law firm, but my heart was no longer in the meeting. I didn't see how these people with their total lack of knowledge about Iraq and, for that matter, what lay beyond the Green Zone, could on the basis of Russian experience play any positive role in developing this country. The idea that the CPA might be staffed more broadly with people of this sort was, quite frankly, terrifying.

CHAPTER 12

Kadhmiya

ON A FRIDAY IN the late summer of 2003, I had a full day off and was
fortunate that my uncle Hummam, to whom I was particularly close, also
had a day off, a rarity for him. We set out for the Holy Mosque of
Kadhmiya, planning to return for lunch with my aunt Zahra.

My uncle Hummam was a senior officer of the Supreme Council for
an Islamic Revolution in Iraq (SCIRI), one of the largest exile-led parties
in Iraq, and he had been particularly close to the assassinated Ayatollah
Hakim. Being a Shi'i religious figure from a prominent Shi'i family, the
Ba'ath targeted him at an early age, and after a prison term in Iraq he
escaped for Iran as a young man in his thirties and had remained there
rising within the ranks of SCIRI until the regime fell.

Iraqi media outlets continually interviewed him, his name had circulated as a potential minister or committee head, and he was widely considered a good person to know. While I knew all of this, I remembered
him mostly as my father's much younger brother, who used to take me to
the mosque in Iraq during our family visits, after which we would visit my
favorite pickle factory, and then finish off by drinking Pepsi in a bottle.
These remain among my fondest Iraq memories as a child, and to this day
I always, when possible, prefer my Pepsi in a tall thin bottle.

Uncle Hummam had been different then—more jovial, quicker with a
joke, more active, willing to jump around a field and attempt to learn the

game of American football. After the changes and the madness that was Iraq over the past several generations, his prayers became longer, his voice deeper, his readings of the Koran more impassioned, his conversation more tuned to God and the afterlife. And the past.

"Your uncle Hussein used to love chickens," he would say. "Mexican chickens and Chinese chickens and French chickens. Every day he'd come to the house with a new chicken, it drove your grandmother crazy." Then he would look down and shake his head. The Ba'ath killed my uncle Hussein in the early 1980s.

Despite the change, I enjoyed my uncle's company as much now as I did then, even if things were different, for him and me, and so I looked forward to our morning together. Kadhmiya was not far from Baghdad's center; at one point it had been considered a separate district but now, given Baghdad's expansion, was effectively a suburb of it. Kadhmiya is not altogether different from the larger Holy Sites of Najaf and Kerbala. It also housed tombs of two of the later twelve Shi'i disciples of Muhammad, the Imams. Inside, the crowds were thinner in number and less emotional. I thought of it as Najaf or Kerbala lite, far easier to visit because of its proximity to Baghdad but not quite the same experience. My uncle and I had gone many times when I was a child and now we had an opportunity to go once again.

My uncle pointed out the way, navigating in a manner that only an Iraqi could understand. He clearly had no idea what particular street we happened to be driving on, but he did have a general sense of landmarks and slowly made his way among them until we were sufficiently close and reached the marketplace near Kadhmiya.

Like Saadoon Street, Kadhmiya's market had deteriorated considerably under Saddam's rule. Unlike Saadoon Street, Kadhmiya was not prosperous to begin with, and the sight of it could readily lead an unsuspecting visitor to believe he was observing a market that had not changed significantly in hundreds of years. Having traveled this road many times with my uncle as a child, however, this would be an absolutely false impression. Kadhmiya was, when I visited as a child, a very different place. The general items sold in the market were more or less the same, as they were in any Iraqi market: basic staples such as fruits and vegetables, simple household goods such as plastic ware and utensils, and, nearer to the shrine, religious trinkets. But the place had changed; the storefronts now appeared to be on the verge of collapse. What was once a semi-paved lengthy road on which stalls, tables, and basic storefronts were erected was now thick dirt, and I, surmised, mud in the case of rain. The wagons pulling goods in various directions needed repair desperately; that they continued to function at all was no small wonder to me.

"Do you remember what this place was like when we used to come, Ammu?" I asked my uncle (*Ammu* is the Arabic name for uncle).

He looked down with the sad thoughtful eyes that I now associate with him, shook his head very slightly, and mouthed a short prayer.

"I don't think I understand what you are doing. Can you explain it again?" he asked, changing the subject.

"Yes Ammu. I am setting up a law firm. Work is thin right now, but it is all about positioning, until things stabilize. I meet with Americans and Iraqi government officials, and try to take on small matters for little money so that when the situation stabilizes, I find myself in a better position. Just the other day I met the minister of trade."

"He's your mother's relative. That's no feat—you've seen him a million times in London. So what, other than meeting people, do you do, is there legal work?" he asked.

"Sure. We form companies and set up agencies and help on the creation of matters such as these."

"And there are people who will pay American money for this? Can't an Iraqi lawyer do this better than you for about $50 a month?"

"Well, yes, he can, I suppose. But if a big international deal comes in, Iraqi lawyers do not have any idea how to answer the client's questions. They've never encountered a big deal, so they don't know what the client wants, and their isolation prevents them from knowing. I am the bridge between international capital and Iraqi law."

"A bridge." He looked puzzled. "If you will accept advice from me, this is not moneymaking time. I think you should do government work, and help the country draft its laws. That's a good bridge for you, between the Americans and the Governing Council."

If there was anything my uncle had, for all the time that I knew him, it was a highly tuned conscience and a deep, almost all-consuming concern for social justice and the public welfare.

We were silent as we negotiated our way around the market.

"What are the characteristics you seek in an ideal spouse, other than beauty?" my uncle asked suddenly.

His question caught me by surprise, and I was not sure what to say in response. I replied in a more characteristic Iraqi fashion. "What do you think they should be?"

"I'm married, it does not matter," he said, with the hint of the insouciant smile I remember from my youth barely crossing his face.

My plan to avoid the question was foiled. I could not possibly remember what it was I said, even five minutes after I said it, though I am sure it must have been entirely incoherent. Had it made any sense, my uncle would have pursued it further, pushing the discussion in the direction he would like it to go. Instead, he asked only a tangentially related question.

"And would the headscarf mean anything to your wife?" he asked me.

"Oh, it's not important to me, Ammu, though I do respect women who wear it of course." I quickly replied, wishing to neither offend his religious sensibilities nor misrepresent my own views.

"I think it should be. The headscarf is a fundamental part of our religion, and without modesty, true devotion to God is very hard."

"Yes, but I cannot force a woman who does not wear a veil to wear one."

A hurt look crossed his face; he seemed genuinely insulted. "The Americans brainwashed you or something. Did I say force? Did I say marry a woman who does not wear a headscarf and force her to wear one? That, I agree with you, is foolish. I said you pick a woman who already wears one. Then there is no forcing, that's picking wisely."

"I see, so you don't believe in compulsion."

"It's not a question of what I believe, it is a question of what Allah orders, and he says in the Holy Koran there shall be no compulsion in religion."

"I never thought compulsion was anything but counterproductive," I added meekly. Some silence followed.

We finally parked the car and started to make our way to the shrine. I suppose I had not sufficiently considered the consequences of the fact that my uncle was a senior figure in a Shi'i religious party, and we were approaching a Shi'i shrine. In Iraq, this is as close as it may come to a rock star at a nightclub. Hundreds came to kiss his hand, and our prayers at the shrine were difficult as many crowded about seeking to talk to him, or at least shake his hand. I was surprised in many ways, proud in others, but mostly disappointed more than anything in myself.

Of course, my situation in Iraq was different from that of my uncle, but we had both come to the country for a reason. He had left Iran in the spring of 2003 to rebuild a shattered political order and reconstitute a legitimate state where none currently existed. Even if my goals were different, I could not help but compare myself to him, and I fell short in the balance. He was right, I thought, as I saw devotee after devotee approach. This was not a place to make money. I made my way unnoticed to the tomb, grasped its rosewater-scented lattice, and mumbled a prayer as the throngs whirled around me. My professional plans were not working and provided me with no satisfaction. I needed to do something else.

Winter 2003: Concerns Mount

CHAPTER 13

Departure and Return

I LEFT IRAQ IN early October of 2003, once it became clear that my attempt to open a law firm had failed. Clients could not be found. I had accumulated only about $5,000 after several months of effort, and the security situation made a turnaround very unlikely. I left to consider other options. I expected a rapid return within a matter of a week or two, but weeks turned into months—two months, in fact—before I was able to put any new plans into effect. The cause of this delay was partly selfish. I could prattle on at length about the importance of being in Iraq to serve the country, about the essential goodness of the Iraqi people, and about the heart and the head, but after a good cappuccino, an afternoon at a proper gym, and an evening at a quality cinema, all of that seemed to be senti-mental claptrap, capable of deferral. Eventually the cappuccinos, health clubs, and movies became less important, and the desire to return became stronger, but that did take, in my case, about nine and a half weeks.

The other, more important reason for my delay was that I was not sure what to do when I returned to Iraq given that my previous venture had failed. I began to review and search, but ironically it was not through any effort of my own but rather sheer happenstance that I found my next posi-tion. An Iraqi-American recommended me to a friend of hers, who recommended me to the International Human Rights Law Institute of DePaul University, which had just won a contract from the U.S. Agency for International Development to rebuild Iraqi law schools in consultation with the faculties of the law schools themselves. I therefore embarked on an entirely different mission, of reconstruction and not commercialism. I would earn a salary, of course, but less than half of the salary I could expect to be paid at a large New York law firm. Nevertheless, given the circumstances, I found the opportunity far more satisfying than anything else that presented itself.

As I prepared for my departure, Iraq seemed to be continuing on the same stunted path, though where precisely it was leading was not clear. Many of the basic services were in roughly the same shape as they had been when I left two months before, the economic picture remained as bleak, and the violence was about the same. If anything, it had increased. I would therefore be returning to what seemed to be increased levels of danger, with more concern for my safety, but with my hope and optimism still alive. Resistance aside, divisions aside, obstacles and difficulties aside, I still hoped and believed in Iraq's future.

CHAPTER 14

"We Got Him"

I WAS AT THE Frankfurt airport waiting for a plane to take me to Jordan when my new boss, David, called out to me. I had been searching for a muffin while we waited for our plane to Jordan, and David was a floor above looking down at me from an escalator. He was shouting urgently, so I rushed upstairs eager to hear what had happened. I feared that my colleague, the third member of our group to enter Baghdad and an Iraqi-American who would head our Baghdad office, had been injured. Why else would someone shout to come quickly, unless there was an emergency involving one in our party? When I arrived short of breath from the climb, David pointed to a television screen. I saw Paul Bremer, head of the CPA and America's proconsul in Iraq, smiling as he said six words I would never forget.

"Ladies and gentlemen. We got him."

He had used only a pronoun, but I knew whom he meant. Saddam had been caught. I smiled, fought back tears in front of my boss of several days, and tried to appear as impassive and professional as I could. I had waited for thirty years for this moment, and yet, here, now, it didn't feel right to say anything. I had to restrain myself; I didn't think David would ever really understand who Saddam was, to an Iraqi. David was an American, a kind, hardworking and decent person, but not one with any previous connection of any kind to Iraq. I would have conversations with Iraqi relatives and friends about this, I was sure, in the next few days, weeks, and even months, but here, now, in the raw moment of the event, it would have to be different.

I was raised in the United States, Saddam Hussein never could touch me, but I was never more scared of anyone than him. He was the only one I thought could reach me. As a boy, I thought I knew my father would always protect me against any axe murderer or armed-to-the teeth maniac that walked into our house. But Saddam? He killed my father's brother, he could easily kill my father, or so I reasoned as a child, and anyone who could kill my father could surely get to me. Other children may have dreamed of witches, vampires, or serial killers, but to me there was only one serial killer that mattered, and nothing could stop him. Not even God, not to a child like myself at the time. I had prayed, and God had seemed, at the time, to a child's mind, helpless.

Then I was young. Now I considered myself rational, sensible, and well educated, yet until Bremer spoke on that day, and against any sense of reason or logic, I was terrified. I could not help but think it; he might come back. The Americans were already jittery over casualties, he had a network, and most important, he had always found a way to come back. He was never gone. We had asked God too many times for that, and we could never bring ourselves to believing that. Perhaps a reasonable man would tell you the pure illogic of such a belief. But that reasonable man would not be an Iraqi. For us, the story of Saddam Hussein began in the nightmares of children and only ended when a colonial administrator ridiculed by some, despised by others, and liked by very few said those three simple words that warmed my heart, and those of millions of other Iraqis. "We got him."

For that Paul Bremer, if for nothing else, thank you.

CHAPTER 15

Rearrival

I RETURNED TO BAGHDAD in my newfound role as reconstructor several days after Saddam had been caught. I had missed my grandmother during my first trip as she had arrived after I left, and so I had not yet joined her in her home in Iraq. This would be our first occasion to do so, and I looked forward to it.

Though the landing was as hair-raising as it had been the first time, the flight was more comfortable in a propeller driven plane that could hold twelve. It was not filled with military men but with the staff of various nongovernmental organizations. Moreover, our landing was not at the military side of Baghdad's airport but the civilian, still closed to the public but at least resembling in some vague sense an actual airport. The scene was almost Kafkaesque in its bureaucratic normalcy in surreal circumstances. As I approached the immigration desk, an American guard asked me to hand my passport to an Iraqi employee who inspected it.

"Where are you coming from?" he asked.

Only one plane landed in this terminal daily, always from Jordan. So I told him, "Jordan."

"And why are you here?"

The plane I had arrived on only permitted passengers working on reconstruction contracts to fly in them. So I told him, "I am working on a reconstruction contract."

"And how long will you stay?"

I had no definitive answer. "A while, I guess."

"Welcome to Iraq." He stamped my passport.

All the contractors behind me received the same questions and delivered the same answers.

We then collected our bags from a regular baggage claim, though a golf cart could probably have held everything on the plane, and passed through customs, where another Iraqi inspected our bags. Other than our group and the substantial airport staff, there was not another soul in sight. This at an airport designed for thousands. It had immigration, baggage claim, customs, and a curbside, but no people. There was even arrival and departure information on a large 1970s style billboard with movable letters, which from the information it contained may have been frozen in time since 1990, when the U.N. closed the airport. The last plane to depart according to the board was headed for Frankfurt.

We sat at the curbside, waiting seemingly for nothing. Nobody came, nobody went, for over an hour. We were supposed to be picked up by someone from the CPA, but apparently they had been delayed. Finally, a man about twenty-four-years old appeared, accompanied by a colleague of roughly the same age, fully armed and wearing a bulletproof vest. They ushered us into their SUV. They were tall, muscular men, with the short haircuts I always associate with military men. We drove off swiftly and the young men locked and loaded their weapons.

"Don't you worry," one said to me under his breath, "we'll blow the fucking heads off of any motherfucking Haji who looks funny at us." I had read a news report indicating that Americans in Iraq often referred to Iraqis derisively as Hajis. This was the first time I had heard it.

"Fucking Hajis, don't know a fucking thing but a gun, well here's one for them," the other said.

"Hey, sit back, man, we can't see out the back," the first one barked at me.

The two men came with us to the hotel where most of the staff were staying, and offended the hotel security personnel by refusing to leave their weapons at the desk.

"So are you guys private security contractors?" I asked, after they had finished exchanging curses with the hotel guards.

I received dirty looks from that.

"We're *lawyers* buddy, we work on the Mass Graves Excavation Project. We help document Saddam's crimes against the Iraqi people," one exclaimed.

Well at least he didn't say crimes against the motherfucking Hajis, I thought. An immediate question came to mind. "You guys speak any Arabic?"

"What the fuck for? We believe in George W. Bush, we're serious Republicans, and we're here to do our part to take back Iraq. Rule of law, baby. Rule . . . of . . . Law," he said, pausing after each word.

I thought maybe he was expecting a high-five after he'd made this statement; it sounded more like the words of an ESPN sportscaster than anything a lawyer investigating crimes against humanity and promoting the rule of law would say. In addition, the gun hardly jibed with the sentiment respecting the necessity of the rule of law. I recalled the words to a '60s song as he spoke, *Yeah you don't believe in war, but what's that gun you're toting.*

"So where'd you go to law school?" they asked.

"Columbia Law School."

"Fucking New York liberals," one said.

"Where'd you guys go?" I asked.

They told me, but it was not a place I had heard of or recognized. I found it easier to deal with these two after this by smiling and paying no further attention to anything they were saying. Finally they left, to my immense relief, with a promise to attend future events we would inform them about, though I at least did not have the slightest intention of communicating with them again.

Shortly thereafter, I left the hotel and had the driver of my new project take me to my grandmother's house, located in the Iraq in which I wanted to be. I arrived late at night. My parents and my brother, Ali, were there as well. Ali had come to work in Iraq, and my parents had come to see the country again after having been away for nearly two decades. As the car pulled up, everyone came out to the driveway to greet me. My grandmother, being older, waited inside by the door. We shook hands and kissed, and each person grabbed one my bags. It was late fall, and a cool breeze was blowing, swaying the branches of the palm trees in my grandmother's garden. I was happy. This was my home now, and I was going to be here for a while.

I turned to my brother Ali. "Hey, how come Abu Ahmed isn't shooting his gun about Saddam?" I asked.

"You mean that neighbor?" he pointed, toward Abu Ahmed's house. "Saddam was captured a few days ago. The guy ran out of bullets yesterday, I think," Ali smiled. Ali would be sleeping in the room across the hall from me. He had already set up a solar projector on the top floor so we could watch movies together. We walked toward the house together, and my grandmother stepped out.

"Come in, Haider, come in," she shouted. "I am so happy you are here! Did you hear about Saddam? They caught Saddam! I just hope they don't release him again!"

CHAPTER 16

CPA Adrift

Because it was funded by the United States Agency for International Development, our new project was expected to coordinate fairly closely with the CPA in implementation, given the CPA's primary responsibility of governing Iraq during this period of time. We therefore spent several meetings with the CPA explaining our plans and processes, how we would work with the Iraqi law schools, what types of consultations we would need with them in order to set up programs for them, what materials we could provide for their library, and whether other infrastructure would be necessary. At one such early meeting, however, we received a suggestion that was telling of the extent of the CPA's actual isolation from conditions in the rest of Iraq.

"I think part of this law school project should involve you guys teaching Iraqi law students the Spanish language," suggested the top CPA official responsible for advising the Iraqi Justice Ministry.

I was aghast. Hardly any Iraqis spoke decent English, and none that I knew spoke Spanish. Some knew French, particularly those who had studied law given that Iraq's Civil Code is largely French in origin. Spain, however, had no significant history or connection of any kind with Iraq, nor did Latin America.

"Sorry, did you say Spanish?" I asked.

"Yup," he replied self-assuredly.

"I see. Let me ask you, why Spanish?" I asked.

"Well, really, if you know something about the Iraqi system, you would know that the Spanish have a civil law system, just like the Iraqis, and the Spanish are participating in the reconstruction of Iraq," he began to explain.

"Uh huh. But wouldn't French be better then? I mean, the code is largely Napoleonic," I said.

"The French won't help, and they want Iraq to fail," he said determined and slightly annoyed at the suggestion. "They aren't here, are they? They could have joined our coalition, they didn't. Fuck them."

I stared at him. I couldn't believe that he was seriously suggesting that in proposing languages of instruction, deep and broad cultural considerations were less important than the question of who helped America invade in 2003. But I said nothing. David and Sermid, who ran our Baghdad office, were with me, and from their glances it seemed they were not eager to engage in a quarrel over this. I knew neither of them would support any kind of Spanish language instruction, but both considered it worthwhile to humor the old man while we remained in the Green Zone and then do what we wanted once we left. Probably the prudent course, even if a maddening one.

CHAPTER 17

Finance Committee

IN ADDITION TO MY work with the Iraqi law schools, soon after my arrival in Baghdad I began to advise the Finance Committee of the Iraq Governing Council at the request of Adnan Pachachi, a member of the Governing Council. Dr. Pachachi was himself advised by my friend Fareed, and Fareed had arranged this opportunity. I was grateful for it. I very much wanted to be more involved in Iraqi policy making and legislation.

The function of the Finance Committee was to review legislation prepared by the CPA in the form of "Orders" and provide input respecting those Orders to the Iraq Governing Council, which could only give advisory opinions respecting the legislation. The impact of my work was, therefore, somewhat limited. Nevertheless, I found preparing Orders quite fascinating as an exercise in cultural relations between two vastly different societies.

The chair of the Finance Committee was Ahmed Chalabi, known as the friend of the neoconservatives and once reputed to be the Pentagon's favorite as the first ruler of Iraq after Saddam fell. His star had fallen to some degree by the end of 2003, as violence raged and the neoconservative vision of Iraq had not come to pass. Dr. Chalabi was also my mother's cousin, though I had startlingly few dealings with him over the years. Nevertheless, other than he and I, very few in the room were bicultural. The others were either Americans who had never seen Iraq prior to their arrival with the CPA, or Iraqis who knew America from recycled sitcoms on bad satellite television. The potential for confusion, misunderstanding, and even mutual contempt was immense, as one session concerning intellectual property made clear.

The CPA official began the meeting by testifying to the benefits of broad intellectual property protection, indicating at one point that Iraq could become like Singapore, a haven for companies who need to protect their intellectual property in an otherwise hostile region.

In response to this, an Iraqi representative shot up his hand in the middle of this session. He asked, in Arabic, "Wouldn't it be better to make software freely distributed and do the opposite of this law? Then we would be a haven for distribution of these things for cheap. That makes more sense than this Singapore stuff you are talking about."

"That is piracy," the CPA representative explained, after her translator told her what had just been said. "That's illegal."

"It's not illegal if we don't have a law against it," added another Iraqi.

Dr. Chalabi cut off this line of questioning. "Guys, we can't have laws allowing software piracy. We need a law that looks more respectable than that."

"But the prices of software might be high then, and how do we import it?" asked another Iraqi. "Why do we need this law, I oppose it."

"Guys, look, CD kabob will continue, piracy won't go away soon, but you can't formally legalize it," Dr. Chalabi said. "Nobody does that. Let's move on."

The Iraqis seemed placated, though the CPA representative looked distraught at the admission of future rampant privacy. She finished her presentation. A few asked questions, then Dr. Chalabi turned to me, the first time he had done so in the entire series of meetings I had attended and asked, in Arabic, "What do you think about this?"

I paused, surprised that he had directed the question to me. "What's the point?" I asked, quietly, so that the translator couldn't hear me. "This woman comes in from the CPA and starts comparing Iraq to Singapore, as if the problem with our being a software center has something to do with intellectual property laws and nothing to do with the fact that there are people riding donkeys who are carrying mortars and aiming them at any tall building they can find. Iraqis have other priorities. Hell, I don't think most of them know what intellectual property means."

I was rambling, and realized I might offend some listeners. I switched to English, "Dr. Chalabi, half of the guys here don't know what intellectual property means. They want a law allowing piracy. We are wasting our time."

"So no objections?" interrupted the CPA officer, looking at Dr. Chalabi. He looked at me, asking if I had anything to say publicly.

I sighed. "I'll write some small comments to you ma'am but other than that, it's fine."

The meeting then ended.

CHAPTER 18

Basra

IN CONNECTION WITH OUR Iraq legal education project, we had selected three law schools with which to work in different parts of the country. These were the law schools in Baghdad, in Suleymania, a city in the north of Iraq, and in Basra, Iraq's only port, lying in the south on the border with both Iran and Kuwait. In order to have a better idea of the ways in which we could help in the process of legal education in Iraq in the context of these three schools, discussions and consultations with the faculty were critical. To that end, in December of 2003, we scheduled a trip to Basra, to be followed in January of 2004 to Suleymania. David, the executive director of the program, had returned to Chicago, leaving Sermid, Zuhair, our office manager, and me to take these trips.

I had never been to Basra prior to this trip. I had not made any deliberate decision to avoid going; I had just never thought of it as being particularly important. I had no family in Basra, Basra had no particular attraction to the casual tourist or the religious pilgrim, and it was not an ideal place to visit during my trips to Iraq prior to the first Gulf War, when the war with Iran had just ended and Basra, the second largest city in Iraq, was a pile of rubble.

Most Iraqis from beyond Basra tended to have the same opinion of the city. The overwhelming majority of my family, whether they were long-term expatriates or Iraqi residents who had never left, had never stepped foot in Basra. Even the idea that I was going to go there received puzzled looks—from CPA officials, family members, barbers, and taxi drivers alike, followed by the inevitable question, What's in Basra?

Fortunately, due to my new position, which involved work with Basra University, I had a good enough reason, and on a personal level, I also looked forward to seeing a part of Iraq I had never seen before.

Our travel did not begin auspiciously. Intending to travel in a two-car convoy, Baghdad's impossible traffic and a dense fog swiftly separated Zuhair and me from Sermid's automobile as we approached the Diyala Bridge that led to routes south of the city. We soon found ourselves alone in the midst of a traffic jam that seemed absolutely surreal.

The entire road had been diverted from the four lane Diyala Bridge to a wide muddy expanse just to the left of the river. There was no road as such, and because of the fog, I could only see about twenty yards in any direction. These twenty yards revealed a landscape of red mud and motor vehicles of every conceivable variety moving in whatever way they could manage, but certainly without lanes or any form of directional order. Rusty trucks stickered with Quranic verses or other Islamic phrases grinded gears and slipped and slid dangerously close to nearby cars, kicking up dank clomps of mud that fell in their vicinity. Busses loaded with Shi'i pilgrims plowed along slowly through the mud as their inhabitants chanted in religious devotion to the Imams. Pickup trucks attempted to force their way through the morass, their drivers screaming expletives at whoever happened to be in their way. Huge semis dragging along prefab houses were in the midst of this chaos, oblivious to anything that might be alongside them. The remaining vehicles were ordinary cars like our own, trying to fill any gaps that appeared, honking and cursing and spinning and accelerating and braking, often at the same time. And everywhere on the ground was a blanket of thoroughly trod red mud several feet deep.

An hour passed before we realized that the difficulty lay in the fact that we had been diverted onto a single lane bridge, and there was absolutely nothing by way of organization to prevent drivers in both directions from repeatedly entering onto the bridge, and being stuck facing each other screaming at each other in the process. By the time we approached the bridge, we heard that one of the prominent Shi'i religious organizations had dispatched its paramilitary units to set some semblance of order, much to the praise of the driver of my car as well as the occupants of nearby cars, all of whom cursed the Americans for causing problems that never previously existed. The American refusal to direct traffic was understandable enough for security reasons, but nonetheless devastating in effect. It was a safe assumption that the Americans had closed the main bridge, and their decision, however well-reasoned, to send us off in this direction without taking further care to organize the traffic earned them many enemies, and the Shi'i religious groups not a few friends.

On the other side of the river, we kept driving, hoping that the nightmare would end soon, not realizing that it was about to start. Another hour later, as we returned to the base of the bridge on the other bank, we saw what had closed it. Someone had detonated an explosive device beside an American tank, and the debris of a Hummer and several Iraqi cars, along with a slightly damaged tank, was visible. Several bloodied and lifeless Iraqi bodies, both men and women, were being dragged this way and that by American forces. One soldier lay on the ground wounded, attended to by several others, and around the perimeter were soldiers standing with guns pointed in the direction of the snarling traffic, fingers on triggers, visibly tense.

Then from behind us, in Jeeps and Hummers and Bradleys, other American soldiers suddenly approached, shouting at the traffic to part ways, leaving their vehicles and jumping over our own to make more progress, firing into the air, with terrifying hatred in their eyes.

Their anger notwithstanding, it was clear to me that the real victims of this attack were Iraqis. We were to learn later that not a single soldier had been killed. No doubt their vehicles had been built to withstand such types of weapons and indeed they did not appear to the naked eye to have been seriously damaged. Not so for the 1970s-manufactured, cheap, and barely functioning motor vehicles that were unfortunate enough to be close to the American vehicles when the explosion occurred. Each of them looked as if the device had been detonated inside their particular vehicle. The only surprise to me had been that the corpses remained so intact. It was a gruesome and nauseating sight, but it didn't even make the news. No American soldiers were killed, there had been a larger explosion in a busy

Baghdad shopping district the same day, so this incident was ignored. It was simply typical of twenty to thirty attacks that were taking place in the country on a daily basis. An entirely banal act of the noble "resistance."

Eventually we passed through all the commotion and several hours later arrived in Basra, checked into our hotel, and fell straight asleep.

CHAPTER 19

Basra II

WE IRAQIS HAVE A saying to signify the passing of a considerable period of time, somewhat analogous to the amount of time that might pass, in idiomatic English, between two blue moons: *After the destruction of Basra.* For example, our meetings have gone well so there is no need to meet again until after the destruction of Basra. Or, I don't see my college roommates very often now that we live in different cities, but I am sure that I will see them again, after the destruction of Basra.

Basra is Iraq's only real port city, with Kuwait lying to her south, Iran to her east, and an often hostile Baghdad-based and non-federal Iraq governing her from the north. Its repeated destruction with some degree of regularity, was taken as a given. This was so even prior to the emergence of Iraq as a nation, as the city lay at the edge of Ottoman-dominated Iraq, on the border with Persia.

But even given the fatalism manifested in the above aphorism, the people of Basra have endured more in the last twenty years than can be imagined. The waves of near total destruction the city has suffered and the subsequent neglect after each wave of destruction became obvious upon entering the city. I wept at the sight of Baghdad suffering from such profound dereliction during Saddam's reign, but the decline of Basra seemed considerably worse. It was less emotional for one, like myself, who had never seen it earlier, but heartrending all the same.

Hundreds of thousands of date palms used to grace the southern reaches of this city, sweeping gently toward the borders with Kuwait and Iran. Now, only harsh desert stood for miles, the Ba'ath regime having razed the date palms in the nine year war with Iran. The Shatt Al-Arab used to be a beautiful waterfront on Basra's eastern edge, where children played and families strolled along the shore as boats could be seen all along the waterway, ferrying passengers eager to leave the city for an hour or two of leisure across to smaller villages on the other side, or up and down the river itself to view the gardens and gardens of date palms. Now, tankers that looked like they were last used more than two decades ago sat cold and rusted at the water's edge. Few ventured to the river to see them, and none would dare go after the hour of six in the evening. As for the other side of the river, that was where the bloodiest battles of the Iraq-Iran war took place, where hundreds of thousands of soldiers on both sides were mowed down in what has been called World War I–style trench warfare but was in fact much worse, given the indifference on the part of either side toward human life. The Iraqi Republican Guard enforced orders to advance on well-fortified Iranian trenches by killing any Iraqi soldier who refused to move into the suicidal hail of bullets. So many bodies were cut down so quickly that there was not enough time to bury them, and more often than not dogs consumed the remains. This, for obvious reasons, was no longer a place that Basra residents tended to go during leisure hours.

Buildings and infrastructure still showed signs of devastation. Lacking the funds to repair many of the roads and buildings, it appeared that the residents of Basra moved their storefronts back into whatever shells of structures remained, and carried on as before. More or less used to this state of affairs, they seemed content that Baghdad had begun to ignore them again, that their police controlled the streets more effectively than the entirely ignored Baghdad police force, and that the pro-Saddam "uprising" currently taking place elsewhere had not reached Basra. They remained hopeful that whatever happened in the center of the country would not cause them further misery. Underneath this, however, lay a barely concealed anger—at the United States, at Saddam, at Iraqis outside of Basra who had been so neglectful of the interests of their port, and at a very unsteady state of affairs following decades of torment.

Yet what angered the people of Basra about the United States more than these attacks was what followed. According to popular legend, on the Iraqi army's return from Kuwait after its humiliating defeat, a frustrated Iraqi captain, in the middle of Basra's central square, named Sa'ad Square, aimed the turret of his tank directly at a picture of Saddam Hussein and fired. And thus began what is known in Iraq as the 1991 Intifada, which swept through the south and north of Iraq. It was widely believed then that the first President Bush, who spoke of the horrors of Saddam Hussein and urged his overthrow, would come to their aid when they sought to do what he asked. That did not happen.

I remember 1991 well. I was a young college student, initially stridently opposed to the war in Iraq but passionately supportive of the Intifada that followed and well aware through family of the devastation wrought by Saddam on those opposing his rule. Those were trying times. General Schwarzkopf's explanation that in fact America was maintaining a position of neutrality struck me as military cant. To bomb a country as extensively as the Americans did, to urge the replacement of the Saddam Hussein regime as they did, and then to stand by as the rebellion took place, knowing who would win in such a conflict and the means the victors would use to cement their triumph was from my moral perspective an absolute outrage.

But I was in the United States and the world went on. Gradually, America's perfidy faded into the background. I had law school to attend, a new city to move to, new friends to make, and I was not going to live in the past forever. Once in a while, I would remember what happened, particularly when Colin Powell was proving so popular in the United States despite his role in the betrayal, but these thoughts quickly faded to the background. Standing in Sa'ad Square, however, the anger welled up inside me again. It is a nondescript square, entirely unmarked, with a gas station on one corner and an ice cream stand on the other. I didn't even know where I was until I asked. Yet once I was told, I remembered everything and was struck by a blinding rage at a memory of the past. In Sa'ad Square, rage and anger at what happened, what America did, over a decade ago are the only things I can feel. I could almost taste the bile in my throat.

The point, however, is deeper than my own feelings. The people of Basra pass by Sa'ad Square every single day of their lives. They felt the effect of U.S. sustained sanctions for twelve years, the same twelve years that I spent going to law school, working for a federal judge, and traveling the world as an international corporate attorney. While they were cut off from the world, their law schools unable to continue updating their libraries, their medical facilities suffering from continual deterioration, their valuables being sold to feed their families, I was accumulating wealth, prestige, and experience. I had the luxury to forget, they did not. So when the United States decided twelve years later to reverse its initial mistake and remove Saddam Hussein from power, for me it was as if only a year had passed, and I expected the reaction to be much the same as it would have been in 1991—overwhelming joy, candies, and flowers. But the hatred had burned deep, the rage never subsided, and the suspicion of U.S. motives was forever embedded. The absolute abhorrence of the people of Basra to the regime of Saddam Hussein, along with hopes that perhaps a Shi'i–led government would emerge from the rubble of the previous regime led to their grudging support of the Americans this time. Never, however, candies and flowers.

Given the past twenty years, it would take a long, long time for this barrier of suspicion to disappear. It won't happen until long after the destruction of Basra.

CHAPTER 20

Basra III

BASRA WAS A CITY gripped by a rising tide of Islamism. Well over 90 percent of the women on the streets of the city wear headscarves, and the walls of the shops are adorned with the photos of prominent Shi'i scholars, some killed by Saddam, others sworn enemies of the Ba'ath Republic: among them, Muhammad Baqr al-Sadr, killed by Saddam in 1980, Muhammad Baqr al-Hakim, killed in Najaf in August, and Muhammad al-Sadr, killed by Saddam in 1999. Islamist women are also given due recognition, of a strictly non-photographic sort. Basra's girls' school has been renamed in honor of Muhammad Baqr al-Sadr's sister, Bint al-Huda, an activist in Islamic women's causes and killed by Saddam along with her brother.

The greatest irony of all, however, lay at the gates of the university itself, where one is greeted with, among other portraits, a large framed photograph of the Ayatollah Khomeini, mortal enemy of Saddam and the United States both. Ayatollah Khomeini had spent a decade attempting to enter Basra, and never succeeded. Now, because of the actions of the United States, his picture adorns the gates of Basra University.

As one ventured beyond the Khomeini picture and into the grounds of Basra University, more evidence of Islamism could be seen. The bearded guards who stopped us just as we entered were almost hostile to our presence. They wondered what we had come to Basra to do. After finding Zuhair's music tapes in the car, they insisted that such tapes be played one by one to ensure that they contained nothing seditious. Zuhair complied, explaining to them with each song that was played who the singer was, what country they were from, and any other identifiable unique characteristics that could be identified. The guards seemed amused by Zuhair's digressions, though not terribly interested in the information he was providing. Our car was searched thoroughly a second time. After this, I, the lone person on the trip without Iraqi citizenship, was made to fulfill one requirement.

One of the guards glared at me. "You! Are you Iraqi?"

"Yes," I replied in Arabic, "I am Iraqi."

"Then recite the Shahada!"

The Shahada is the Muslim profession of faith, which has nothing to do with Iraqi citizenship or nationality. Nevertheless, I had no inclination to argue.

I began, "I testify that there is no deity but God, and I testify that Muhammad is the Apostle of God."

"And?" he continued to glare. I knew he wanted the uniquely Shi'i addition.

"And that Ali is near to God."

"Enter!" he said, and pointed.

As we advanced toward the College of Law, we noticed statues that had been erected at the university had had their heads removed. A woman without a headscarf was a rare sight indeed.

The college itself was a drab building devoid of facilities of almost every kind, including chalkboards, desks, chairs, tables, and whatever else might be considered standard in a university setting. Some of these fixtures had recently arrived at the school, but the situation was still plainly inadequate. In light of this, the faculty welcomed our presence as a potential source of revenue to improve their law school, but they were unsure of our motives. While all of them apologized for the treatment we had been subjected to at the entrance gate, they asked pointedly whether we had come to Basra on some sort of American project to remove any mention of Shari'a, the Islamic religious code, from their curriculum.

When we informed them that we neither sought nor intended to do anything against the will of the university faculty, they relaxed, though they reiterated the point several times throughout our meeting that the country's laws, and the university's curriculum, must be largely based on the Shari'a. They also let us know that studies of other legal systems were acceptable and, in fact, to be encouraged. I did not mention the Spanish language proposal, however. As we were preparing to leave, one of the faculty members spoke up.

"Professors Sermid and Haider, we need something we haven't yet discussed," said Wasit, clearly one of the more progressive and thoughtful members of the faculty.

"Please, tell us," Sermid said.

"Some of the top students in our classes are women. They want to get master's degrees. They deserve master's degrees, and some deserve PhD's. But the Ministry of Higher Education will not give us permission for graduate studies. Tell them you will fund it and I think they will agree."

"I don't think we have the funding," Sermid explained. "I can talk to the CPA and USAID, but sometimes I am not sure they listen. They might say there is a graduate program in Baghdad, tell the women to go there. And of course I know . . ."

Howls of protest interrupted him. A more conservative professor, Ali, said, "Our women aren't going to Baghdad unaccompanied!"

"Not everyone has a relative in Baghdad," another added. "What about the ones who don't?"

"And there are cultural and social norms they have to respect," chimed in a third.

"We will see," I told them. "We don't expect the other things you requested will be a problem, including of course the Shari'a books you wanted."

"The Americans will let you buy us Shari'a books?" asked Wasit.

"Yes, I cannot imagine they would object to that," said Sermid.

"But the Americans won't let us educate our women here in Basra?" said the younger professor. "I don't understand. I thought Americans liked women being educated."

"They do," I replied, "but they think women should be able to travel."

"Well, here in Iraq they won't even if maybe they should, so if they don't let us open a graduate school here, then we can't educate our women at that level," Wasit interrupted mildly, but with a slight tone of indignation.

"Yes, Professor Wasit, you are right," Sermid said, "but we have to explain that, and besides, our budget is dedicated to other things."

"Okay," said Wasit, "but explain it. The Americans have to understand something about this country if they are going to try to run it."

CHAPTER 21

Car

ALMOST SIX MONTHS INTO my residency in Baghdad, at the start of 2004 and between our Basra and Suleymania trips, I purchased an automobile. This was an inevitable development; Baghdad, like Los Angeles, is a large city geographically where people of all incomes live in a house with a yard (there are fewer than 31,000 apartment units in a city of five million people), and a car was necessary to get around. I could have attempted to master Baghdad's nearly unfathomable public transportation system, but this seemed less than appealing for several reasons.

First, I doubted that the current government exerted sufficient control to collect fares from the buses. As a result, I suspected that the system was not so public in that most of the fare went to the fortunate driver in whose possession the bus happened to be on April 9, when the former regime fell. Also, as far as I was able to gather from casual observation, the system involved vehicles of various types going in every conceivable direction and charging every conceivable fare with no indication anywhere as to what the fare or the route was supposed to be. If I were to ask the driver, I would get an answer, but unless the answer involved the recitation on his part of the exact location where I wanted to go, I wouldn't really have any idea whether it was the right bus, given my general ignorance of the city. This stemmed partly from my relative newness to the city, partly from the fact that so many roads had been closed by the Americans that the proper route was often hardly a direct one, but mostly because finding a Baghdad road map was difficult, so I did not have the opportunity to study one. In addition to these problems, asking a bus driver for the proper fare was extremely foolish, as it would advertise my ignorance to him and guarantee that he would respond with a heavily inflated price. I decided rather quickly that purchasing a car was a better option.

Iraqis were not predisposed to make fast decisions in purchasing items such as automobiles, a result I think of the large amounts of idle time they tended to have, their financial limitations, and the severe consequences that could often follow from making any sort of rash decision in a totalitarian society. I had found this to be a problem often enough at the universities, where we could not do so much as purchase shelves for a law school library without either going through numerous channels for approval, or, in our case, bypassing this process by claiming that we were acting on direct orders from Paul Bremer himself.

When going to buy the car, I brought along Abu Mustafa, a nephew of our family's housekeeper who I hoped to hire as my personal driver (thereby perpetuating in practice the class system which I have vocally opposed in theory). We began our search with a conversation.

"Abu Mustafa, I have to have a car very, very soon." I said. "It is urgent."

"You mean like in a month? It seems fast but maybe we can spend time looking and we will find one. I have a cousin actually who is selling his car."

"Actually, not in a month, in a week," I said. Silence. "Don't worry," I added, "I accept full responsibility. I just want your advice. I will assume authority for the decision."

"Okay, as you wish then." Now that Abu Mustafa could not be held responsible for a mistake, he relaxed noticeably.

Baghdad car dealerships were organized much like all other forms of standard commerce in Iraq. It was, to my mind, an unfathomable system wherein each car dealer congregated with every other car dealer in select areas, so that buyers needed only to walk a small, tightly packed street to find a large number of dealers and a large assortment of cars. From the point of view of the consumer, the system worked quite well for obvious enough reasons, but I had to wonder why the car dealers chose to place themselves among dozens of other competitors selling precisely the same thing.

By the standards of the rest of the Iraqi market, the car market was fairly well developed. The cars were clean, the roads and stores were clearly marked, and the signs of dilapidation and decay that existed throughout many other markets in Iraq were nowhere to be seen. Still, this was not an American dealership. Cars were tightly packed within the lots themselves and double- and triple-parked on the road outside them, so that a single file of vehicle traffic was permitted to pass on a road that was either deeply packed dirt or barely navigable mud, depending on the weather. Additionally, because there was no clearly correct direction of travel, cars were frequently facing each other and drivers blared their horns at one another, each gesturing vigorously at the other to move, until a dealer's assistant casually sauntered out and tried to adjust the locations of his automobiles to allow the cars to pass each other. This usually required another assistant of another dealer to move his cars, and considerable time transpired before traffic advanced. Not yet having a car ourselves, we were like the other pedestrians, left to dodge traffic from wherever it came and make our way forward among the dealerships.

The cars at this particular upscale center were priced approximately between $3,000 and $9,000. At the lower end of the spectrum are the Korean cars (Opel and Daewoo) and the upper end consisted of later-model German cars (Mercedes and BMW), though nothing I found had been manufactured before the year 2000. Still, by Iraqi standards, this was upscale. Most cars on the street were in considerably worse shape than the cars we found on display.

The most popular car in Iraq is, in fact, a far cheaper model than any Opel or Daewoo we could find. It is the Brazilian Volkswagen, which has a long and storied history in Iraq. Apparently, Volkswagen at some point in the early 1980s decided to begin manufacturing a lower end model of the Passat from a factory in Brazil (to distinguish it, of course, from Volkswagen's many high luxury models). They looked very similar to any other Passats I had seen, though given the many complaints about them I suspected they were not nearly as reliable. How so many of these cars managed to find their way into Iraq remains a mystery to me, though the common explanation was that Brazil required Iraq to purchase large numbers of them to compensate Brazil for providing weapons to Iraq during the war with Iran. Somehow the explanation struck me as less than entirely satisfactory, if nothing else because it seemed hard to believe that the Brazilian government would prefer that Iraq pay Volkswagen in exchange for weapons supplied by the Brazilian government. But whatever the cause, the Brazilian Volkswagen soon became a virtual symbol of Iraq. One could not travel anywhere in the 1980s in Iraq without seeing a new, handsome, recognizable hatchback with the unmistakable decal dominating the lower part of the rear windshield reading "Made in Brazil." The cars were cheap, but plentiful, symbolic of a people shaken by war but still seeing themselves as upwardly mobile.

Brazil stopped manufacturing these particular cars in the late 1980s. Nonetheless, fifteen years later, Brazilian Volkswagens still dominate the Iraqi landscape. The cars were now rusted and worn, their windows usually did not function, they had nothing approaching climate control, and in many cases their frames looked as if they may have been in many an accident. Thus they were symbolic once again, but this time of the devastating neglect to which Iraq had been subject over the past decade.

By contrast, the cars in this dealership were all "new," manufactured in the 1990s, and most had effective climate control, power windows and brakes, and other modern amenities that were more or less standard in the United States. Ironically, of all the amenities, it was the air conditioning that was often lacking in the automobiles, in a country where the summer temperature often exceeded 120 degrees, and even more ironically, it was often in the higher-end models where the absence was found. I suppose it demonstrated another well-known, long-standing characteristic of Iraqis: an insufferable predisposition toward ostentation, at times verging on the vulgar. The car mattered, but the air conditioning, which nobody could see, was less important.

I had little use for such showiness, partly because I liked to think myself above it but more importantly because the security situation made this type of display extremely unwise. A $400 Brazilian Volkswagon would almost never be stolen, but a $12,000 Mercedes was a considerable risk. For me, the balance needed to be somewhere between those two, something that was comfortable but at the same time did not run a high risk of theft.

In the end, I settled on a 1997 Daewoo Prince for $4,050. I was unsure as to why the dealer had been unwilling, after much negotiation, to lower his price another $50, but he insisted on $4,050, and I was not going to let the final $50 break the deal. Some relatives were concerned for me because they still found the car far too expensive and thought it ran the risk of being stolen, but I simply could not have proceeded much lower without a serious detriment to my comfort level.

Unfortunately, I could not actually own my car. I tried to register it in my name, consistent with the foreign investment law promulgated by the CPA, but then found that nobody would allow the car's license plates to be fully registered without my having Iraqi citizenship papers. My efforts to get those papers had not been successful, and my waving a six-page foreign investment law signed in English by Paul Bremer around the registrar I knew would get me nowhere. This was the CPA's crown jewel, its proudest piece of law to date, and about which its personnel boasted endlessly. In theory, the law permitted foreigners to own virtually anything in Iraq, including cars, and this had proved highly controversial.

But most of the debate about the law seemed academic. In reality, I couldn't even register a car in my name, much less an oil refinery. In the end, I was forced to "sell" the car to my cousin and have him register the license plates. This, as well as my lack of an Iraqi driver's license, could present some difficulties in a lawful society, as a policeman would soon realize that I was driving, without a domestic license, a car that was not registered to me. But in Iraq, a short explanation and a handsome bribe would cure that problem.

Now that I had the car, finding my way about the city was becoming easier, but not without its challenges. Most problematic for me was the curious bend the river took in the middle of the city. There was a square just before Freedom Square where, if one stood facing the Karrada district of Baghdad, one could have turned left and after 600 yards crossed the suspension bridge over the river Tigris to the Green Zone, turned right and immediately crossed the two-story bridge over the Tigris into the Saydia district, or turned around and after about a mile crossed the Jadriya Bridge over the Tigris into the Harthiya district. Three directions, three bridges, one river. For someone as directionally challenged as I am, this presented enormous complications.

Street names were another source of difficulty, though I was starting to adapt to them. The main problem was that the names of the streets on the street signs bore scant resemblance to what Iraqis called them. There was a street that ran through the heart of Karrada that Saddam Hussein chose to call Yasser Arafat Street. At some point after the invasion, someone in the largely Shi'i neighborhood placed placards on the street declaring it to be "Imam Mahdi Street," named after the twelfth, hidden Imam, or leader, of Shi'i Muslims, whose appearance would set in motion the chain of events leading to Armageddon. Most likely, some troublemaker tore down one or more of those signs and replaced them with a sign declaring the street to be "Omar Ibn Al-Khattab Street," after the second caliph of Sunni Islam, so hated by the Shi'is that very few Shi'is would ever name their sons Omar despite the relative popularity of the name throughout the Arab world. Those signs lasted one hour. In a silly act of Shi'i defiance, another street in the Karrada district soon took a Shi'i name, Safinat al-Najat, or the Ark of Salvation, an appellation given to the martyred Imam Hussein. Yet despite the plethora of signs and slogans, I had never in my life heard either of the two streets referred to as anything but Inner Karrada Street and Abi Nuwas Street, the same names that were in use long before Saddam took power. Signs bearing those names, however, were nowhere to be found.

Though I had initially intended to make use of Abu Mustafa as my driver for all purposes, I began after no more than a week to rely on him less often during nonworking hours, choosing to drive myself instead. There were obvious risks to driving in Baghdad at night on my own, but I had become more of a fatalist, in line I suppose with the temper of the region as well as the reality of life here. Ultimately, my life was more subject to the whims of fate than any precautionary actions I might or might not fail to take.

CHAPTER 22

Suleymania

SERMID, ZUHAIR, AND I took our second trip in connection with our project in January of 2004, this time to the city of Suleymania, with the same purpose as our trip to Basra; namely, to engage and consult with the faculty in the College of Law respecting areas where our project could assist in the legal education process. Suleymania was worlds removed from Baghdad's chaos and Basra's devastation. Deep in the northern Kurdish region of the country, surrounded by mountains, and well beyond the reach of the current violence, Suleymania was calm, peaceful, and relatively prosperous.

The Kurds were well aware of the relative placidity of the region, publicly attributing it to the fact that they had been free of Saddam Hussein for the past thirteen years, but privately attributing it to the inability of the Arabs generally to interfere in their affairs. For the most part and with some justification, the Kurds tended to be very distrustful of Arabs entering their territory. *Pesh merga* (Kurdistan's historic guerrilla units that now function as a principal security force within the region) asked us to register our names at two checkpoints, and searched our cars at several more on the drive from Baghdad. Our Kurdish driver helped to ease tensions, and we soon noticed that English, while far less understood than Arabic, resulted in our receiving considerably more respect by security officials. From then on, at any checkpoint or with any policeman, I became an American guest of the University of Suleymania and was more often than not allowed through with minimal difficulty.

The Kurdish distrust of our presence even reflected itself in the mosques, where we could not pretend as easily to be American guests of the university given that we were praying in an obviously Muslim manner. Those in the mosques eyed us suspiciously and followed us around rather closely, until it became clear to them from the manner of our prayers that we were Shi'i, at which point tensions swiftly dissolved. That this took place in largely Sunni mosques in largely Sunni Kurdistan is no small irony—akin to a suspicious and distrustful Protestant congregation being relieved that the guests who had just entered their church were Catholics—but entirely in keeping with Iraq's current political reality. Both the Shi'a and Sunni Kurds had felt marginalized, abused, and mistreated by every previous Sunni Arab-dominated Iraqi regime, and the Kurds, therefore, tended to be more kindly disposed to the Shi'a.

Outside of the mosques, Islamic fervor did not appear to be a major force in Kurdistan. Headscarves could be seen, but tended to be the exception, not the rule. Groups of young men and women walking together were common, alcohol could be found almost anywhere, and the thick full beards and chadors that were the sign of the deeply devoted were rare.

When I looked on the streets of Kurdistan, when I saw children playing safely beyond dusk, when I saw the shopping areas and parks that were secure if not terribly developed, and when I witnessed among the city's residents a certain satisfaction with the way things were and a hope that they would remain this way, I had hope for the rest of this tattered, ruined nation. It may have taken thirteen years, economic development may still have been in its infancy, and corruption may have been rampant, but Kurdistan was safe and happy. It was at least a first step.

CHAPTER 23

Suleymania II

IN THE ARAB PARTS of Iraq, the Kurds were regarded, in jokes and ordinary conversation, like Poles once were, unfairly, in the United States—as well-meaning and friendly people but fundamentally stupid and especially lacking any sort of common sense or street intelligence. If an Arab were to make three rights to go left, for example, someone might have told him that he was driving like a Kurd.

I of course was not a believer in such silly stereotypes and attributed them mostly to the unfamiliarity on the part of Kurds with the Arabic language, which could have appeared to non-contemplative native speakers to be a form of stupidity. So I regarded it as a matter of some irony that our Kurdish driver, in order to reach our hotel, deliberately passed the front door of the establishment, and then made three successive rights to try to park the car along the left side of the hotel, despite the fact that ample parking appeared to be available along the front. Not finding a parking spot at that location, he made four successive right turns to end up in the same spot and seemed somewhat surprised that there was no parking there, where he had been not a minute earlier. He then made another right back to the front of the hotel, which he had already passed twice, and was relieved to see that parking was in fact available there, as it had been all along. Zuhair and I looked at each other puzzlingly.

"Kaka (the Kurdish word for Sir), you are driving like a—" said Zuhair.

"A what?" asked our driver.

"A Turkoman," Zuhair quickly replied, wisely refraining from making the reflexive Kurdish stereotype that could have meant trouble for both of us.

The Turkomen, another of Iraq's ethnic groups, have never been the subject of stereotypes of this sort. Nevertheless, our driver seemed rather amused and pleased that the Arabs had started making fun of the Turkomen, partly because he assumed that meant they were leaving the Kurds alone for once, and partly because there are some significant frictions between the Kurds and Turkomen in certain parts of Iraq, particularly Kirkuk. Throughout the remainder of our time with our driver, he made repeated comments about someone or other behaving, driving, acting, dancing, and even walking like a Turkoman.

"Look at that restaurant called MaDonal. It is supposed to be McDonald's, but those Turkomen can't spell. And they can't cook either, the real McDonald's is much better," he said on one occasion. Another time, "What is that child, a Turkoman? Why is he carrying the milk like that? It's spilling everywhere." Once, he even shouted, "Stupid Turkoman driver. Pull over, let a Kurd drive!"

I smiled uneasily at each comment, unsure of what other reaction was appropriate.

We soon found that our driver was not the only person in Kurdistan who, to use our driver's preferred phrasing, had a Turkoman's sense of direction. One time, we asked an older fellow for direction to the hills.

"Go right," he said, pointing left.

"Maybe his Arabic is weak," I told Zuhair. "Sir, do you mean left?" I asked, pointing left.

"No, no. *Right,*" he said again, pointing more urgently to the left. Right was indeed the correct direction.

Suleymania had stunning vistas in its hills. Beyond the many mountains before us lay the border with Iran, and beneath us nestled in a placid valley unaware of the nation in which it happened to be sitting was the center of the city. The air was fresh and crisp, devoid of the diesel fumes that dominated most of the rest of Iraq, the wind brisk, and the entire scene altogether refreshing. After a cumulative twenty weeks in lawless, violent, and unstable Iraq, this almost felt like Switzerland to me, though this comparison would be ridiculous to anyone who had not spent much time in Baghdad. Sermid, Zuhair, and I only lunched in the hills, but I felt considerably different when I returned, happy to know that there was refuge in this troubled land. Iraq really is a beautiful country, rich in historical tradition, natural resources, culture, and religion.

The only blight on the landscape from the hills came courtesy of Saddam Hussein's regime, which burned the hills of their evergreen trees in order to limit mass defections to neighboring Iran. Among Saddam's well-known but somewhat less publicized crimes were the outrageous acts committed against the environment. From the oil wells he set ablaze in Kuwait, to the several-thousand-year-old marshes he drained in southern Iraq, to the destruction of Basra's palm trees, to the burning of Kurdistan's evergreens, Saddam stood as one of the world's worst environmental criminals ever. A more complete study of his environmental devastation deserves to be made.

In the meantime, the Kurds were replanting the trees, but the trees remained in their infancy; they were still too small to affect the landscape, yet were large enough that I could imagine what the place would look like in a decade or two. It would be a stunning sight, assuming nobody came along to cut them down again.

CHAPTER 24

Health Club

SOON AFTER RETURNING FROM Suleymania, I joined a health club. Being a regular user of fitness centers in the United States, I had gone a considerably long period of time without a trip to the gym, and this had more than once been a source of annoyance to me. Baghdad was not an easy place to live, and I had frequently become frustrated with the harsh and seemingly endless difficulties the city presented on both personal and professional levels. It was at those times that I needed a gym the most.

I hadn't immediately joined a health club because of the complete lack of appropriate facilities and equipment in the places I had seen. In part the problem was cultural; Iraqis, my relatives included, could not even begin to understand why I would be interested in such an odd form of leisure. I remember visiting my uncle Nawfal after work hours, as I often did, typically without advance notice as per Iraqi custom. My uncle Hummam was visiting at the same time. The three of us, accompanied by Nawfal's daughter, my cousin Rana, were drinking tea and chatting in Nawfal's garden as the sun sat low on the horizon. It was a beautiful late afternoon, I was enjoying it in wonderful company, and I began to talk about my life. I disclosed to them my plan to join a health club and lose weight using the Atkins diet. There was a moment of silence after I finished.

Then my uncle Hummam began to speak. "I just want to make sure I understand what you are saying, Haider," he began. "You are going to eat nothing but meat, which costs money, and then spend more money to go running around on a machine?"

"Well, when you put it like that . . ." I interjected.

"It's not a question of how you put it," my uncle interrupted, "it's a question of whether or not this is what rich people do when they have too much money. Spend money eating too much, and then spend money to lose weight that you gain from spending money. Can't you just eat less?"

"Even then I wouldn't be in good health," I protested. "The Prophet Muhammad, peace be upon him, said that a sound mind lies in a sound body."

Rana spoke up. "Of course. We aren't arguing this. But what is so great about this running on a machine business? Swimming pools are nice, just play around in one of those." She smiled at the thought of a pool. "It's very refreshing, especially in the summer," she added.

"You swim?" I said skeptically. Rana wore a headscarf, so the idea that she would put on a swimming suit struck me as absurd.

"They have ladies' day, you know," she replied curtly.

"In Iran we used to go climb the mountains, or go for long walks, this is a very healthy and important thing to do," my uncle Hummam said. This was a favorite refrain of his, how heavenly life in Iran was prior to his coming to Iraq. "But paying to climb stairs that aren't even real on a silly machine makes no sense at all." Then he paused, and added, "I always thought they did that in the West to meet women."

My uncle Nawfal, who usually played the role of my defender in these situations, interrupted at this point. "Would you leave this boy alone, he gave you the Prophet's statement, he is trying to live it his own way, and it's his money anyway. You'd think there were no problems in Iraq the way the rest of you go on about his joining a health club."

Nawfal, being a businessman who owned his own Iraqi radiator plant, seemed to understand American individualism and consumerism, where a person could do with his money as he pleases, better than most Iraqis. For most Iraqis, how a man spends his money is a matter in which the community very much takes interest. Thankfully, Nawfal was the oldest of my uncles and for this reason his word was final, particularly because we were in his home. His age relative to my uncle Hummam, who was the youngest of my grandmother's children, mattered much more than the position of influence my uncle Hummam had managed to attain over the years. As a result, my uncle Hummam and Rana fell silent and the conversation ended.

Unfortunately, in my quest for a health club, I soon learned that the best Iraqi gyms might charitably be compared to junior high school weight rooms circa 1978 rather than anything to which I was accustomed in twenty-first century America.

The fitness center I investigated first was essentially a large square room with a wooden floor that looked like it might have been barely suitable for holding a ballet lesson or learning how to dribble a basketball, but it did not seem to me to be much good for anything else. There were three stained, dank, off-white walls (whether deliberately off white or only appearing so because of grime, I was not sure) and a fourth wall with a filthy floor-to-ceiling mirror. A bench press was casually lying on one side of the room, and leaning on it was a weight bar. Smaller weight bars were strewn about, as well as weights that were supposed to be placed neatly on a rack along one wall but had likely been not anywhere near that wall in weeks.

As for aerobic machinery, there was what passed for a treadmill. It creaked slowly into motion, never seemed to get up to more than four miles an hour, and it achieved that speed only with a great deal of groaning and effort. And then every time my foot pounded on its fragile belt it slowed down noticeably. Tension-based non-electric bicycles that predated the modern spin cycles by a decade were also available and indeed recommended because they would work through power outages. Nobody had ever heard of a Stairmaster. The room was dark, mildewed, and rank. The locker room was filthy. I could only use the facilities four days a week. It was closed on Fridays and on two other days the club was reserved for women, though I certainly knew no women who would be interested in exercising in a place like this.

My first reaction on entering this particular gym, therefore, was severe disappointment, although carefully masked so as not to offend the staff that was well-meaning and helpful. My driver, however, was quite impressed and beamed throughout the entire visit, and actually gave me a confused look when I asked if there were any gyms that might be nicer. What could I possibly mean, he asked. This gym "had everything," he insisted. Even Uday was known to come here on occasion.

A frequent saying I came across in Iraq was that a particular outlet or store or neighborhood "had everything." After spending many months in Iraq, I understood this to mean that the store in question had almost everything that such a store might be expected to carry in Iraq at the time, but whose selection would be considered paltry by the standards of the United States or even other large cities of the Middle East. A grocery store that had everything is better than others in Baghdad, but not impressive by Western standards. Similarly, a gym that had everything was better than others in Baghdad, but looked like the one I had just visited. I came to despair every time I was told of some place that had everything, given that I knew I would find something with far less than what I considered to be "everything."

In any event, being unable to find a better gym than that the one I had just seen, I considered a membership at the Hunting Club. The fitness facilities, I was told, were somewhat nicer than those at any private gym; the membership fee for Iraqis was quite low ($150 to join, $6 a month thereafter); and in addition to a gym, there was a heated indoor pool, two tennis courts, and, of course, most important to Iraqis though of little importance to me, I could then be a bona fide member of the Hunting Club. I could take foreigners to eat there (though I never found the club's café to be comparable to restaurants outside the club), and I could attach a decal to my car showing the world my new elite status. All for $6 a month.

The only problem being, of course, that I had to be an Iraqi citizen to obtain such a favorable fee. The membership prices for foreigners were four to five times higher, and while the exorbitant $30 monthly fee for foreigners could be handled, I was not eager to pay more than $500 to join when I lived on about that much monthly. I realized that this meant that I now had to increase my efforts to obtain Iraqi citizenship, both to take advantage of this discount as well as to be able to register my car in my own name.

In theory, Iraqi citizenship is easy to obtain for a child of two Iraqis. I should need only to appear at a particular government office, bring my father's Iraqi citizenship papers and my own birth certificate, and then leave with my own Iraqi citizenship card entitling me to Hunting Club discounts and other as yet unknown benefits. Unfortunately, things were never that simple in Iraq. When I went to the appropriate ministry to file for Iraqi citizenship, problems began immediately. I went with my brother, Ali, who had just started his own business in Baghdad, buying and selling a variety of goods that were not readily available in Iraq but that he thought could be useful, among them water coolers with filters to deal with the poor quality of Baghdad water, motorcycles to negotiate the city's snarling traffic, and solar powered equipment to deal with the power cuts. Ali had just begun this endeavor, and business to that point had been slow. He came with me to get his own Iraqi citizenship papers. A clerk scrutinized our applications.

"Doctor, you two were born in the United States?" he asked.

"Yes, so?" Ali replied on our behalf.

"Well, your birth certificates have to be in Arabic. English is not our official language. Your parents should have known that, and had the birth certificates written in Arabic."

"I don't think they have Arabic birth certificates in America, but I can translate them," I said, trying to be helpful.

"I don't know, it's rather irregular and we're having trouble these days," the clerk replied.

"Can I help you with your trouble?" I asked, knowing what he wanted. I handed him 10,000 dinars, or $6.

"Okay, you are my brothers and fellow Iraqis, I will help you, dear brothers. Go to a legal translator and get them translated and come back to me. I'll take care of it. Abu Ahmed is my name. God be with you."

This took a few days, as a "legal translator" was not easy to find. Finally I did find one, and he turned out to be a translator who charged twice as much as the market price for affixing a seal on his translation with a stamp. Ali gave up and assumed there had to be a better way to handle this. As for me, I returned with my legal translation in hand, but Abu Ahmed was busy. He referred me to his friend, Abu Ali.

"If you are not Iraqi," he smiled, "then I am not Iraqi. You will get your card soon. But we cannot do it with just this translation. You need your father to come with his papers and swear before a judge that you are his son. Then the testimony and the translation of the birth certificate go to the office outside the Green Zone, they stamp them, you bring them back here, and then we process everything to get you your card. Very simple, two weeks maximum, if you can spend the mornings on it."

"But my father is not in Iraq," I protested.

"Oh, what a problem, this creates trouble," he said. I knew he was looking for a bribe, so I gave him some money. He smiled again and said, "Listen, as your brother and friend, I'll tell you what court to appear at, but go with your uncle and then the judge will accept it. I am married to his daughter, and he will help."

"I know it creates trouble, but can we bypass all of this? I can help you for your troubles," I said, indirectly trying to offer more money to avoid this.

"We are a government of laws, everyone must follow the law," he snapped.

Apparently, from his reaction, it seemed that this was not something I could bribe my way through entirely. It seemed that some institution, until that moment undetectable, and referred to by Abu Ali as "law," had a role to play.

I left the government offices grimly certain that I would not soon be a citizen of Iraq. If my life changed such that citizenship was a more important goal for reasons that did not relate to Hunting Club discounts, naturally I would reconsider putting in the time and effort, but at the time I saw no benefit that justified this amount of effort.

My family, friends, and nearly everyone else with whom I came into contact (even the government clerk, much to my surprise, who was hoping to add another Shi'i to the voter rolls by making the process as simple as possible) were puzzled by my decision.

"It's just another two weeks, Haider, what is the problem?" my cousin Suha, aunt Zahra's daughter, asked me when I dropped by my aunt's house unannounced immediately after the incident. We were sitting around the table eating an Iraqi staple that was particularly popular in the winter—rice and an okra and lamb stew. Aunt Zahra made it well, though no one was as expert as Sa'diya.

"He needs Wasta," said Ahmed, Suha's husband. "Wasta," which translates roughly as "influence," is an Arabic term that refers to the shady types of relationship-based dealing that dominates the region. Wasta is not bribery, exactly, any more than a politician who accepts a lobbyist's invitation to a football game is necessarily doing so in exchange for one particular vote. The parties do not exchange money for a specific transaction, but they do trade commodities or favors in a more indirect fashion.

"This guy said he'd help him. He said two weeks," Suha retorted. "But to be safe, why don't you use your cousin Nuri, he has Wasta. He is your relative, too, family can always be trusted."

"But if this man said two weeks, why not stay with him. It's two weeks, are you that busy? If you are, then make it three, one day go to work, one day do this, and go to work in the afternoon. What is the problem?" Suha's brother Ameer chimed in. Working half days for three weeks apparently did not seem to be a problem for an Iraqi.

The dramatic rebalancing of the value of time versus money had, I was discovering, reached near absurdity in Iraq, and not just for the obtaining of official documents. A month before the citizenship incident I had needed a coffee grinder. Abu Mustafa spent a week looking into the coffee grinder market and determining the best brands, another week searching through stores for those brands and trying them himself, and the final week negotiating the best price, which turned out to be 10,000 dinars, the price of nearly everything "expensive" in Iraq. Three weeks, one six-dollar coffee grinder. When I told this story to my family and acquaintances in Iraq, they were uncertain as to the point, and smiled weakly. For them, this was precisely the manner in which a person went about buying a coffee grinder. I suppose, however, that this is no worse than the opposite extreme displayed by so many overworked New York corporate lawyers, who would rather pay $500 for a tie for their father on his birthday than spend any time looking for a more appropriately priced or more suitable gift. Still, neither approach struck me as desirable.

At any rate, given the obstacles, I was unable to find a gym or join the Hunting Club at Iraqi prices. Determined to reestablish fitness as a priority in Iraq, I decided to check with the "nicer" hotels, in particular the Babylon Hotel, to see how their facilities fared. At this point, my standards for acceptability were dropping fast.

The Babylon Hotel had no gym. It did have a mini weight room and a smaller and somewhat cleaner square room with a mirror, but there were no exercise machines of any kind. There was, however, an indoor pool with warm water, an outdoor pool for summer swimming, and tennis courts. This would have to do. I paid my 150,000 dinar annual dues (approximately $110) within fifteen minutes of seeing the facilities.

The Babylon gym facilities seemed to me to be another apt metaphor for the state of Iraq. On the one hand, the essentials seemed fine. There were locker rooms, an entrance to a pool, an area for massages, a Jacuzzi by the pool on the right, large bay windows overlooking a palm tree-lined garden, three outdoor tennis courts just beyond to the left, and refreshment centers by the pool and in the garden. It should have been lovely.

But the locker rooms were aged and filthy, and the repeated mopping of the floor by the staff seemed to do little good. The refreshment center looked like a 1950s soda pop counter, with shake machines in place of juice mixers and an espresso bar. This would not in itself be a bad thing, except that the shake machine did not seem to work. Instead, a single mini-bar–sized refrigerator served as the refreshment center, providing some soft drinks when it was staffed, which was not often. The Jacuzzi was filled with pool water, the water jets and water heater did not work, the windows were so dirty and scratched as to be nearly impossible to see through, the pool was heavily chlorinated (which was probably good given the appearance of the pool floor). Overall the place looked like it could have been impressive at one time, but it was no longer.

Basic improvements should have been possible. The refreshment center could have served a wider variety of drinks and be better staffed. The windows could have been replaced. Everything could have been cleaned more often. These would be rather modest measures indeed. However, it did not seem as if many cared, other than the few foreigners using the facilities, mostly businessmen or aid workers. Iraqi guests and the management and staff alike seemed content enough as things stood. The hotel already "had everything."

CHAPTER 25

Generator

Several days after joining the health club, I needed to return a generator that was not installed properly. I had been placed in charge of handling the purchase and installation of this generator for the office of our legal education project, and because we wanted a generator that was large enough to power an entire office, this was not an easy task.

Most generators in Iraq are rather small and capable of no more than lighting a room, and possibly powering a television and computer. They cost anywhere between $100 and $500 and can be purchased in almost any Baghdad neighborhood. But generators of this sort were useless for appliances that use more power, among them refrigerators, freezers, space heaters and—most important in the Baghdad summer heat—air conditioners. These appliances would overwhelm the generator's engine and cause it to sputter and ultimately shut down. Thus in a Baghdad home, when power is turned off, its inhabitants engage in a ritual wherein they shut off all major appliances and then start the generator to power mainly the lights and television. I had become accustomed to this and even assisted my relatives in making sure that the appropriate appliances had been turned off when power was cut.

But this was no way to run an office, and thus we decided for the purposes of work that we would spend the $20,000 necessary to buy a very large generator that could power everything we needed, including air conditioners. Such a generator had to be delivered by flatbed and then lowered onto our property by crane; it could not be lifted any other way. I arranged for this. However, soon after delivery it became apparent that the generator would not function, and so the next morning I called the seller to request that something be done to fix it. Nothing was done.

As a result, I had to make several trips to the generator seller, call daily to demand assistance over the next week, and ask my brother, Ali, to go to a dangerous part of town where the generators were sold and where I had purchased it in order to insist that the seller bring a crane to return the generator and fix it. This took an entire day, during which Ali walked into the seller's office and refused to leave until the seller made arrangements to pick up the generator and make the necessary repairs. Eventually, through Ali's admirable efforts, a crane and flatbed truck came to pick up the generator at our office, at 5 p.m.

The drivers of the crane said they were concerned about traveling with the generator at night and requested that I pay an additional fee for their agreeing to do so, ignoring the fact that my brother had left at 7:30 a.m. to get them and they had made him wait the entire day before the crane appeared.

"I have to pay? You delivered a bad generator. It does not work. Why should I pay for moving it back?" I asked.

"This is how it is in Iraq; it is the way we do business," one of them replied, matter-of-factly.

"The way you do business is you deliver a generator broken and then I pay $500 to go back and get it fixed?" I continued my protest.

"We did not do this on purpose. Do you think we would do this on purpose?" the other asked angrily.

"No, of course not, you are good friends and brothers. Iraqi brothers. But I cannot pay, I am sorry," I said immediately, hoping to defuse conflict while at the same time holding to my position.

"You must."

"I cannot. Do you want me to call the seller himself? I will tell him. He knows my cousin Ali," I said.

"Please do," one of the drivers replied.

I called the seller who said he was happy to take it back for free if the drivers agreed, but that he had no control over them. I again spoke to the drivers who said the decision was actually not theirs; it was the seller's. Then I had my cousin Ali talk to the seller to see if he could talk to the driver. After three hours of negotiations all agreed that the generator would be taken back and fixed at no charge, save a small tip for the drivers. I was pleased with the outcome. I accepted the delay with equanimity as the price for living in Iraq.

The drivers left with their crane and my generator. I followed behind in my own car, for if I had learned anything in Iraq it was never to let anyone drive away with $20,000 worth of equipment. We were approximately halfway to the manufacturer's location when the police stopped us the first time. They asked for the generator paperwork and I produced the receipt, my passport as identification, and my international driver's license. They had no idea what the license was and handed it back to me. The other material they scrutinized more closely.

"These papers are wrong, sir, they aren't the right ones. You stole this generator," the policeman said.

"Really, I did not, sir. This is the receipt. It's stamped, you see. I assure you it was a legitimate purchase. I can bring the owner of the unit if you would like," I replied.

"No, I won't believe him. I think you stole this from a government ministry," the policeman insisted.

"I swear it was purchased. Really. How can I convince you?" I asked.

"Where is your Iraqi identification?" the policeman asked, changing the subject.

"I do not have any with me, this is a U.S. passport," I said.

"That proves you stole the generator, it is against the law for Americans to own equipment like this. No legitimate dealer would sell it to you," the policeman declared.

"There is a foreign investment law now that allows foreigners to buy whatever they want."

"I don't care what the Americans say, this country is not for sale. You can't buy generators, that is the rule here." Then he smiled, "But you do seem like a nice person, and you are Iraqi really. Maybe you bought it from someone and thought it was not stolen. I should help you. Do you want me to escort you to your destination? I think you will need a police escort. Otherwise you will get stopped again."

I immediately replied, "Actually, an escort is not necessary, thanks so much for the offer. Can you just write me a note? I know this will take time from your important duties, and I will honor your time." This is standard Iraqi jargon to suggest that I would pay him.

"It is trouble, and as you know we are busy fighting terrorists and keeping the country safe," he told me. After a short discussion, he agreed to a bribe of 40,000 dinars, or $25, to compensate him for taking time out of his schedule fighting the terrorists to write my note.

By 9:30 p.m. we were on our way again, and by 9:45 we approached the suspension bridge. We were not crossing the river, indeed we couldn't because the Green Zone lay on the other side and the suspension bridge was closed to all non-Green Zone traffic. However, we did need to pass along the riverbank either under or over it in order to proceed. For reasons that I will probably regret for some time, the driver with a crane and a generator almost ten feet tall chose to pass under the bridge. Predictably, the crane could not pass, and we were stuck.

Because the suspension bridge was an entry point to the Green Zone, American soldiers guarded it. They emerged suddenly from the darkness, cut us off from behind, and bellowed at us to get out of our vehicles and lie flat on our stomachs on the road.

"Get out of the motherfucking car and on the fucking ground you motherfucking asshole!" one soldier shouted.

"Shut your fucking mouth before I blow a hole through your faggot ass!" a second one screamed.

Another soldier forced my head down on the ground and shouted, "Eat the pavement motherfucker!"

They searched our pockets for weapons and opened the generator doors to see what was inside. Cars approaching, unsure of the cause for the lights and commotion, slowed down and stopped. The soldiers started to shoot vaguely in their direction and the cars sped off. One soldier told another how this demonstrated that the only language that Iraqis understood was force. As if they had tried other means of persuasion in this instance and it hadn't worked.

Eventually my passport was found and the soldiers let me up from the ground. Several of their guns were still pointed directly at me, with red laser beams that I assumed indicated the line of fire flashing back and forth across my chest. I began to explain the situation with the generator. Curiously, in contrast to the Iraqi police, they seemed more interested in making sure I had a driver's license, and when they saw the Ohio license in the wallet they had pulled from me, the conversation took a different direction.

"You're from Ohio? Me too! I'm from Sandusky!" said the soldier who had minutes earlier threatened to blow a hole in my faggot ass.

"Damn Midwest, nothing good there, just a bunch of fucking cowhumpers," remarked the one who had begun the shouting.

"Yeah well, our mothers don't fuck us like they do in South Carolina," responded the soldier from Ohio.

I intervened. "So can we have this conversation without weapons pointed at me, do you think?"

The weapons dropped. "Yeah sure, move on through, you're good to go Ohio boy, and don't come under here with a truck like that, man, or you'll get yourself killed. Man, are you lucky I didn't shoot your mother-fucking ass."

The police stopped us at a second checkpoint about fifteen minutes later and told us to pull over. Before they approached, I noticed the generator drivers clearly agitated, talking rapidly to each other.

"Their mothers are the whores, not ours!" said the first. "Did I say something to them? No, and he says this about my mother. My *mother.*"

The second said, "A thousand blessings on Osama Bin Laden. I hope he kills more of them and their whore mothers and whore sisters. Race of dogs and pigs."

"God's curse on them, the pimps," the first said in response. "Lay me on the ground and then insult my family, too. Wild dogs are more civilized than Americans. They're only rich because they have no morals and steal the money of honest countries. Who brought Saddam? They did, the brothers of whores."

"You know they always talk that way," I cut in. "They talk that way to each other. They don't take the term 'motherfucker' literally, like we Iraqis do."

"Because their mothers are all whores and they are the bastard children of whores, that's why they say that. Tell them that when you see them, and then tell them Abu Mahdi hopes they all die tomorrow by Osama's hand," one of the drivers replied in anger.

Just then the policeman came over. I had no energy to deal with him and so immediately offered him 40,000 dinars for another note. He accepted it, though he seemed slightly disturbed that I had not even attempted the common courtesies that precede the paying of bribes. We were finished in five minutes. Given how light traffic tends to be at that hour, because no sane individual travels late at night in Baghdad, I was home shortly after 11 p.m. It was a twenty-minute journey, completed in three hours.

I could not sleep that night, partly because I thought I had almost died and partly because I could not help but read broader lessons into this very personal experience. I wanted to believe that the ordeal was all a product of bad luck; namely, that I happened to buy a generator from the wrong company and run into the wrong police officers and gotten surrounded by the wrong U.S. military patrol. Unfortunately, however, I could not bring myself to accept this. The generator seller came recommended by my cousin Ali, and never in my experience has a vendor behaved differently than he. Iraqis have told too many stories about their police force for me to think of them as anything but ineffective and corrupt. The CPA pointed proudly to the raised salaries of Iraqi policeman from $1.50 a month to $300 a month, arguing that the increase in pay made bribery unnecessary. Iraqis said, and I was starting to agree, that the only effect was to increase the price of a bribe. And as for the American soldiers, my encounters with them now were almost always tense and unnerving even if not always at gunpoint, so much so that I tried to avoid them whenever possible. Whatever the reason, and I was sure it lay not in the characters of the soldiers, they were turning on Iraq. And at each pistol pointed in the direction of a nearby car, at each insult, at each occurrence of ill-tempered behavior, the population was turning against them.

CHAPTER 26

Attack on an Uncle

"The Americans shot at me!" I heard my uncle shout urgently as he entered my grandmother's house.

I ran downstairs from my bedroom. My grandmother was also making her way over to the kitchen where my uncle was pacing and nervously looking at his car and impatiently waiting for us to enter the kitchen.

"Remember when you said it's all rumors? It's not rumors it's true, they just attacked me," my uncle said to me. "They shot my car, it has to be repaired now."

"What happened?" asked my grandmother, approaching on her cane. She was slightly hard of hearing but was among the most perceptive women I knew, notwithstanding this, and was thus well aware that something awful had happened.

"The Americans shot at me, Mother!" shouted my uncle, so she would hear.

"Which Americans? Are you hurt? You have to go to the hospital! *There is no strength and there is no power but in Allah the High and Magnificent,*" my grandmother said excitedly, quoting the Koranic verse most often recited in times of distress. "Sa'diya, call the hospital!"

Sa'diya, the housekeeper, remained seated. "Auntie, they didn't shoot him, they shot the car." Sa'diya always called my grandmother Auntie.

"Grandma!" I shouted. "They shot the car, not my uncle Isam."

"The car? All praise is due to Allah, Lord of the Worlds. Sa'diya, don't call the hospital." Sa'diya remained seated. My grandmother sunk into her chair, her head in her hands. "Every day, it's worse."

My uncle then began to tell his story. "I was at an intersection, there was some sort of explosion. One of the improvised explosive devices they have in cars. The Americans were near me, just in front of me, I couldn't get away from them. They shot. They shot and shot and shot. Everywhere, anywhere, they didn't care. They could have killed somebody. They almost killed me. They ruined my engine. Can I get compensation? Look at the bullet holes. One even came through the windshield!"

He gestured toward his car. There were bullet holes in the windshield and rear window.

"Don't they know there are people on these roads?" he continued. "It's a traffic jam, what do they think, the bomber will stand up for them and do a little dance and say 'it was me, it was me.' They're really stupid people . . . much more stupid than the British. Basra is quiet because the British are much better administrators, the Americans only know about their big guns. They think they will wave around their big guns and everything will be like they want. Can I get money for this? All they have are their big guns, any place they invade they destroy, except Germany and Japan, but those two are very resourceful. The Americans are stupid."

Given his state, I wasn't sure if he was making a political statement, directing a request to find out about compensation, or just relating a story about the attack. I'd never seen him this emotional before, and I was certain that his feelings about the American presence were quite different and more nuanced than this. Who could blame him for his emotional state? The bullets that hit his car could have hit him. I did not interrupt.

"I counted at least twenty-five shots. I bet they shot at least one person. They don't care, they're stupid. Everyone in that traffic jam hates them, and they think they can solve that by shooting more people. They lost in Vietnam, they aren't doing anything good in Afghanistan, they ruined Lebanon, and now they are here to learn the same mistake."

"Where did they shoot the car?" my grandmother piped in.

"The windshield and the windows, Mother!" my uncle shouted. "It needs to be fixed, it will cost me thousands!"

"I will pay," hollered my nonworking grandmother, a woman who must rely on her children for support.

My uncle ignored the comment and asked me again about compensation.

"Americans," muttered the immobile Sa'diya.

Later on, I went to find out about whether my uncle had a claim, but this was a pointless enterprise. The first sergeant I spoke to laughed in my face, another hinted that perhaps my uncle detonated the device and therefore deserved the shots, and a third gave me a pamphlet about winning the hearts and minds of Iraqis. Nobody seemed competent or able to deal with the issue I had raised.

Yet I deemed this to be of the highest importance when considered on a scale broader than merely my uncle. Demoralized, angry, and inadequately prepared soldiers frustrated by daily attacks against them had begun to vent their frustrations with shocking levels of violence on the streets. This deserved attention that it was not receiving. The U.S. media, in their never-ending campaign to "support the troops," and the U.S. government, desperate to keep public support of the war high, had not reported on these matters at all. And as for me, I was frightened for the future of this country.

CHAPTER 27

Two Conversations with My Neighbor

IN AUGUST OF 2003, I had been having tea with Abu Ahmed, as I often did late at night when I was not ready to sleep and the danger of Baghdad made travel beyond my immediate neighborhood unadvisable. We would sit in his garden, often with my cousin Ali, and discuss all things imaginable, his electric fan whirring in back of us in the stifling heat. Abu Ahmed served us tea flavored with cardamom in tiny tulip shaped glasses with copious amounts of sugar. Tea throughout the country was prepared and served in this fashion, and I always associate it with Iraq. Outside of Iraq, I have never been able to replicate the taste or experience. The simplest café stand in Iraq seems to have better tea than anything I have found abroad.

On this particular evening, as the three of us sat near the fan in a vain attempt to remain cool in temperatures exceeding 100 degrees, Abu Ahmed had something specific on his mind.

"Doctor Haider, I would like you to come with me to a meeting," he said.

"What meeting?" I inquired.

"We Shi'a are having a neighborhood meeting, we want to tell the American captain we have to hold elections for the neighborhood council. His name is captain Ted. Do you know him?" he asked me.

"Ted what? Why would I know him?"

"Captain Ted, that's his name, Doctor Haider. I thought you might know him from America."

"America is a big place," Ali tried to explain.

"And Ted is a common name," I added.

Abu Ahmed nodded, uninterested in this piece of trivia. "Anyway, Captain Ted appointed a neighborhood council but he appointed only Sunnis. And Wahhabis, too, they are all Wahhabis and they ignore the Shi'a. We need an election to make it fair. Will you come?" Wahhabism is an extreme and puritanical form of Sunnism, based largely in Saudi Arabia, which declares the Shi'a to be heretics, though Iraqi Shi'a had begun to use the term casually with reference to any Sunni whose views they found distasteful.

"I guess. What do I need to do?" I asked.

"Explain it to Captain Ted. He is a good man, I think. He hates Saddam and Ba'athis. Tell him he accidentally appointed friends of Saddam and Wahhabis and America's real friends are the Shi'a."

"That might be a little extreme," Ali said. "But I think you should come. He will understand you better than us."

"Fine," said Abu Ahmed. "Just explain it to him, and maybe we can have an election. Tell him we want him to monitor the election, too, not the Sunnis. They'll cheat. He is honest."

I remembered this conversation well when I saw Abu Ahmed in February of 2004, shortly after I had returned to Iraq after a two-month absence. I saw him crossing the street near my grandmother's home so I pulled over.

After some pleasantries, I asked him, "So how is Captain Ted, did he ever do that election?"

"No, he left, and besides I don't care about talking to the Americans anymore." There is no work, I need to feed my family, and all Americans do is talk about Saddam. Saddam Saddam Saddam. He is in jail. I have no food—which is more important?"

"I understand, the economy is terrible, isn't it." I said with concern.

"They were supposed to improve our lives. What do we have? Electricity, none. Water, none. Security, none. What have they done? Tell me, what do we have?" Abu Ahmed asked with resentment and anger in his voice.

"Satellite television, I guess. Mobile phones?" I tried to add helpfully.

"Neither of which I have or can afford. I need work. You know, if the terrorists came to me now and gave me money to shoot Americans, I'd do it," Abu Ahmed said loudly.

"Be careful, try not to talk this way," I said. I looked around, hoping there was no nearby military patrol.

"Why not? Are they my cousins I am shooting? No. I would kill myself before I kill an Iraqi, but who are they? If someone pays me, I'll do it," he declared a second time, even more loudly.

"I don't know, you could get yourself killed doing this," I said.

"I can also die starving. Besides, they'd have to pay me. I wouldn't be doing it out of devotion to the cause, only if they gave me money. I need work!" he shouted.

That was the last significant conversation I had with Abu Ahmed. His understandable anger and frustration led me to think it would be better to avoid him, and so I did. In late 2005, he was killed in a random act of violence that had become all too prevalent on Baghdad's streets.

CHAPTER 28

Ashura

IN A BETTER WORLD, this chapter would be about the unfortunate security situation that prevented me from seeing my first Ashura commemoration in Baghdad—the first Ashura commemoration that had taken place in Iraq in my lifetime.

The Ba'ath had prohibited, or at least severely restricted, the commemoration of this most important of Shi'i religious holidays for obvious reasons. What we are commemorating is the death of Muhammad's grandson Hussein, called by the Shi'a the "Leader of the Martyrs" and the rightful leader of the Muslim community, which at the time in Shi'i legend was in the hands of a tyrannical, usurping, and unjust caliph, Yazid. The cries that day, to the usurping caliph, of *far from us is your indignity* and *the oppressors shall see what punishment awaits them* would naturally disturb Saddam Hussein; the historical parallels could readily be drawn between him, a Sunni dictator seeking to subject the majority Shi'a of Iraq, and Yazid, the murderer of Muhammad's grandson Hussein. So the commemoration was banned for thirty-five years. To compare it to the banning of Easter for Christians is no exaggeration.

I have seen commemorations to Hussein in the United States, Britain, and Iran, but never in Iraq where the original indignity had taken place, and never at the tomb in Kerbala. It was with a mixture of happiness (ironic given that the commemoration itself revolves around mourning and grief) and anticipation that we Shi'a looked forward to Ashura in

March of 2004, when we would be free to commemorate as we wished. Still, there was a palpable sense of foreboding as well. The country was not safe. The Americans had proven themselves incapable of protecting it, or unwilling to do so. Al-Qaeda had suggested they would seek to provoke us in a civil war with our fellow countrymen through incendiary attacks, and nothing would be more provocative than an attack on this occasion. My brother and I had discussed the matter, and decided that we would participate in some of the evening celebrations in our paternal grandfather's home, and would certainly be involved in the massive cooking preparations that would take place the day before, but we would not go to the holy sites themselves, as it was too dangerous.

The food preparations on the night before Ashura in 2004 revived generations-old traditions that had been banned for more than two decades. They were a sight that warmed the heart. Food on the day of Ashura basically is of two types: a lamb and lentil stew known as *qima* and a porridge known as *hareesa*. Families prepared these dishes the night before Ashura on the streets of Shi'i neighborhoods in pots large enough to hold a person. Families would share these foods with each other the next day.

Meanwhile, on that same night, in the streets of Baghdad and at the holy site of Kerbala itself, processions of black-clad men wearing headbands with the script "O Hussein," and women covered head-to-toe in black chadors, marched through the streets. Children dressed like the men scurried back and forth between the two groups. Cries for the legends surrounding the dead Imam were heard, men walked and hit their chests rhythmically, men and women alike wept frantically and urgently for the orphans and widows of Kerbala—for Fatima the daughter of the Prophet and mother of the murdered grandson, for the Leader of the Martyrs' sister, Zainab, who carried the tale of the injustice throughout the Arab lands, ensuring that the stain which hung on the name of the Umayyad dynasty for this killing would remain forever.

And, as the news reported, in a custom more honored in the breach, many of the men and even some of the children carried with them sharpened knives tied on links of a chain. They then threw the chain on which the knives were hung over their backs in hard succession, cutting themselves in the process. Some fathers cut the foreheads of their very young children with razor blades, and the children, sometimes as young as two, cried uncontrollably as blood poured down their faces. Some believed that this would endear them to the grand martyr himself. The scene was frenzied, bloody, and somewhat frightening, though less so from where I was, which tended to be some distance away from those who were actually hurting themselves. The more extreme varieties of commemoration are not encouraged by our clerics, and nobody I knew chose to partake in the actual bloodletting, instead keeping themselves a fair distance away from it. Still today, nobody criticizes the practice, and no cleric dares to issue an outright ban. I can only hope this will change.

All of this we witnessed, in sorrow and mourning as was the custom in honor of the dead grandson, but also with a strange mix of contentedness. We were free on the streets of Baghdad to practice our religion for the first time in decades. The blood was excessive, the fear was pervasive, the crowds hesitant, but each cry, each wail, each thump on the chest was a cry of freedom, at last, from a savage tyranny that had at once seemed unending.

On the streets that night I ran into Abu Abbas, the friend of a relative. He was busy preparing *qima* with his family. "Look at these pots, look at this one, Professor Haider."

"I see it Abu Abbas, it's great."

"No, look, this other one, see how big it is. And watch, if you touch the top, it's not hot. Touch it. Try it."

"I don't really need to touch your pots, I believe you."

"And this one is even bigger, look at it!"

I wondered how long we would discuss his pot collection. I felt that perhaps my time was better spent watching the throngs in commemoration.

"I found these after my father passed away, Allah's mercy on him. I had never seen them before, but I knew what they were for. Ashura. Now I can use them."

Abu Abbas had on an apron that his uncle had brought him from England, which read, "The chef is in, everyone else out," and it was stained with the *qima* he was preparing. We walked along together for a bit, he beating his chest more vigorously than I. He wept deeply as he heard over a loudspeaker the story of Zainab bidding farewell to her brother Imam Hussein for the final time before he left his tent on the night of Ashura.

After the story came to an end, Abu Abbas wiped away his tears, smiled, and asked about my family. I could not tell if he was mourning the dead Imam or celebrating his freedom to commemorate. I didn't know which I was doing either.

I should be writing more about this. I should also be writing about the processions I watched on television the next morning as they culminated in a large gathering at holy sites in Baghdad and Kerbala, and reenactments took place of the events in Kerbala itself. Some unfortunates were conscripted to play the role of the soldiers in the caliph's army, charged with the task of murdering Imam Hussein, though in this case they were in greater danger, as the audience spent a fair amount of energy damning them to hell, cursing them, their parents and their offspring eternally, and in extreme cases throwing shoes at them. I should be writing about my feelings that day, those of mourning for a hero of my childhood, those of joy that we could breathe again the sweet air of freedom in Shi'ism's home, those of disappointment that security concerns kept me at home watching it all on television.

But then the "insurgents" struck again and for me everything changed—forever. The so-called Islamic resistance on that day, never regarded by me as a positive force, became my deepest enemy.

Mortars and grenades and suicide bombs were planned and arranged throughout holy sites in Iraq to ensure the maximum damage to human life. Dozens were killed in Baghdad, dozens of others in Kerbala, the site of the original injustice against Hussein. On television, all that we could see were bloody limbs, terrorized people running frantically, buildings falling apart, ambulance sirens blaring, and chaos everywhere. We could make no sense of it, though we knew the substance of what had happened. On its holiest day and at its holiest site and at various places throughout the region, Shi'is were attacked for no reason other than because they were intending to practice their faith in freedom for the first time in decades. I have never been more despondent or more frustrated in my life. More than this, however, I was angry.

I was angry at the Americans, and the very thought of watching a single

U.S. Army or CPA spokesman express regret and outrage at the attacks turned my stomach. Though they insisted that they would shepherd the country to freedom and democracy, they had proven themselves time and again unable to provide the one elemental service a sovereign must provide: security. If this was how they wanted to rule, they were better off going home. Nothing good could come from this type of governance. It was not governance at all, only its illusion to satisfy a discontented American public.

I heard the CNN spokespeople, I heard the experts explain how impossible it was going to be to protect so many people in so small an area, and I could only think one thing—if it was the Olympics, if it was the anniversary of September 11, if it was the Oscars, if it was the Super Bowl, an event not one-tenth as important as Ashura, America would have found a way. Whatever the problems, whatever the obstacles, the U.S. would make sure its people were protected. But when it came to Iraq, they sounded like Yasser Arafat. It was no surprise to me that the tanks that approached the mosques after the attacks were greeted by hails of rocks and shoes. The same reaction, I surmised, that might have greeted Arafat if he arrived at a Tel Aviv café after it had just been bombed.

Yet the Americans did not actually commit the crime, and therefore my anger was more directed at those who almost surely did: Osama Bin Laden, Ansar al-Islam, Abu Mus'ab al-Zarqawi, al-Qaeda, Taliban, Saudi Arabia, and the remainder of this confused, murderous, ragtag set of supposedly Muslim maniacs who have extended their wave of destruction to levels that I would not have imagined any human being, let alone any Muslim, could contemplate, that of murdering fellow Muslims in the midst of an Islamic ritual.

Whatever notion any of these fanatics may once have had regarding the return of Islam to its fundamental principles, primitive and silly as it was, has been lost with the pounding of their mortars at the walls of mosques, the explosions of their automobiles amidst crowds of civilians, and the sacrifice of their children to suicide for no other reason than to kill the children of others. The immediate reaction of most Iraqis I knew was adamant denial of Islamic complicity, and insistence that no person who did this acted as a Muslim and within the traditions of Islam. (CNN misunderstood the sentiment when expressed thus, seeming to think that the statements of witnesses that the perpetrators were not Muslims implied some sort of Jewish conspiracy rather than a simple statement that anyone who committed such an act was not moved to do it by the tenets of our religion. It was not, I was sure, the last misunderstanding I would hear relayed on American television.)

I went to the Ashura commemorations later that evening as I had committed myself to do; it never occurred to my brother or me that we would not. Before the events of the day, it was a matter of participating in an important religious ritual, but now it was political, and personal, and nobody was going to scare me into staying home. I saw Abu Abbas that night, and understandably he was crushed. His hopes for a grand Ashura celebration had been destroyed; something he had waited his whole life had been denied him for one more year. Looking at him—his downcast eyes, wearing the shirt he had on the night before, his cheeks streaked with tears—I remembered an image from a school educational film that would stay with me forever. It was of a young black man in a southern cafeteria sitting down and asking to be served while some rural whites poured ketchup on top of his head and jeered at him. He looked at them despondently and asked, "Why do you hate me so much? I just want lunch." I saw that same look, of incomprehensibility, of confusion, of despair at such an overwhelming injustice that seems entirely unprovoked, on the face of Abu Abbas that night.

Spring 2004—Failure

CHAPTER 29

Falluja

I SPENT A MORNING in April of 2004 at Baghdad University. As part of our education project we agreed to help the university build a court in the law school that would hold mock trials for educational purposes. The university itself avidly supported the idea, although not in the manner we had anticipated. The faculty wanted to build the room to hold mock trials for *real* attorneys and judges. We, who were less enamored of Iraqi hierarchies that relegated students to passive recipients of information, proposed an approach common in U.S. law schools, wherein the students themselves would act as the attorneys in the mock proceedings. The faculty considered this madness and dismissed out of hand the idea that the students would learn anything from making a mockery of a trial proceeding.

I returned to our office in the early afternoon after a long and bitter negotiation to find our office manager, Zuhair, sitting at his desk looking glum. Zuhair and I had known each other for quite a while by April, but mostly on a professional level. I genuinely liked Zuhair, but this was the first time I felt comfortable enough to approach him and ask him what the matter was.

"Did you see the news? Did you see what they did in Falluja?" he asked me.

I knew what he was talking about. Falluja had been at the core of the terrorist insurgency almost from the start of the American occupation, when U.S. soldiers killed over a dozen Fallujans as they gathered for a demonstration at the war's end to protest the American presence in their town. It is a small town populated almost exclusively by Sunni Arabs, with about 300,000 residents. It is also extremely conservative, thereby being predisposed in some ways to violent and extremist Islamic movements, and staunchly opposed to the American presence. On the day I spoke with Zuhair, four security contractors (effectively soldiers, though paid much more handsomely) were driving through Falluja and were killed by a rocket-propelled grenade that caused their car to explode. Their charred remains were dismembered, dragged along the ground, and hung on a bridge over the Euphrates River, as thousands of townspeople sang and danced to this sickening spectacle. It was among the most nauseating sights I had seen yet.

"You know what they are going to say about Islam and Muslims. I'm not going to let anyone say anymore to me that Fallujans are good people. They are not good people. The whole town was cheering," Zuhair said.

It was a feeling I think many Iraqi Muslims and Arabs felt. We have been through a great deal over the past decade, watching one horrific act performed in our name after another. Whether it was the *Achille Lauro* or September 11, the Entebbe hijacking or the Riyadh bombing, we found ourselves repeatedly on the defensive, attempting to explain our religion and our culture on our own terms. This had never been easy; we never found the media entirely fair, and the terrorists rarely made our case any easier. They made the news, but the overwhelming majority of us who paid our taxes and lived our lives and owned our homes and contributed meaningfully to society did not. I suppose this was inevitable, a pain that each of us had to deal with in his or her own way, a pain I had learned to accept growing up as I did.

"'What hurt me the most was what they said when they did it, Zuhair. Did you hear?" I asked, deciding to share some of my own feelings.

"Yes, I heard."

"With our souls, with our blood, we will defend you, Islam' is what they said." This was a chant popular with the former regime, except "Saddam" was the last word of the chant, not "Islam."

"I heard." Zuhair looked too sick to have much of a discussion. It was the way I felt as well. "They're going to say everywhere that this is Islam," he continued, "and since those guys are talking about Islam, who can blame the rest of the world for hating us.

"You know what they should do, Professor Haider? Since the whole town is on camera dancing? It goes like this: We surround the town and we cut off the electricity and everything except emergency supplies. Nobody goes in or out for any reason other than an emergency. Then put up the pictures of all of those guys cheering, and say we want these guys, all of them, or the town stays under siege. Not good people, Professor Haider." He then walked out, saying as he left, "I know this idea isn't a great one, but we have to do something. This is crazy."

Finding nobody else in the office who was thinking much about work given the circumstances, I went home only to find more glum faces. Particularly my grandmother, who was as angry as I have seen her. She was sitting in the kitchen, staring out the window next to the door. Ali, my cousin, sat facing her, and his back was to me as I entered. My grandmother turned to me as soon as I came in the door.

"Do you know who we are?" she shouted at me. "We are the cradle of civilization! We had the world's first laws and the world's first empires! We are Mesopotamia and the land of Ali, the son of Abi Talib, whose speeches are the pinnacle of eloquence."

This type of speechifying is very typical in Iraq. I almost never listened to the first thing anyone said in a meeting in Iraq because it was almost always a lengthy and irrelevant exposition along these lines. However, I had never heard anything like this from my grandmother, the least pretentious person I knew, and certainly not in as emotional a fashion as this.

"I know, Grandma," I said. Ali sat silently, apparently lacking the energy to continue this discussion further.

"Who else in the world knows?" Who thinks of our mosques, our historic universities, the gardens in Babylon?" she asked. "Do you know what we are now to everyone in the world?"

"People don't judge a whole civilization by the acts of a few," I tried to say. She ignored me.

"I have seen rabid dogs treat corpses better than those people did. This is shameful. And you know what they'll say on Al-Jazeera? They'll call those people heroes."

She was right. The idea that anyone on a pan-Arab station would regard such unspeakable savagery against American security contractors as anything but heroic was unlikely. Something was rotten in our world, and that day we could almost smell it.

"I'm going to go lie down. Please don't turn on the news. I don't want to hear anymore," she said as she left.

And with that, Ali got up to return home. As he walked out the door and without turning around, he shouted, "They should wipe out Falluja. We've already got a zoo."

CHAPTER 30

Moqtada

"THE WAR IS OVER," I announced as I walked into the kitchen of my grandmother's home one Friday in April of 2004. Ali, my brother, was sitting at the table while Ra'ad leaned against the refrigerator. Sa'diya was in the back of the room cutting vegetables. She looked up as I entered, and my grandmother, nearby in her favorite pose, stared blankly out the window where she could see the yard. I wanted to make my announcement public so that when the war finally did end, maybe years later, everyone would remember that I had predicted it first. I wrote to my friends shortly afterwards, to ensure an even greater circle of witnesses.

"America has lost Iraq," I continued.

"What, because of Moqtada? That guy is worthless. He claims to be a man of religion with his black turban and God knows what. He's an idiot." Ra'ad, perhaps the most secular among us, said this.

"A popular idiot, Ra'ad," I responded. "A popular idiot cleric," I continued. "A popular idiot cleric from the Sadr family," I concluded, making reference to his unquestioned family pedigree.

"A thug and not a real Sadr," Ra'ad responded. "Didn't he kill another cleric? They should take him down."

"Moqtada, Moqtada, let the guy get lost," Sa'diya added.

"The Americans can say what they want, they started this," Ali said. "They created the crisis with this guy."

Ali was absolutely right. The April 2004 troubles in the Iraqi south began when the CPA decided to shut down Moqtada's newspaper, a paper with a circulation of under 100,000 that, outside of those vendors carrying exclusively Shi'i religious material, nobody seemed to carry and nobody read. I spent the last several months poring over newspapers and magazines from various parties to gather a sense of what Iraqis of all stripes were thinking, and I only saw the newspaper twice. I never bought it.

After the closing of this largely unread paper came the arrest of Moqtada's top deputy for a murder committed a year before. Moqtada reacted by announcing a demonstration at the entrances to the Green Zone. The CPA closed the Green Zone in anticipation, the U.S. consul warned of a "high probability" of violence, and each Green Zone entrance was manned by armed guards on top of every tall building. They were pointing weapons at the demonstrators, and someone in the military command sent tanks to the gates. The tanks ran over two of Moqtada's demonstrators, soldiers killed others, the U.S military attacked Moqtada's centers of authority, and seven U.S soldiers lost their lives in the ensuing violence. Then the fire began. City after city throughout Iraq's south erupted in rebellion, and coalition forces proved unable to quell them. America could not have made a more foolish mistake. I pointed this out to Ra'ad.

"He's still a thug," Ra'ad said.

"Nobody is telling you that you're wrong, Ra'ad, the question is what to do about the guy," I said.

"What kind of Sadr is he anyway, Haider?" my grandmother asked. "The other Sadrs wrote volumes of books on Islamic law and theology, but this jackass can't write his own name. I don't think he could possibly be as popular as you think."

This was my grandmother. A woman born in an Iraq of a different era, sister of one of Iraq's most prominent businessmen, wife to a minister, world traveler, and respected by all within her milieu. That there could ever be a mass of undereducated, frustrated, violent, and poor Iraqis who looked to Moqtada as a leader did not seem possible to her. It was woefully evident to me, however. President Bush could speak with as much machismo as he wanted about how Moqtada needed to be arrested, but the president was powerless in this regard. He no longer controlled the south, Moqtada did. And like in the U.S. election, nobody ever wins without the south.

CHAPTER 31

One Year after the Fall

ON APRIL 9, 2004, the first anniversary of the fall of Saddam Hussein, I took my first vacation from Iraq, though only for a week to go to the warm and safe beaches of Sharm El-Sheikh, Egypt. Driving to Jordan was at this point entirely impossible. The roads going west from Baghdad had all been closed; I had to fly. Over the course of the past year, the Americans had been slowly closing road after road within the city, and now this had spread outwards. I could not go west because America had made enemies with the Fallujans before the war ended, nor could I travel south because America had now made an enemy of Moqtada. There was not much to see east of Baghdad, at least until one reached the border with Iran, so essentially I could only go north toward Kurdistan through the dangerous and volatile but still safe enough to be accessible city of Kirkuk. Otherwise, land travel was more or less impossible, and air travel restricted to authorized personnel, among them myself because I was working for a project run by USAID. Most residents of Baghdad were trapped in a city that grew more dangerous by the day.

The recent flare-ups only pointed to a wider problem: The occupation had failed. One year following liberation, and security was worse than it had ever been. One year following liberation, and electricity remained no better than when I first arrived in Iraq. One year following liberation, and crime remained rampant. One year following liberation, and sewage remained untreated, roads unpaved, basic services not provided for, telephones in many areas remaining in disrepair, and mobile phones too expensive for most residents. One year following liberation, and too little had changed. As a result of these considerable failures, America had lost its credibility. Without that credibility, progress seemed impossible.

There was a time when many of us thought that we would remember April 9 as Liberation Day, when the statue personifying the evil that had ruled us for so long came crashing down. At the very least, we would go to Firdous Square on that day, where the statue once stood, and dance in the emptiness that is there, waiting to be filled with the hopes and dreams of an oppressed people finally unshackled. This was now impossible.

Firdous Square was closed on this April 9, an American Hummer warned any who dared to approach that they would be killed. Nobody would come even if the square were open. Relieved as all Iraqis were to be rid of Saddam, few viewed it as the day in which Iraq was liberated from tyranny, but rather the day on which a tyrannous ruler met his just end and a wrongful occupation began. April 9 would never be celebrated here. Another day will have to be chosen, one less associated with the end of one nightmare and the start of another.

So I chose to leave Iraq on the first anniversary of the fall of Saddam Hussein rather than sit at home and reflect on the disappointments of the past year. I was to meet two old friends from Hong Kong in Sharm El-Sheikh. I hoped to forget entirely about Iraq during my absence and to use the time reminiscing about my past life, far from the chaos and uncertainty in which I had placed myself.

Baghdad's chartered flights left from a different wing of the same airport in which I had arrived on Independence Day, once called Saddam International Airport and renamed Baghdad International Airport, or BIAP (long I), in U.S. military speak.

Like everything else, the airport had shown absolutely no improvement from when I first arrived in July of 2003. In fact, the road leading to it had deteriorated considerably. What was once a green, shaded, divided highway lined with palm trees on each side had become an unsightly array of bulldozers and concrete dividing walls reaching as high as six feet, with tanks occupying the dividers and positioned along each side of the highway. Nervous soldiers with obvious twitchy fingers guarded the American military vehicles and convoys. They pointed their weapons toward the cars closest to them as vehicles went up and down the road. And in the place of the grass and palm trees that were once there, everywhere was ugly brown upturned earth, rocks, and tree stumps.

Sadly, despite these security precautions, the road from the airport to the center of Baghdad remained one of the most dangerous in Iraq at that time, with convoys attacked daily. We traveled this road at speeds exceeding 100 mph to get through to the airport checkpoint as quickly as possible, hitting a brake to slow the car to less than 40 mph if a convoy appeared ahead of us. Every Iraqi had learned to stay far away from American convoys, and with every day the distance between them and us only increased.

Once past the checkpoint, the airport was as it had been when I first arrived, more resembling a military base than anything capable of handling regular civilian traffic, and clearly in no position to be reopened to the public soon. Now there was a passport control, a snack bar, a duty free shop, and a Burger King somewhere, I was told. Other than this, nothing had changed. But I had changed. Fully armed nineteen-year-olds who could kill me in an instant no longer attracted my interest, nor did the ubiquitous sandbags, concrete barriers, tanks, mounted automatic weapons, and other military paraphernalia that had so intimidated me on my previous flights. That was humdrum by April 9, 2004.

Surprises did await me at the airport, however. The neighborhood where the airport stood, Abu Ghraib, was on the road to Falluja and was a veritable hotbed of anti-American resistance. On this first anniversary, it was literally in open rebellion, and from the airport terminal we could see huge clouds of smoke rising from oil fires lit by the insurgents in Abu Ghraib to shield them from attacks from helicopter gunships.

The scene was surreal. I sat in the passenger terminal of an abandoned airport sipping tea, looking at the view outside. Helicopters hovered about 500 meters from where I was sitting, circling thick plumes of black smoke below them. At the same time, in all sorts of directions were what I thought were bullets and artillery shells being fired. I could only judge by the sound and the light (the smoke prevented us from actually seeing anything). The loudspeakers announced that there would be a short delay in our flight as the battle continued, stated matter-of-factly like some sort of minor weather disturbance. When we finally did get clearance to take off, the fight had died down but it had not ended. From the walk on the tarmac to the plane, it was evident that smoke continued to rise, but in less copious amounts, that helicopters continued to fly, but at higher altitudes, and that guns and artillery continued to be fired, but only intermittently.

Though I knew we would take off from Baghdad as we had landed, in a spiral, and though I knew from experience that the landing was considerably more sickening, this ascent was very tight, very fast, and absolutely terrifying. There was not much distance between the Abu Ghraib insurgents and us and, assurances from the plane staff aside, I couldn't easily convince myself that a well-aimed artillery shell could not reach us. None did, fortunately, and soon enough we were at a safe altitude, heading west out of Iraq.

CHAPTER 32

Abu Ghraib

I HAD AN ELDERLY aunt, Amina, who lived near the suspension bridge where U.S. troops had searched me during my ordeal returning the generator. Amina was in poor health, and so I tried to pay her a visit whenever I could. Every time I did, she was gloriously happy to see me and would ask me to spend the night, an offer that I always declined. My visit in May of 2004 was no different except that she seemed curiously preoccupied. We were sitting in her living room with about four of her grandchildren, all young men, and my uncle Nawfal who had also come to visit.

"Haider, you know these pictures which we sometimes see on television of Abu Ghraib. Are they real? It is really shameful," she said.

The comment stunned me, because to describe something as shameful, or *aib*, to use the Arabic word, was a considerable insult within Iraqi circles. An Iraqi does not use such a word lightly.

"Those guys at Abu Ghraib are all Wahhabis from Falluja. They probably deserve it," said Hussein, the twenty-year-old husband of one of her grandchildren.

"Wahhabi" and "from Falluja" were starting to be used by the Shi'a to mean "Sunni." Clearly the Abu Ghraib detainees in May of 2004 were suspected of being part of the insurgency and were overwhelmingly Sunni, but there was no way that anyone could know if they were Wahhabi or Fallujan just from the pictures.

"Then find them guilty of something or put them on trial maybe," my aunt said to him. "What is this shamefulness? These pictures are terrible, who does this to people?"

My uncle Nawfal added, "I never thought the Americans would do something like this. I did think from the beginning that they came for our oil. I didn't think they would respect our traditions, culture, and religion—but this? Your aunt is right, it's shameful."

"It doesn't surprise me," May, the eldest grandchild, spoke up. "I always thought the Americans were very smart with their lasers and bombs and technology. Then they come, and heavens! Barely a single one has any sort of refinement."

"That's true," said Ahmed, her brother. "No refinement at all, most of them did not go to college. Who builds them all their technology then?"

"Come on guys!" Nawfal interrupted. "Do you think Americans with college degrees and PhDs are the ones they pick to send over to this sewage pit of a country? They send the people who don't know anything. I've been to America, most Americans are very smart."

"Actually, it's a volunteer army," I said. "They send the people who sign up, they don't pick anyone."

"Yeah, yeah, so they don't 'send' them, but the idiots who have no other choice are the ones who 'choose' to go, I bet," said Hussein, who clearly seemed the most anti-American of the bunch.

I later learned that Hussein had joined Moqtada's Mahdi Army to the strong objections of our family, most of whom continued to regard Moqtada as an uneducated thug. Soon thereafter, he demanded that his wife no longer show her face in public, another development that led to strong familial discord.

"Well, whoever is here, it's pretty shameful," my aunt concluded.

If these were the feelings of a Shi'i household that was, on a relative scale, favorably disposed to the Americans, I wondered how the rest of the country was feeling.

CHAPTER 33

American Embassy

As PART OF OUR USAID-funded law school program, my associates and I decided to bring the senior library staff and heads of various law departments at Iraq's most prestigious law schools to the United States in the summer of 2004 so that they might gain some exposure to the American legal system. All those we invited were eager to take advantage of the opportunity. We set about determining the procedure by which visas might be obtained for the participants.

We learned that for an Iraqi to visit the U.S., he or she first needed to travel to Amman, Jordan, to apply for a visa and pay a $100 application fee in addition to their travel expenses to Amman. At the time, there was no possibility of obtaining a visa through Baghdad, even for a university educational program sponsored by the government of the United States. American foreign policy involved convincing the Iraqi people that America sought its best interest, yet America wouldn't let Iraqis apply for a visa to visit America from their own occupied capital.

In Amman, embassy staff interviewed the applicants and then decided if they were, in the words of the embassy, "qualified" to enter the United States. If rejected, an applicant went home and received no refund on any expenses incurred. If accepted, an applicant returned to Baghdad and then went back to Amman later to collect the visa. As a consequence, no Iraqi could possibly travel to the United States for any purpose, including cultural, educational, or religious exchanges, without considerable outside sponsorship. The process alone, including travel costs, would easily exceed $1,000, almost half of which had to be expended before a visa decision was made. Few organizations were willing to spend that kind of money on what was considered a remote possibility.

Moreover, Jordanian security services and, in fact, a fairly broad sector of Jordan's population, native-born and Palestinian immigrant alike, held Iraqis in a fair amount of contempt, and their treatment of them could at times border on the appalling. This was, unfortunately, not widely publicized. Nevertheless, the phenomenon of ill treatment was a principal cause for a fair number of political positions taken by Iraqis that could perplex Western journalists—such as why a nation whose population demonstrated such vehemence toward the state of Israel showed no interest in taking measures of any kind that might alleviate the suffering of Palestinians. Many Iraqis considered Israel to be a racist, occupying, and illegitimate government that oppressed their Arab brethren, the Palestinians, but then nearly all Iraqis felt that their Arab brethren probably deserved it.

In any event, Iraqis were loathe to travel to Jordan, let alone travel there twice, and after having arrived with the Iraqis and having seen how Jordanian officers treated them, I could see why this was so. One officer took the travel documents of one of the departmental heads at Baghdad's College of Law at the airport. He made the elderly man spend two complete days at the head offices of Jordanian security with ill-mannered, ill-tempered, and offensive security personnel who interviewed him at length to be certain he was not a security threat. Ultimately, he was released.

When we went to the U.S. Embassy for our visa interviews, it turned out that a young man about twenty-four-years-old, who looked annoyed before anyone had even spoken to him, was responsible for the nine individuals I had brought with me. He rejected without consideration unmarried applicants, so three of our party of nine could not go to the United States. They included the chief librarian at Baghdad University, Iraq's oldest and most prestigious university, and certainly its most well endowed. She protested.

"She's not married, so she is not qualified," the twenty-four-year-old said to us.

"Why does my marital status matter?" the librarian asked. "I am in charge of the library of the largest law school in Iraq. One of the conferences to which we are going is about law libraries. The American government wanted Iraqis to come. Who will you send?"

"Someone qualified," he said.

"I have eighteen years of experience, how can I not be qualified?" she asked.

"I don't care about your work experience," he said angrily, as if she were distracting him with irrelevancies.

I interjected. "Excuse me, but you keep talking about qualifications and she is only pointing out her qualifications."

"I am not hiring her," he said, "only interviewing her for a visa. For which she is not qualified. She has no ties to Iraq, and she could be going to America because she wants to settle there."

"But I know nobody there, I have no work there, I have no family, and my English is poor," she insisted.

"Exactly, those are the other reasons why you are not qualified. Bring the next applicant!" he said.

"Hearts and minds indeed," I muttered, turning away to find the other applicants.

We cancelled the Iraqi participation in the conference. Too few of our applicants were "qualified" for a visa. And the war remained lost.

CHAPTER 34

Jogging

As was befitting the benighted times in Iraq, my thoughts in the spring and summer of 2004 tended to focus on failures, incompetence, deceptions, disappointments, dark matter indeed. But while such a focus was unavoidable, it is nonetheless necessary at times for all human beings, irrespective of their condition or circumstances, to find something to provide them relief in trying times. I could not live in blackness forever.

To that end, and at considerable risk to myself, I took my first run in the Green Zone in the early summer of 2004, before the 130 degree heat of July and August rendered the notion of outdoor exercise a fool's errand. The danger in May lay not in the run itself, though normally a man running around anywhere in Baghdad would attract a fair amount of attention (unless of course he were being chased by a larger man, or at least a man with a larger weapon, in which case it might be regarded as commonplace). However, my route was entirely inside the Green Zone. I was not the only runner in the Green Zone; three women passed me on my run wearing only sports bras, Lycra shorts, Walkmen, and sneakers, an uncommon sight elsewhere in Iraq.

But danger there was nonetheless. Outside the Green Zone, an ethnic Iraqi Arabic speaker like me could blend in readily and avoid being targeted, to some reasonable degree at least. Within its Berlin-like walls, safety generally reigned, as Iraqis generally could not gain entrance, and even Americans could not enter with their cars unless they had a badge.

It was the transition between zones Green and Red that was trouble-some. Once I neared the blast walls of the Green Zone in my car, it was perfectly clear where I was headed, and those small telltale signs that made it obvious that I had not until recently been a resident of this country for the past several decades, signs which would be entirely unheeded less than a mile back, suddenly become noticeable to all. I wore a seatbelt, I had a goatee, the expression on my face, the cut of my suit, the style of my hair—everything started to seem different, and the looks I received shifted suddenly from what were once indifferent glances to hostile glares. The change was remarkable, in the space of five minutes I had been trans-formed from an ordinary Iraqi into the face of the enemy.

It was not always thus when entering the Green Zone. To be sure, there was in the past a danger of some sort of attack on my person; those per-ceived to be working with the United States were targeted by some. How-ever, there was a time when the insurgents really were limited in their numbers and means, so that the entry was considerably less tense and fraught with danger, notwithstanding the occasional car bomb. It was very different now. The general population may not have been in broad uprising, but it was fairly obvious on entry to the Green Zone that their sympathy did not lie with those who entered.

In any event, once safely ensconced in the Green Zone, I found an appropriate place to park my car. This took some effort, because with each attack the areas in which cars, such as my own without vehicle passes, were permitted to park were reduced, so that all of us were now piled in what appeared to be to be a pit of pebbles just outside the Convention Center. Then I ran.

I began, as noted, at the Convention Center, just across from the Rashid Hotel. The Rashid was perhaps the only decent hotel left in Baghdad by the time the former regime fell, Baghdad's other five star hotels having long been degraded through the sinister combination of Saddam's criminal neg-ligence toward anything in Iraq that was not built for or used by him and debilitating U.N. sanctions. The Rashid's most famous ornament, a mosaic of the first President Bush's face displayed prominently on the floor in the central lobby, was removed by the American forces soon after their arrival. The hotel was now occupied entirely by the occupation forces and was not open to the public. It was also the target of frequent mortar attacks, as it lay dangerously near the entrance to the Green Zone. My badge got me inside, and at times I did venture into it for a cigar or for the pirated DVDs sold in the lobby, but for the most part I avoided the place. It was too stark a reminder of the most negative aspects of the occupation. Armed and jackbooted twenty-year-old boys tracking dirt around Baghdad's finest hotel was not something I cared to see very often.

My run continued deeper into the Green Zone toward the building where the Iraqi Governing Council met. To say that the population of Iraq, which was by and large patiently supportive of the Governing Council at one time, has been greatly disappointed by their performance would be a terrible understatement. Their most recent fiasco was the selection of a new flag for the country, a paradigmatic example of some of the problems of the Governing Council in the collective opinion of the general population.

A variety of artists of Iraqi origin submitted designs for the project, and the winner was the brother of the Chair of the Governing Council's Flag Committee, a man who had not stepped foot in Iraq for over thirty years and an atheist openly contemptuous of the Islamic faith which most Iraqis held very dear. Moreover, Iraq had no government come June 30, and the Governing Council, rather than address this, was engaged in lengthy debates about a flag. The flag itself was extremely unpopular as well. The reds, greens, and blacks that dominate every flag of the region were absent, as were the typical broad stripes, prominent stars, and bold contrasts. Instead there was a white background, two blue stripes, a small yellow stripe, and a big blue crescent in the middle of the flag. It resembled no other flag I know, save, vaguely, the flag of Israel.

I had not seen the new flag flying anywhere since it was announced. I had, on the other hand, seen a number of the old flags fluttering about, many more than before. I was actually relieved by this; there was a time months ago that nationalist defiance took the form of a picture of Iraq's heinous dictator. The flag was a considerable improvement.

The Governing Council building was a bit off of the road, and former Gurkhas guarded it. Access was strictly limited. I looked inside and could find nobody there; they may have been deep in the building. The Gurkhas eyed me suspiciously as I neared, and so I kept running.

I turned a corner and came upon Celebration Square. The square was meant to celebrate Saddam's "victory" over Iran in what he termed the Second Qadissiya War (the First Qadissiya War being the original Arab victory over the Sassanian Empire of Persia that lead to the Islamization of modern day Iran). Two major monuments dominated Celebration Square, one architecturally impressive in my view and the other grotesque in the extreme. I passed the impressive one, promising to return to it on the way back, and proceeded to the grotesque monument, a parade ground which was the dimensions of, though considerably larger than, a football field. On each side of the parade ground stood a set of two arms cast from the arms of the dictator himself, each emerging from the earth holding a sword aloft vaguely in the direction of the other so that the swords were crossed over each other high above. One set of crossed swords constituted the entrance to this monstrous parade ground, and the other the exit. And most repulsive of all, hundreds of real helmets of dead Iranian soldiers who had fought in the war surrounded each arm at its base. Bullet holes and other vestiges of violence appeared on many of the helmets.

I had seen this monument once before, in 1990, after the war with Iran and before Saddam's invasion of Kuwait. It made me sick then, and angry now. A well-known Iraqi dissident and very good friend of mine, Kanan Makiya, has called on the monument to remain as a symbol of Iraq's darkest era so that we would never forget. I could not agree. I could not bear to look at it for the rest of my life. Moreover, it was unnecessary; I needed no monument to remember what happened in Iraq.

Unable to tear down this monument dozens of stories high, much as I would have liked to, I took the Prophet Muhammad's advice that the believers who could not correct a wrong with their hands should correct it with their tongues, and so I spat at it, condemned the man who built it, and continued on around the parade grounds to the other end. Along the way I passed the building where the Revolutionary Command Council (RCC) once sat. The RCC was in theory the authority responsible for all legislative and executive authority in Iraq during the Saddam era, though in fact it was Saddam alone who ruled, and the RCC was one of the many tools of his unchallengable authority.

The RCC building was to become the locus of the Special Tribunal that would try members of the former regime, a fitting irony indeed given that the larger criminals (Tariq Aziz, Uday, Taha Yasseen Ramadan, "Chemical" Ali) were all at one time or another RCC members. Work seemed to have begun, or at least cranes had been put in place to do something. I just had not seen them do anything yet at the time of my jog.

I finally came to the other end of the parade ground monument and stood almost directly between the two swords over my head. Two Iraqi policemen eyed me suspiciously, until I showed them my U.S. badge, then they waved and sat down again. An Iraqi flag, the old one again, flew in front of the place where they sat, almost midpoint between the swords and slightly behind them. I stood for a moment, and then turned back. I had had enough of the swords, and the run had already taken almost three quarters of an hour.

On the return, I passed by the monument for which I had considerably more respect, the Tomb of the Unknown Soldier. The tomb itself is fenced off and two Iraqi policemen guard the entry. Not being foolish enough to attempt Arabic with these individuals who obviously spoke no English (occupation aside, anyone who knows anything about the world is aware that it is better to pretend you are white if you want access to something), I muttered something in English, flashed my badge, and kept running. In Hong Kong this sort of thing never bothered me. Now it seemed to me that there was something fundamentally wrong with acting like a foreigner in order to receive better treatment.

The Tomb of the Unknown Soldier was a large, fifty-meter wide, solid, circular, gently upward sloping structure with a hole at the summit. Inside the hole lay the tomb itself. I took to the side of it and ran up, by this time fairly exhausted from the heat and the length of the run and determined to make this the very end of it. Breathless by the top, I looked forward. The tomb was just ahead of me, with flowers only a day or two old laid by its side. Nobody was supposed to be here, access was very limited, so only the cleaning staff or the police could have left the flowers.

In front of the tomb was some nonsense quote, no doubt by Saddam, though his name had been scratched out, about how the mothers and fathers of the martyrs whose bodies were never found could find their family's sacrifice here, where the unknown soldier lay buried. Empty words indeed, and emptier still in light of the small amount of compensation Saddam offered to those whose spouses and parents died in the war. In the rest of the world, Saddam's payments of $25,000 to each Palestinian suicide bomber were *prima facie* evidence of his support of terrorism, and indeed they were, but to Iraqis, they were first and foremost a criminal diversion of precious resources. The number of families struggling to survive because of the loss of a breadwinner in one of Saddam's many wars was staggering. To Iraqis, this was where Iraqi money should be spent.

When I finished paying my respects to the interred, I looked out from the top of the monument to the city of Baghdad. The river Tigris flowed nearby, the Palestine Hotel stood by its banks, with the suspension bridge lying gently over the river further downstream. Some of Baghdad's most famous mosques dotted the landscape, and they had just begun a call to prayer. Gardens of palm trees were visible near the horizon. Sometimes, at times like this, despite the war, despite the violence, despite the hopelessness, and despite the occupation, I never wanted to leave.

I would have stayed longer but it was time to return. I walked back to the car. The T-shirt, shorts, and sneakers came off, and on came the cotton shirt, dress slacks, and polished shoes worn by Iraqis. While normally I preferred not to change into clothes likes this after a run and before a shower, it could not be helped in this case. There were few things more dangerous than to be driving around Baghdad in obviously American clothing. I combed my hair, took a drink of water, and drove out of the Green Zone.

CHAPTER 35

Victory of Sorts

DURING THE LATE SPRING of 2004, with the advent of a single soccer game, some semblance of the world I had left behind in the United States returned, despite my considerable and growing distance from America each passing day. The precise occasion was Iraq's match against the Saudis, a game with immense consequences for the Iraqis because a victory would qualify them for the 2004 Olympic Games.

Iraqis of virtually every segment of society awaited the match with nervous anticipation. An excited pre-match buzz dominated nearly every conversation and even the underfinanced, understaffed, and overworked Iraqi press attempted, on tenuous grounds, to attach immense global significance to the match.

Thus it was that for one day, Baghdad was not the war-torn and devastated city of my ancestors. Instead, it was like my hometown of Columbus, Ohio, prior to the annual game with Michigan, or the city of London prior to the World Cup match with Argentina, or the island of Manhattan before the Subway Series. War and death could wait. Right now there was a game, and we had to win.

To understand why Iraqis were so enthusiastic about their team, it is important to note that the nation once did have one of the prouder and more competent soccer teams in the Middle East. However, as with so many other things, the previous regime managed to destroy this reputation and bring Iraq to the basement of Middle Eastern clubs. The Hussein family was, it seemed to me, an anti-Midas sort; the gold they touched turned to crap.

At some point in the 1990s, Saddam decided to place the management of Iraq's national sports enterprise in the hands of his son Uday. Uday chose a rather unorthodox technique to improve the performance of the most important element of that enterprise, the soccer team. He beat and tortured underperforming players, shaved the head of every team member after a poor showing, and interfered in game management by telephoning team managers in the midst of matches and demanding that particular substitutions be made. Not surprisingly, these methods were less than effective in motivating the team, and the team's performance deteriorated rapidly.

As the Iraqi team improved its performance after the fall of regime and came ever closer to Olympic qualification, Iraqis forgot the dark past and began to focus on a more hopeful future, at least inasmuch as sports were concerned. One final obstacle remained by June of 2004—the pestersome Saudis, who thought that Uday or no Uday, our team was no match for theirs. Needless to say, we thought otherwise, and longed more than anything to see our team demonstrate that on the pitch. I am no soccer aficionado, so any description I might give of the match itself would be woefully inadequate. More interesting to me were the fans, the Iraqis, urging the team to victory. The game took place at night, and by this time Baghdad was no place to travel in the late evening, much less to congregate in large numbers to watch a soccer game. I watched the game at my grandmother's home, with Ra'ad, Sa'diya, Ali, and my grandmother.

The conversation, which so often centered on Iraq's troubles, was of a wholly different nature.

"You know what the problem with our team is, they are too slow, and that fellow there doesn't know how to hit the ball properly. Who is he anyway?" Sa'diya asked.

"My mother, the eighty-year-old grandmother coach," said Ra'ad in exasperation. "Listen, you don't understand this game. We're talking about soccer here, so just keep quiet."

"I understand that my son doesn't have manners, and that he should learn to get some," Sa'diya retorted.

"Would you two leave it alone? I'm trying to figure out if we're going to win or not and all I hear is your yapping." shouted my grandmother.

"Gooaaallll!" the commentator shouted. Iraq had scored. Ra'ad, Ali, and I jumped up and shouted. Sa'diya in her long black flowing robe began to dance and the neighbors could be heard doing the same. Gunfire that seemed to come from Abu Ahmed's house pierced the nighttime silence.

"Goal? Iraq scored and I missed it with Ra'ad and Sa'diya bothering me. This time you two shut up so I don't have to miss anymore of this game," my grandmother ordered.

The match carried on, Saudi scored only minutes later, and the match remained 1–1 throughout. My cousin Ali called to check in from his house. He was too nervous as the time began to expire to watch on his own, and could not come to our home for fear of missing a goal. Zuhair called and told me that the Green Dragons, as he was wont to call the Iraqi team, would surely win the Olympics if they could beat the Saudis, seemingly ignoring the fact that even the best of the Middle Eastern teams were no match for those of Europe or Latin America. One of the professors from Suleymania called, as well, to inform me that the substitute who had entered the game, Younis Mahmoud, was from Kirkuk, a city only two hours from Suleymania in Iraq's north.

"Who?" I asked.

"Younis Mahmoud, Professor, he just came into the game a while ago."

"Never heard of him," I responded.

"Only four minutes left, looks like a tie for us. Not bad," said Ra'ad to nobody in particular.

"Professor, I'm happy an Iraqi sub is from your home town. I should go though," I said.

"Of course . . ." he started to say.

"Look! Ball free!" Ali shouted, "It's an empty goal!"

Shouts everywhere, everyone stood, and suddenly an Iraqi player appeared and dropped the ball into an empty net for the go-ahead goal. The player, it turned out, was the Kirkuk substitute, Younis Mahmoud.

"Congratulations, congratulations!" my grandmother beamed, smiling at all of us. "Iraq wins! Iraq wins!"

Ra'ad, the burly house guard with a gun always at his side, looked like he was about to cry. I could understand why. Finally, Iraq won. Not Saddam's falsely claimed victories, not a victory by the United States on behalf of Iraq, but a single pure, unchallenged, and unassisted victory for the nation. A small victory perhaps, but one desperately needed by a population growing weary of repeated defeat. As for me, I couldn't hear myself think from all the gunfire around us. I was even inclined to shoot along with them, though I never did. I did, however, dance along with the Iraqis in the streets of my neighborhood, and was quite surprised to see some Americans soldiers dancing on their tank. Lit by floodlights and given wide berth by Iraqis, but cheering along all the same, they shouted in their thick U.S. accents, *'ash al Iraq,'* or Long Live Iraq. I thought that if this were the dominating image that Iraqis had of American soldiers, rather than of stern men pointing big guns at them, things might have turned out differently here.

The pictures that appeared later on television and in the newspapers, of Iraqis in their homes watching the game, were moving indeed, and gave hope to a nation desperately in need of it. Black-tented elderly women who I would not have thought would recognize a soccer ball, children who could recite every player on the team and their relative strengths and weaknesses, the paunch bellied men, second-guessing every decision the coach had made and questioning the skills of each player, Kurds in national costume, Arabs in long white robes, western-dressed secularists and staunch Islamists, all fixated on a game. They cheered and sighed and prayed and hoped that their team would be victorious, as desperate for victory as fans would be anywhere else, different only in the most superficial of ways.

The reality of Baghdad life settled in soon enough after the match. Soccer fans in Baghdad do not have the luxury of the nearly obsessive devotion of their counterparts elsewhere to celebrate until the early hours of the morning. We need to stay alive. But even while returning to my car and my armed driver the next morning, in selecting a route different from one I had taken before yet which kept me on busy roads, and in taking care to ensure that I did not get anywhere near a U.S. military vehicle that might be a target, my spirits were lighter. It seemed it would be years before Iraq could right itself, and before then we were headed for a long period of horror and misery. But still, we had won.

CHAPTER 36

Suleymania Redux

MY FREQUENT TRIPS TO Suleymania took on added meaning by the early summer of 2004. I continued to go to Suleymania as part of our law school reform project, and it remained safe, peaceful, and friendly to Americans. By contrast, between Abu Ghraib, Moqtada Al-Sadr's uprising, the barbarity and tenacity of the uprising, and increased ethnic division, Iraq outside of the Kurdish north seemed to have hurtled into an abyss. Because of this, we were far more successful in implementing programs in Suleymania after our initial discussions with the faculty than we were elsewhere, and this increased our frequency of travel to the north.

I no longer drove to Suleymania. The road from Baghdad to the beginning of the Kurdish-controlled region beyond Kirkuk was simply too dangerous. Kidnappings, car thefts, and murders happened on a daily basis there, though it was not even one of the most dangerous roads in the country. Moreover, I often traveled with Americans—David would often come, or another person working on our project from our Chicago-based office. They often helped with aspects of the project with which I was involved, among them preparing for a summer program in which students could participate in practice-based law workshops, such as moot courts and observation of forensics, so that students would have a better idea of how the law operates in practice. We had hired a law librarian, Kimberli, who traveled with us as well, and she was helping to expand the collections of the various law schools. However, this limited my ability to travel by road, as I was not foolish enough to sit in a car with a person who would have to pull out an American passport as identification at each of the many checkpoints on the way to Kirkuk. To be kidnapped or killed would then no longer be a disturbing possibility; it would be something approaching a near certainty. Instead, we used an alternative route, by flight to Kurdish-controlled Erbil, and from there by road to Suleymania.

The road to the Baghdad airport, the airport itself, the checkpoint, all remained as it had been over the past year, except worse. Bulldozers continued to uproot palm trees, areas of upturned earth expanded, there were more tanks, and the checkpoint was no longer as simple as it once was. We were often required to wait at the checkpoint for as long as several hours, easy stationary targets for a suicide bomber.

The extent of the wait at the checkpoint was, much like entry to the Green Zone, entirely ad hoc. Sometimes soldiers waved me through without any search after I showed a badge through a window. On other days, guards moved me and the other Americans traveling with me to the front of the search line and then searched us, a process that took about fifteen minutes. On particularly unlucky days, we had to wait for a period of hours along with the many Iraqis seeking entry on a daily basis. This was rare, however, and generally we entered more quickly than the Iraqis, as a result of which we frequently reached the airline desk before the Iraqi airline employees who were required to wait in the longer, exclusively Iraqi line.

Spiral ascents and descents remained the norm for flights leaving Baghdad and entering Erbil, followed by a three-and-a-half hour drive to Suleymania along narrow, winding mountain roads. But this did not create a great deal of trouble for us, as our world changed as soon as we arrived in Kurdistan. For one thing, we almost never saw a U.S. soldier, other than a few enjoying some days of rest in a safe area where the population welcomed them. Instead, the *pesh merga* maintained security as they always had. Relative to the American efforts in the rest of Iraq, the Kurds had proved remarkably successful at policing. In Kurdistan, we walked through the town at virtually any hour we pleased, spoke whatever language we wanted on the street, and carried our American passports as identification.

The ride to Suleymania was always astonishingly beautiful. Mountains reached upward in all directions to the sky, some so high that snow still remained on them, and creeks ran down their sides containing crystal clear, icy water, a welcome respite in the 110-degree heat. Kurdish goat herders and shepherds in their traditional dress (checkered head scarf wrapped entirely about the head and above the neck, and loose baggy pants below the waist) dotted the mountainsides, moving their animals from one place to another between vines of grapes. I had always been told of Iraq's natural beauty in the north, but like most Arabs, perpetual conflict had prevented me from seeing it.

At night, after the long drive to Suleymania, a few work meetings, and a pleasant dinner outside later in the evening, I generally retired to my hotel. When I reached my room on the top floor, I would go to my terrace of the five-story building (a skyscraper by Iraqi standards), which afforded an excellent view of the city. There were the lights of the city, a dark area where a city park lay, and near it, an amusement park with a Ferris wheel clearly visible and dominating that corner of the landscape. And beyond the city were the dark, tall mountains reaching upwards and surrounding it on all sides, as if protecting Suleymania from the evil that lay just beyond. I would lie back in a chair, pull out a Romeo and Juliet cigar I had saved for just such an occasion, and smoke it. It was the closest thing I had to relaxation in Iraq.

CHAPTER 37

Mondays at the Reef

I WAS NOT LONG in Baghdad before it became nearly impossible for a Monday to pass without lunch at the Reef. A relative who was starting his own business in Iraq and who had arrived in June of the previous year initiated the tradition a little more than a month before I arrived in Baghdad.

I had no idea what the Reef was when I made my first Monday trip to it in the summer of 2003. The name, for a longtime scuba diver like me, was positively intriguing, and I longed, even then, for the company of people who had been raised in the West. The string of disappointments that befell post-war Iraq had hardly begun then, and I allowed my imagination license that I would no longer indulge only a few months later. I wondered whether the Reef was some kind of rudimentary and recently built yacht club—boats on the Tigris, seafood, a view of the sunset over the river, with palm trees in the foreground gently swaying in the breeze as the crescent moon came softly into view. I was mildly disappointed when I discovered that the Reef was in fact nothing more than an Italian restaurant.

"Excuse me, sir?" I once asked a waiter, when I had arrived early and was waiting for others.

"Yes sir?" he replied.

"Why is this place called 'Reef'?"

"Because it is designed like a Reef!"

"It is?"

"Of course!" he exclaimed.

"Reef, you mean a coral reef?"

"Of course not," he said, surprised at the question. "Does it look like an ocean to you? Reef. Al-Reef. Arabic."

Suddenly I understood. "Oh, Reef, like Arabic from village. I see. But it does not look like a village either."

"The owner used to go to Italy in the summer in the 1970s. He went three times in fact, each time for a week. So he knows Italian villages well, you see."

"I guess. I like the oak tables. I like the piano player too. Can he play something other than a Britney Spears song on it, though?" I asked.

"On your orders I will have him play what you like, sir. You prefer Christina Aguilera? Backstreet Boys?"

"Never mind, I'll try the lasagna today," I told him.

The Reef, as Italian restaurants go worldwide, would accurately be described as mediocre. The food was acceptable, the décor respectable, the service excellent, and the price reasonable. But in the context of Iraq, it may as well have been Rome.

I looked forward to those Mondays, when about six to eight of us would gather to talk about our work, our hopes, dreams and fears, life abroad, the latest film release (which none of us would get to see), the last trip we had taken to Europe, basically anything that struck our fancy. Some who gathered worked for the Americans, and some despised the American presence in Iraq. Some found their home in what they hoped would be a burgeoning private sector, and others were members of nongovernmental organizations or represented individuals on the governing council. Most were Shi'i, some Sunni, one was Kurdish, and several were of mixed descent. But more important than what divided us was what united us: hope, along with increasingly nagging fears and doubts as time went on and America failed to set Iraq onto a course toward stability and prosperity. Though the analogy is not entirely accurate and indeed somewhat saccharine, the gatherings always reminded me of *Diner, The Breakfast Club, St. Elmo's Fire,* those movies of my generation that explored the value of camaraderie when facing an uncertain and potentially terrifying future.

But as Baghdad started to change, so did we. A few in the group joined the government and never made it because of security reasons. Some left the country. The rest were just too terrified to continue showing up or had relocated to the Green Zone. That left me on my own every Monday at the Reef, with my *International Herald Tribune.*

The situation was not entirely unpleasant. I enjoyed the weekend *Tribune,* which was effectively Friday's *New York Times* but abridged, and I had the opportunity to observe the Reef's standard clientele more closely when alone. It was mostly Baghdad's upper crust society, those you could once find at the Hunting Club, which was now largely empty for fear of terrorism. The other patrons of the Reef were young unmarried couples on a date, quite taboo in Iraq, where men and women were not expected to have encounters with one another prior to marriage unless others were present. Mixed gender groups, particularly inside universities, were not uncommon, and two students of the opposite gender might speak briefly alone on the street, or before or after a class, but a date was, in Iraq, entirely unthinkable. I was not accustomed to seeing so many women with their backs to the rest of the restaurant, obviously seated in a way meant to shield their identity to the fullest extent possible while their respective dates faced the other diners, scanning nervously for any sign that someone had identified them.

But such trifling entertainment aside, I had lost something in my colleagues' absence, and at times it was difficult to continue to go because unpleasant and difficult memories of where Iraq was only a few short months ago and where it was by the late summer of 2004 would invariably come to mind. Moreover, security officials working with USAID continually told me that the type of regularity exhibited by my weekly trips was unwise and that I should not go to the Reef anymore for fear of kidnapping; or that if I did go I should vary the routine by changing the day, but I could not and I would not. It may seem like a small sacrifice to forgo one restaurant, or at least to change the day on which I went, but it was not.

Throughout the spring and summer of 2004, I had gradually restricted my activities to a point that resembled house arrest. I could not leave the house after sunset, I often could not make it to the pool, I could not go to the Hunting Club at all, I could not frequent areas where large groups gathered, including most restaurants, and I could not see a movie or go to the zoo, walk in a park, or engage in any other recreational activity out-side of the home. This was my one single indulgence, one paper and one pizza, and I could not imagine doing without it.

In America, this might be considered a defiant gesture against and tri-umph over nihilism, of "not letting the terrorists win," as is said so often by our nation's politicians. But anyone exposed to this type of danger with this frequency and intensity, I think, would disabuse those more romanti-cally inclined of such silly sentimentalism, as the wellspring of this obsti-nacy stemmed not from some desire to triumph over forces of evil, but from a very basic physical and psychic exhaustion. Simply stated, I had reached a point where I could not take any further steps to avoid death; the entire affair was too draining. When I reached that point, I was nei-ther afraid nor brave, but simply tired. I could do little more than thrust my hands in the air, ask a beneficent God for mercy, carry on with life, and, for at least the time it took to eat one pizza, forget that I just might die before I had finished.

CHAPTER 38

Yet I Remain

As the situation worsened in Iraq, many friends and relatives asked me over and over again what compelled me to remain. The threat of danger was continually getting more precarious, particularly for U.S. citizens. The level of hostility toward the United States crept slowly and steadily higher and fear tinged with disgust had replaced hope as the dominant emotion that gripped Iraq's exhausted populace. The bustle that characterized post-war Iraq, the small businessmen that had once sought to expand their very limited operations, the returning scholars who dreamed of founding larger educational institutions, the graduating students who looked forward to a bigger and brighter future were, by and large, gone by the summer of 2004, either killed by terrorists, hiding in their homes, or, if they had means, living abroad.

Businesses still functioned and, of course, schools were open and life went on, but the crowds were fewer, the places of business closed earlier, sales decreased, and the eagerness that once showed on the faces of men, women, and children had disappeared. Even my cousin Ali, who had remained in Iraq throughout the Saddam era and who had held out such hope for the country, was thinking about leaving.

So then why was I, of all people, still here? I was still able to work with the universities, but the extent of my efforts was limited due to security, as students would not show up to class and visiting lecturers would not come to campus. Professors had little motivation to address these problems, and nobody at the university wanted to admit that they were assisting in our project because it was funded by the American government. In addition, I was in constant danger of being abducted, for ransom or for perceived political advantage. And most important, I shared the psychological exhaustion that I saw manifested in my fellow Iraqis. I had to force myself to exercise, to write, to work, to visit relatives, or to do much of anything other than sleep and watch the news. I lacked energy, and it grew worse by the day. I wondered at times how long I could allow myself to continue like this.

Unlike many others, as an American who had lived most of his life in the United States, I had a choice. I could leave my job and go. I suppose there was an element of honor, bravado, or machismo (the precise term being dependent on the perspective of the observer) related to the fulfillment of an endeavor I had set out to accomplish.

But all else aside, what mattered to me most was that I still believed. Intellectually, I knew it was a delusion at this point, but some part of me could not dare to face the horrible reality that existed. Somehow I thought Iraq would pull through, even though every sign indicated otherwise.

I believed in this land rich with oil through which the two rivers flowed, the home of the gardens of Babylon, the gates of Nineveh, the Abbasid palaces of Baghdad, and the holy shrines of Najaf and Kerbala. I believed in its history and its traditions and its religion. I believed in its importance to its neighbors and to the world's mightiest players, who could scarcely afford to leave it in the disarray in which it was. I believed in my grandmother's tomatoes and okra, in Abu Ahmed's tea with cardamom, in the lamb on the spitfire prepared at every large party, and in the grilled fish cooked on the banks of the Tigris. I believed in the sunset over the Euphrates viewed from the plains of Kerbala, in the mountains of Suleymania, and in the swamps of the Ahwar. I believed in the music of Nadhem Al-Ghazali, the poetry of Abi Nuwas, the theology of Muhammad Baqir al-Sadr. And more than anything else, I believed deeply, and without reservation, in the goodness of the people living in this blighted land—in their resourcefulness, their ingenuity, their intense desire for a better life, and their inherent ability to rise above what separated them and work together to create a better land. In spite of the terrorism, in spite of the American blunders, in spite of the crime and the hate and the war and the death and the looting, and in spite of the obvious, I still believed.

CHAPTER 39

Food

IN THIS COUNTRY, LONG deprived of just about anything else for decades, the consumption of food had become the premier source of entertainment and recreation. This was obvious to me immediately—everyone always wanted to go out to eat or arrange for a lunch at someone's home and, either way, I consumed too much. If we went to a restaurant, I had a difficult time controlling my food intake, as the portions were so large that the plate was effectively a one-item buffet that could never be finished. My favorite dish, lamb on rice, typically included more than a pound of lamb and three types of biryani, each containing two to three cups of rice. This was not to mention the endless supply of bread and Arab appetizers that were automatically included as part of any meal and that were served family style, so that dozens of plates were passed around filled with hummus, tabouli, baba ghanouj, salad, potato salad (called "mayonnaise" here), and countless other Eastern delicacies before the main course had even arrived. I have tried, but never have I left an authentic Iraqi restaurant feeling anything other than slightly nauseous from overconsumption.

Meals in the homes of others tended to be the same, or even worse from a health perspective. Unlike American homes, where a mother tells her child to consider the starving children in China to get the child to finish eating his food, in Iraq nothing could be more embarrassing to the host than the idea that his guests would eat all of the food on the table. Instead, an Iraqi host would place a cornucopia of culinary delights on the table that would be enough for three times the number of guests who had been invited.

On one occasion, I was at the house of my elderly aunt Khadija when she noticed that my plate was half empty.

"Haider, you haven't eaten a thing, give me that plate!" she said.

"No, Auntie, really, I am very full. I finished one plate and then even had a smaller second serving," I replied.

"That's not enough. Here, give me that plate!"

"Auntie, honestly, I have had quite a bit. I'm getting fat."

"You can start your diet tomorrow. Here, give me that."

"Auntie, tomorrow I am invited to Ammu Mahdi's house, and he'll do the same thing."

"Then the day after you start your diet. Give me that plate."

"I'll serve myself, Auntie."

"Okay, I am watching you," she said, and turned to resume an earlier conversation.

Iraqis also considered it quite rude to agree to be served a second time, or even a first time, unless someone insisted. It would be unimaginable for an Iraqi to walk into my home, and if I asked him what he wanted to drink, for him to say he wanted a Coke. This would be akin to an American walking into someone's home and, after saying hello, walking over to the refrigerator, opening it, and pulling out a Coke. An Iraqi behaving properly should say he wants nothing, and then be offered a choice, Coke or coffee, for example. At that point, a response in favor of one or the other would be acceptable, though even then a guest might say he does not want anything, in which case a host should just give him Coke or coffee.

I learned this the hard way in the United States, when several Iraqis came to my parents' home when my parents were not at home, but were expected. I asked the newly arrived guests twice if they wanted help with their bags, and twice they refused. As they approached the house, my mother arrived and saw me walking alongside them without a bag in my hand while they struggled with theirs. She chastised me severely for my rudeness. I later learned the customary Iraqi practice, which is to simply grab the bag without asking and refuse to relinquish it once taken. Nevertheless, I continue to believe to this day that a grave injustice was done to me on that occasion and remind my parents of it, though my father's response was that this injustice works both ways, as he nearly starved in the United States during the first year of his arrival. Nobody in West Virginia, where he first lived, forced him to eat at dinner parties and his polite refusals to take more meant he ended up watching everyone else enjoy second and third servings of food while he sat quietly wondering how quickly he could excuse himself and go to the nearest McDonald's.

In any event, a person in Iraq could hardly avoid overeating on any occasion where food was served. This was Iraqi tradition. The development that seemed to have taken place over the past decade, however, was the extent to which eating had usurped any other form of social occasion. The lack of recreation and social and community activity other than food consumption developed as a result of a debilitating combination of a totalitarian regime that sought to keep its population from forming any type of social or civic organizations not under government control, and the crippling U.N. sanctions that did nothing to alleviate the population's misery or provide them alternative recreational activities. Because of a bungled occupation whose administrators had failed to provide the most basic level of security or the slightest improvement in elemental public services during the period of their administration, broad social gatherings that might have taken the place of a meal (parties, dances, museum outings, trips to the zoo) were still impossible.

In direct consequence of this unfortunate series of factors, Iraq must have had the largest population of obese individuals relative to the general population on earth. I had never seen such enormous girths on so many men, in particular. Were not so many other needs so pressing, a study should have been commissioned concerning the resulting costs that were likely to arise in Iraqi society in light of such obesity. The American Midwest, where I was raised and which seemed to have substantial obesity problems of its own, was a diet colony relative to Baghdad. Midwesterners may gorge on fatty and unhealthy foods, but at least they go to a fairground or an amusement park to do it. Life in Baghdad was built exclusively on consumption and a sedentary lifestyle. In this, Saddam Hussein had thoroughly corrupted his people.

Ironically, despite the ready abundance of vast quantities of food and the plethora of establishments serving it, I felt deprived of choices that might be available to me elsewhere. The food may have been plentiful in quantity and high in quality, but it was hardly diverse. Virtually anything other than Iraqi meals (and in some limited cases mediocre Italian or bad Chinese food) was almost entirely unavailable. While I deferred to nobody in my appreciation of Arab and in particular Iraqi cuisine, eating it almost exclusively for nearly a year had been quite taxing. I craved the variety available elsewhere in the world.

To that end, my brother and I began to host an international meal on Friday evenings, attended by Sa'diya and Ra'ad, as well as my cousin Ali and sometimes my uncle Isam. The search for ingredients was not always easy, as the number of stores that carried the ingredients we wished to purchase was limited, the ingredients were expensive, and the availability of any particular item was never assured. Consequently, the menu depended largely on what we managed to find. I found it ironic that in a religious Arab and Islamic city such as Baghdad, it was easier, had I wanted it, to purchase a beer than to buy a carton of ricotta cheese. That the ricotta cheese carton cost as much as twelve beers ($11.17) was ironic as well, though I was more annoyed than amused by this.

Aside from the costs, I enjoyed the venture and was happy that we had managed it despite the substantial difficulties involved in procuring what we needed by way of ingredients. My grandmother, on the other hand, could not begin to understand why two men would take this task of food preparation upon themselves, and suspected it was because of some failure relating to the food she provided for us. She was less than enthused, but over time began to tolerate it.

Before our first meal, which was Mexican, she asked us directly, "Do you not like the food Sa'diya prepares? That's the problem, I am sure. Sa'diya! See what you have done! You've driven the boys to cook!"

"No, Grandma, Sa'diya cooks great food. We just want some things that we are used to from home," I said.

"Sa'diya can make you Mexican food. Right, Sa'diya? I've been to Mexico, I can help her." Sa'diya rolled her eyes.

"Grandma, it's okay, we can do it ourselves."

Her offer to have Sa'diya cook Mexican food reminded me of an earlier occasion when we had searched the house for dates and could find none, and my grandmother and Sa'diya argued about who should climb the palm tree in our backyard to get more. The idea of two women well above eighty climbing a date palm while Ali and I sat and watched was a source of much amusement to us.

"Yes, Grandma, we can do it. Just on Fridays. Every other day we can eat Sa'diya's food because it is very good," Ali said.

My grandmother shrugged and then shuffled to her chair at the table with an air of slighted resignation, thereby giving her approval. Next, Sa'diya took her seat, and said, "Why are we eating Mexican food anyway? This is Iraq, not Mexico." This was a relatively positive reaction from Sa'diya, however, as compared with her review of Chinese food a few weeks later. "God help the Chinese," she said, "if they have to eat this stuff every day."

CHAPTER 40

Swimming Pool, Outdoors

IN WHAT STOOD AS the greatest improvement in my personal and recreational life since the purchase of my television in August of 2003, my health club's outdoor swimming pool opened at the start of June. While the indoor pool had remained open and would stay open throughout the summer, the onset of the heat had driven many people to the pools throughout Baghdad. The Hotel Babylon's health club pools were no exception, and lap swimming was impossible most of the time given the limited space.

The problem was partly one of crowds and partly one of culture. Iraqis approached swimming pools as they did traffic intersections, preferring the freedom and independence in having no rules whatsoever to the kind of order that developed nations favor. In the case of traffic intersections, there were no lights or signs (or at least none to which anyone paid the slightest attention), and people got through an intersection entirely on the basis of their independent judgment as to how much traffic there was opposing them, how large the opposing cars were, and whether or not they had already yielded to enough cars while waiting. So there was no reason that the car turning left yield necessarily to oncoming traffic; which car yielded was largely a matter of implicit negotiation between the two approaching vehicles, and for the most part they worked it out.

These rules did not apply if a police officer was present directing traffic, but this was rare and occurred only when an intersection was particularly busy. At all other times, even if there happened to be a police officer at the intersection, he preferred to sit quietly in the shade with a newspaper, letting the cars make their way through the intersection until his intervention became necessary—mostly when the traffic no longer moved and the sound of the honking horns began to interfere with his newspaper reading.

Swimming pools in Iraq were similar. There were a few lap swimmers, but no separate swimming lanes set up for them. Nor was it clear to any Iraqi why a lap swimmer moving back and forth in a straight line across a pool was not at fault if random teenagers happened to run into him or even jump onto him in the course of swimming or leaping into the pool. For this reason, I avoided busy swimming pools, and so between this and the security concerns involved in taking the road to the pool, I was rarely able to swim.

So it was with a great deal of anticipation that I awaited the opening of the outdoor pool at the start of June. For the most part I was satisfied with the results. Swimming in the late afternoon remained impossible due to the demand for both pools at that time, but the late mornings were an ideal time to swim. Temperatures exceeded 90 degrees by 10 a.m., thus the elderly men that inhabited the pool at that time stayed indoors, and the younger crowd never arrived until after school ended.

Like much of the rest of the health club, the outdoor pool would have been impressive if it were better maintained. It sat in a garden along the Tigris River, though in Arab custom, walls blocked any view of the river, the hotel, and the street outside so that Iraqi women could frequent the pool on Tuesdays and Saturdays and swim in private, when men were prohibited from entry. The precaution was largely unnecessary, as Iraqi women placed a good deal of emphasis on remaining untanned, given how unattractive Iraqis considered a tan to be, and no woman would go into the sun to swim as a result.

Despite the lack of a river view, the garden was decent. Palm trees lined the perimeter, there were flowers and bushes, and the grass was well kept. Aside from the garden, the pool area was in considerable disrepair. The water was not filtered well and therefore murky, the pool chairs were in poor shape and lacked cushioning of any kind, and the pool deck, made of concrete, seemed to have been laid decades ago and not improved since.

But in the cool water, if I tried hard enough, I could focus on the greenery of the garden surrounding me and it almost seemed like I was somewhere else. During the course of a swim, a particularly low flying helicopter, an explosion in a neighborhood not too far away (the Green Zone was across the river, directly opposite the Babylon Hotel), gunfire, or something else was always there to remind me where I was. But for at least some short period of time, I could almost forget and relax in a way I had forgotten I could.

I usually left the pool by 11 a.m., before the crowds arrived, but if I had morning appointments and could not get to the pool before noon or 1 p.m., I would leave just as they began to enter. I did not mind, so long as I had finished swimming. I found it entertaining just to sit in the shallow area of the pool and watch the children, adolescents, and even young men in their twenties splashing about, enjoying themselves. The rules limiting horseplay in the pool that I experienced as a child in the United States were absent here; all of the Iraqi youth ran on the deck, jumped in wherever they liked, dove in the shallow end, held each other underwater, and did all of the things I was strictly prohibited from doing in my childhood. There was a lifeguard, but he seemed to be about as busy as most policemen at traffic intersections. He sat comfortably in his lifeguard chair, some distance from the pool where the shade was, and kept to himself. Once, I heard a whistle blow, and I turned in astonishment toward the lifeguard, assuming someone must have done something truly awful to merit a whistle from a fellow who barely paid attention. It turned out the lifeguard hadn't blown the whistle; some kid had brought one to the pool and was playing cops and robbers with his friends. Not surprisingly, this made no impression on the lifeguard. In a way, it all made sense, given the fatalism to which many Iraqis subscribed.

I told my cousin Ali this story over tea at his home later that day.

"Haider, what did you expect exactly?" Ali asked.

"Well, I thought the lifeguard would stop them, it could be dangerous," I said.

"If he falls, he falls, it is the Will of God. Are we going to make children sit at a pool and do nothing?"

"I used to love the pool, but we couldn't do any of the things they do here," I said.

"No running or dunking?"

"No, it is dangerous," I said. "People want to protect their children."

My cousin shook his head, distressed. "It is the Will of God, you can't prevent what God wills. I guess it's not much worse than us though. I thought we were deprived, but it seems you were too. You never had a swimming pool a kid can enjoy because Americans think they can beat fate. But they can't—they can only close down swimming pools."

CHAPTER 41

Departure

ALONG WITH MANY OF my Iraqi colleagues with foreign citizenship (as well as those few non-Iraqi expatriates who remained), I would depart Baghdad before the June 30 handover in order to escape the madness that the Americans and the new Iraqi government promised us. A year prior I would have been incensed by the announcement that it was best for expatriates to leave Iraq temporarily, given the dangers. It would be like the New York Police Department asking the residents of Manhattan to move out of their homes on an American holiday because of the likelihood of a terrorist incident. But in the year that had passed for me in Iraq, during which the security situation in Iraq had progressively deteriorated, and during which the Americans clearly demonstrated that they either lacked the will or the means to do anything about it, I had become accustomed to information of this sort, and reacted by making preparations to leave.

I would be leaving for about a month, and thus my one year anniversary of arriving was marked by self-enforced exile. I had no choice. The ominous threats by the insurgency and the feeble reactions of the supposed authorities made it impossible to do anything else. However, I would leave with a heavy heart. On my last two trips out of Baghdad, I looked forward to the respite, to good restaurants and a comfortable bed, to U.S. magazines, and freshly brewed coffee and a doughnut. This time, while I would have all this at my disposal, I would not be so unabashedly happy about it. This time, it was not entirely clear to me that there would be anything to go back to in a month. If the direst warnings turned out to be accurate, disaster could befall this land very soon.

I did not necessarily expect disaster at the handover, but for the first time it could happen. It might not be impossible for the insurgents to cause enough trouble to enable chaos to rule, in relatively short order. The thought of running from the country I cared about so dearly when this might happen felt contemptible. In my head, I knew I was no soldier and nothing could be achieved by staying. In my heart, I measured myself against the Shi'i martyrs that were the heroes of my youth and found myself wanting in the balance. I was a coward, cravenly ducking into a rat hole septic tank in some desperate attempt to stay alive, all principles and dedication to rebuild be damned. I felt sick, and weak, and less than a man.

A good night's sleep was impossible partly because of this and partly because a good night's sleep was never possible in the summer given the power outages. The electricity turned off after it was on for two hours. The temperature in my room then skyrocketed; night after night I woke up in a pool of sweat and headed downstairs to turn on the generator, and then came back up to a room that was gradually being cooled once again. Four hours later, I had to turn the generator off; I was alerted to this by the neighborhood watch banging on our front gates. And I lived this way because I was, by Iraqi standards, rich. Most Iraqis could not afford a generator large enough to run an air conditioner. They had to remain awake for hours waiting for power to return, which would then enable them to enjoy another precious two hours of sleep.

I felt unworthy of my air conditioning and the privilege that allowed me to flee while so many I loved were staying behind, in the heat, in the dark, in the precarious and uncertain reality to which Iraq has been consigned. When the electricity cut off at 2 a.m. on my last night preceding my departure, I left it off for about thirty minutes, until my grandmother complained about the heat. As I went outside to run the generator, I thought about who was going to do this after I left, not even remembering that I had already arranged for the street guard to assume these duties. But I was her eldest grandson, and as an Arab who had been taught from childhood the importance of family and respect for elders, I felt additional embarrassment and shame for leaving my grandmother, a weak ninety-one-year-old woman, in the hands of hired help. She and her country deserved better than me.

As I turned on the generator that night and stepped outside the gate of my grandmother's home, an extremely dangerous thing to do in the middle of the night, even in a residential neighborhood, I took my last look at the neighborhood, possibly for a long, long while. I could not hear a thing but the roaring of generator engines. The half moon shone serenely above, and the palm trees and houses everywhere were illumined by its soft and gentle light. Less well-to-do families were sleeping on their roofs. There was nothing on the street. An American helicopter flew low, drowning out, just for a moment, the roar of the generators. This was Baghdad.

A rooster in the empty lot behind us distracted me. Its owner had been squatting for a month now, and unlike in America, where a resident called the police to remove the offender in such circumstances, nobody dared to turn out the unfortunate soul who lived in the cardboard hut he had constructed, nor did they care to. He had become a guard in the neighborhood and helped us find a carjacker who had stolen several automobiles. In this community, the only action that I could consider with respect to the rooster, and one I might have taken had circumstances permitted me to remain, would be to buy it, donate to its owner a much quieter turkey, and enjoy a dinner featuring a cooked nocturnal rooster that didn't seem to know dawn from midnight.

As I looked around the neighborhood, it seemed more than ever that this country was on the verge of collapse, and this terrified me. I was scared that all of the work I had done would come to nothing. I was scared that all the friends and relatives I had here would be subjected to ever greater dangers, and I was scared that my faith and my people would for decades to come be unjustly cemented in the eyes of the civilized world as agents of heartlessness and terror. The failure could be complete and absolute, almost everything I deem sacred submerged in its murky depths.

Whether sustained by Iraqi frustration, Ba'ath resources, or the delusions of radical Islamism, the forces of instability and chaos had strengthened to the point that they had managed to gain the upper hand by my one year anniversary in Iraq, preventing any true state from establishing itself and all but putting an end to any hope for the nation. In Falluja, Baqubah, Ramadi, and even Najaf, the state had simply ceased to exist. Elsewhere, terrorists appeared ready, willing, and able to strike at will against Iraqis and Americans alike. We Iraqis saw a curtain expanding across our nation, the forces that President Bush had called evil were advancing, slowly reaching their goal of sowing so much chaos that the government and nation of Iraq would effectively disappear, just as the country of Afghanistan had for so many years. Iraq was failing, America was retreating, and somewhere in a dark mountain cave, Osama was smiling.

PART II

Marriage, Election, and Beyond

Summer 2004: Hope and Despair

CHAPTER 42

Return to Baghdad

IN THE EARLY PART of August 2004, after a hiatus of nearly six weeks, I returned to Iraq to continue my law school reform project. I was still an employee of DePaul University, which managed the project, and the project continued to receive all of its funding from USAID, including the amounts necessary to pay my salary.

I was bound for Suleymania, where our project would be holding a workshop for recent graduates of the law school, introducing the law students to the realities of practicing law, as well as providing a crash course on the principles of American law. I was responsible for managing this and for providing the lectures on American law.

I continued to debate whether it was wise to remain in Iraq and I often pondered ways in which I could leave while causing minimal disruption to the current project. At the same time, I clung to my increasingly faint hope that Iraq would somehow find a way back to stability and normalcy, and that in the meantime I could continue to visit my family in Baghdad.

I had no illusions of being able to return to my life in Baghdad and my grandmother's home in the immediate future; the situation was too dangerous. This precluded my ability to advise the new government as I had the previous government when I served on the Finance Committee. After all, the national government operated from Baghdad. Instead, I would remain in the north, for the most part in the Kurdish-protected enclave. Even so, I could not bring myself to sell my car or bid farewell to my relatives or empty the room in my grandmother's home, which had been my home for over a year.

When I initially landed in Baghdad, I went immediately to my grandmother's house, where my grandmother, Ra'ad, and Sa'diya were all staying. They were all there to greet me, as was my cousin Ali.

"It's getting bad, Haider, I worry about you," said Ali, nervously, after some idle talk.

"Don't worry, I won't stay long this time, I'm leaving for the north soon," I reassured him.

"What?" my grandmother exclaimed, "You just got here ten minutes ago and you are already leaving!"

"Yes, Grandma, I have to, it is getting very dangerous here and I have a U.S. passport, you know."

I expected an argument. If there was one thing I knew my grandmother had looked forward to, it was my return to Baghdad. My mother had mentioned this several times while I was home in the U.S.

But there was no such protest. Instead, she said, resignedly, "Go. Go, it's better. Get out of this place. It gets worse every day." Then she began to shuffle toward her bedroom, her head down, paying no more attention to the discussion.

I called out after her, "Don't worry, Grandma, I'll try to come for short visits." She kept walking.

"I'll only worry when you come visit. The rest of the time I'll just miss you and be sad, which is better than worrying," she said.

During my brief stay, Baghdad appeared the same as when I had left. The spotty electricity, the overpriced and low-quality mobile phone service, the unbearably slow Internet connections, and the appallingly poor security had not changed. However, this short stopover was not so much an opportunity to reflect over failures past and present, but more an exercise in short-term nostalgia, to bask in the city's warmth, or stultifying heat, and remember how things were the last time it was this hot, a year earlier when had I lived in a city of hope and optimism. I went to the pool, visited my aunt Zahra nearby as well as my elderly aunt, and stopped by the offices of attorney colleagues to say hello.

My aunt Zahra was particularly happy knowing I would leave soon for

Suleymania. "Finally, you are starting to make sense. I couldn't understand why you kept insisting on staying in Baghdad. This is a lost cause now, and there is no reason to put yourself in danger unnecessarily."

"Why are you still here?" I asked.

"It's our fate, we can't leave anymore," she said. "I left Scotland forty years ago. I can't go back to living in the west again—all those drunken people fighting each other. You are different. Go."

"Yes," her daughter Suha said, "go and come in peace." This was a famous Arabic greeting.

"No," my aunt said, "go in peace and, God willing, don't come back here."

Despite the depressing conversations, I enjoyed the sojourn, even if it was fleeting, so fleeting I could barely remember the details only hours after leaving. It was almost surreal, so that it seemed more like a dream or a memory than an actual presence. I was there again, living my life again, driving my car, going to my health club, visiting my relatives, joking, laughing, and acting as if nothing had changed. Except, of course, that everything had.

As I told my grandmother, I planned to return in a month's time, for perhaps a week. These sorts of brief visits would have to do, for now.

CHAPTER 43

The Suleymania Grind

BY THE MIDDLE OF August my life had settled into a pattern in Suley-mania. Lacking much else to do, everything revolved around the seminar our project was hosting. I woke up around 9 a.m., spent an hour or two on administrative and other tasks related to the project, took an hour's walk (just about all I could do in terms of exercise, unfortunately), bought a newspaper, checked my e-mail, and arrived at the university in time for the start of the workshop. I usually stayed until the end of it and then had dinner with a few of the judges or professors, and was home around 11 p.m. to watch a movie or read a novel.

Though this was tiresome in many ways, I was not dissatisfied. I was much safer than I would be in Baghdad. The air was cleaner, the water fresher, the mountain views more inspiring than anything I had seen elsewhere in Iraq. And it was hard to imagine having more professional independence than I enjoyed currently. But I was not terribly productive. It seemed nothing could be achieved with efficiency in Iraq. A meeting with Professor Saman, for example, with whom I was becoming close during my stay in Suleymania, would invariably be endlessly delayed, and, once the meeting finally happened, very little was achieved. And Professor Saman was without question one of the smartest and hardest working people I knew in Iraq.

On one occasion, I went to visit him in order to prepare for a conference we were hosting for Iraqi law professors to take place in Suleymania in about two months' time.

"Come in, Doctor Haider, come in," he said.

"Thanks, Professor Saman, I came because we had an appointment, at eleven-thirty, right? I am sorry I'm fifteen minutes late."

"Of course, do not worry, come in, come in."

Three faculty members, in addition to the professor, were there. They stood to greet me and carried on with their conversation. They were discussing politics. I did not follow the conversation too closely because I was anxious to get on with the meeting. I waited nearly an hour before that particular conversation ended.

"Professor, we have to go. Doctor Haider, it was nice seeing you," two of the three faculty members announced as they left.

The third, the oldest of the three, remained seated. "Professor," he said, "Listen to this line of poetry." He read from a book he was holding.

"Beautiful! Where is that from?" asked Professor Saman.

"Rumi. Here is another."

This carried on for another twenty minutes. I was in a hurry, and bored, all at the same time. Finally, the gentlemen left close to 1 p.m.

Saman turned to me. "Sorry, Professor Haider, what were we supposed to be talking about? Ah, the conference, right."

"Yes, let's try to wrap it up in the next half hour, if at all possible," I said. "I have an appointment with the dean." I needed to see the dean of the law school as well, to discuss a separate program.

"Today? He is out of town today."

"He did not tell me!" *This meant I would have to come back again and lose another morning discussing Rumi and Arab politics,* I thought to myself.

"Why would he suggest today?" Professor Saman asked, almost rhetorically.

"I suggested it, and he agreed."

"Oh that's different, no wonder," Saman said, relieved to have resolved the mystery. "He would never be so rude as to *tell* you he cannot make an appointment you propose."

"Instead, he just won't show up?" I asked.

"Right. Listen, it's late, we are past regular working hours by almost thirty minutes, and I am tired. Plus we are coming back from four to eight for the afternoon seminar. Let's have lunch, and we can discuss our agenda tomorrow. I tell you, these military hours are exhausting. We did so much today, didn't we?"

I returned the next day to meet with Professor Saman and a second professor, Anwer, with whom I had a previous appointment. I was also hoping to meet the dean as well, given his absence the day before. However, I was not entirely optimistic I would be able to pull off a miraculous three meetings in a single day. When I arrived in Professor Saman's office, there was a heated discussion going on about Iraqi politics in the 1950s and Saddam's killing of the Barazani clan. This discussion involved an economics professor who had dropped by unannounced. I again paid little attention to the discussion, frustrated at my entire lack of progress with our work, or any work, over the previous two days, and waited for him to leave. Mercifully, after only forty-five minutes, he did.

I began my long-awaited meeting by asking the professors if they had created an agenda for the conference we were to discuss.

"Professors, we were really hoping for an agenda from you guys on this conference, and we have nothing. I've been looking for the past two days to develop it and we have not seemed to have gotten anywhere," I said.

"Doctor Haider, you see how busy we are. It's 11 a.m. and we've met those professors you just saw, now we meet with you, and then the dean wants to see us. Then you have this seminar you make us attend from four to eight, and we're exhausted. When would we write this agenda?" asked Professor Anwer.

"Okay, okay, what are your ideas, I'll write them down for you," I said.

"You have no time either!" Professor Anwer exclaimed.

"I'll do it after eight, or tomorrow morning, whatever." *Or*, I thought to myself, *I will not drink tea and discuss Arab poetry for six hours tomorrow and do it then.*

"You are not a man, you are a machine!" Saman exclaimed proudly. "This is why these Americans are so much further advanced, Professor Anwer. This is what we need to do!"

I could tell he was earnest, without precisely understanding how deep the inefficiencies in his own society ran.

"Thank you, Saman. Now your ideas?"

They looked at each other helplessly. This required initiative, and if there is anything that Iraqis seemed to have learned from the Saddam era, it was that initiative could get a man killed. It was always better before taking action, therefore, to ensure that one's superior had approved of it.

"Should we get permission on this?" asked Anwer. "We'd better see the dean."

"Well, fine, though he already knows about the conference. We've been planning it for months. But let's see the dean," I replied.

The dean was with a judge, causing us another hour long delay. While we sat in the dean's office, the judge and the dean discussed poetry, politics, and other topics of no relevance to the university or the judiciary. Finally, the judge left and the dean turned to us. I explained the situation, and the need for an agenda.

"That's a great idea," he said, "but it's 3 p.m. already, and I'm exhausted from the long day. Come by tomorrow and we can do the agenda, for sure."

I didn't return, but instead wrote the agenda myself that evening and sent it to them via my driver. I understood later from Professor Saman that the dean was irritated about my having set an agenda for the conference without consulting with them adequately.

CHAPTER 44

Ali Beg

SOMEONE WHO HAS TRAVELED as much as I have is accustomed to disappointments and disillusionments of various kinds when arriving at a supposedly impressive tourist destination that for one reason or another fails to impress. Still, nothing quite prepared me for my late August sojourn. I had decided to take a daylong trip with Professor Saman and several recent graduates of law schools in Suleymania to what were billed as some of Kurdistan's natural wonders, and among Iraq's most important domestic tourist destinations.

The day began early, the younger graduates were eager to get on the road as quickly as possible. I was out of bed before 7 a.m. and we were outside city limits well before 8 a.m. I was not entirely awake when the trip began, but as the minibus we had rented began to fill and the excruciatingly loud, pumping, repetitive, and seemingly unending Kurdish music began to pour forth from speakers all around me, sleep became a distant memory.

The young Kurds, like their Arab counterparts, were full of boisterous energy, behaving more like teenagers in this respect than like recent college graduates. The voices were loud to the point of shouting, there was frequent shifting of chairs, everyone danced furiously in their seats to the sound of the increasingly annoying music, and any sort of sensible conversation was impossible. One of them who had since joined the police force was particularly active, jumping so high in a rather unusual dancing maneuver that he nearly hit the roof of the bus on several occasions. He was a tall, slight man, with a policeman's close haircut, and though he couldn't speak a word of Arabic, he repeatedly looked over at me and smiled, particularly when he introduced a new move into his dance repertoire. There were allegations in Kurdistan that police routinely struck criminal suspects to induce confessions. I wondered if this jovial, excessively friendly and seemingly late-blooming adolescent would be capable of violence of this sort. It seemed incongruous, but then I think it would always seem incongruous to imagine a person doing such things.

We eventually reached our first destination, a waterfall, after about two hours. Though the Kurds had promised me that this was one of the earth's great wonders (an image of the falls appears on the back of the 5,000 Iraqi dinar note), it was not a site I found particularly noteworthy. Perhaps a pleasant place for a picnic or a day trip, but on a global scale this simply did not compete. The falls could not have been much more than thirty feet in length, the breadth no more than fifty feet, and there was nothing special that distinguished them from the myriad other waterfalls I or countless fellow Americans have seen in our lives. It was also overdeveloped and littered, with a café and wooden chairs so close to the falls that they disturbed the view, and a fair amount of trash had been casually thrown in and around the falls.

To Professor Saman, however, this was a place of awesome beauty. He longed for Iraq to stabilize so that a site like this could be visited by Americans and Europeans, bringing much needed tourist dollars to Kurdistan as a result.

"Imagine how wonderful it would be, Professor Haider," he said in all sincerity. "Americans could come here and see this. The world could see how Iraqi Kurdistan is the most beautiful region in the world. We should be one of the world's top tourist sites, but look what Saddam has done to us."

I nodded, thinking to myself that unless Saddam had shortened the waterfall and filled it with the litter I saw, it was hard to see how he was to blame for the relative lack of interest among the world's tourists in this supposed natural wonder.

We left the waterfall early, long before the hordes arrived, and made our way in the throbbing, pulsating minibus to a second location, Jundiyan, where other crowds had gathered; some Arabs from nearby Mosul, but mostly Kurds enjoying the day off. It was at this point that the trip began to take a turn for the worse.

In some way, perhaps, Jundiyan might be an impressive natural wonder. It is basically an underground river that bubbles to the surface halfway up a mountain. The water gently flows down around the site in a stream, meandering left and right and over stone stairs and downward further to the valley below. In my first glimpse, however, I could barely recognize the stream. What I saw was a trash pit teeming with tourists through which filthy water resembling raw sewage ran, carrying the garbage to those unfortunates further downstream. The site was, without question, the dirtiest tourist spot I have seen in my entire life. To the left and the right of the stream, tents had been erected and divided into sections where groups sat, played music, barbecued, engaged in games of chess or backgammon, and otherwise entertained themselves. These were picnic areas, somewhat sheltered from public view, presumably to shield the women, or those more conservative women, from the prying eyes of strangers. The result of shielding the picnic area from the public was that the picnickers could not see the stream, but this was of little concern to most, our rambunctious group included.

The refuse from the cordoned tents was tossed into the stream. Volumes of chicken bones, unconsumed food, pita bread, coke cans, juice boxes, and other refuse casually made their way downstream. In the midst of the flowing water, parents allowed children to swim, coke and watermelon sellers cooled their wares, and everywhere around the site were heaps and heaps of garbage. The waste, the products of the vendors, the vendors themselves, and the crowds and crowds of people forcing their way up the narrow ravine to the source of the water overwhelmed whatever natural beauty the site might have had. I found the whole scene repulsive and depressing. Areas like this, according to those native to the land, were Iraq's crown jewels, at least in terms of natural wonders. My father had described places like this to me, yet I could not find any place to rest my eyes that did not turn my stomach.

"Professor Haider!" Saman interrupted my thoughts as I was staring at the stream and the filth working its way through.

"Yes, Saman," I said, grateful to focus on something else.

"You know what Saddam Hussein once said?" he asked.

I expected another story about Saddam's cruel tyranny and how it had ruined Iraq for decades to come. This was true, of course, but a refrain that was growing tiresome, even for someone like myself with so many relatives dead at his hands. I shook my head.

"He said, "Kurdistan is God's Heaven on earth. God's Heaven on earth," he repeated.

I looked at him, wondering if he was being sarcastic, but could find no hint of irony in his voice or his expression. I looked over at the others who were gazing with equally sincere wonder at the stream of garbage. The policeman caught my eye and began gesturing wildly at the mountain before him, shouting, "Juana! Juana!" (Kurdish for beautiful.) *Were they blind*, I wondered.

My companions looked like they were actually enjoying this, and their happiness made me so angry and frustrated I needed to walk away. And I did. When I returned they were noticeably subdued. I assume I had offended a few of them by leaving on my own, but I could not help myself. All I could think of while watching them smile at this site was the bus ride home nearly every day in junior high school, the older children in the back taunting me, always with the same name, "filthy little desert nigger." I would hold back tears, determined not to let them think I had paid attention. On those rare occasions where I could not prevent myself from crying, I would provoke a fight with one of them, so that they would think it was the physical abuse that caused the tears. Now, the first word, filthy, kept repeating itself over and over in my head. I couldn't help but wonder, were they right? Are we a dirtier people?

We eventually left Jundiyan after much singing and dancing and eating and, unfortunately, littering on the part of my colleagues, and stopped by another, slightly more impressive but no less filthy waterfall called Ali Beg. Trash again, vendors everywhere using the water to cool their goods, tourists everywhere, washing their hair, doing their laundry, climbing over rocks, and having lunch and throwing unused pita bread into the falls again. I had had quite enough by that time, and at our last stop around 10 p.m. at the Dokan River, it took my remaining energy to leave the minibus. I may not have left at all, except that the minibus was supplying the music for the young Kurds who incredibly seemed to have lost none of their energy in the preceding fourteen hours and were playing repeatedly a well-known quick tempo Iraqi song, "Al-Purtuqala" ("Woman Wearing Orange"). Without exaggeration, I had already heard the song thirty-five times on this trip and hardly wished to remain in the vehicle to hear it again. We stopped at the banks of the fast-moving river, and I waded in the icy cold water for a bit, until half-eaten food thrown from someone upstream got caught in my legs, at which point I put on shoes, stood at the shore, and waited for the day to end. It finally did, at 1 a.m. I'll never go again. I was called filthy too many times to be able to handle much by way of evidence in support of the charge.

CHAPTER 45

Flight from Baghdad

IN MID-SEPTEMBER OF 2004, I took a brief trip back to Baghdad to visit my grandmother and to do some work in our Baghdad office. It was my last such trip. The day after I arrived, I woke up in my grandmother's home to see on CNN what I thought was the Baghdad office of our legal education project, and the generator we had purchased. Accompanying this was a news report indicating that assailants had abducted three foreigners from this location, at dawn, and were taking them to Falluja.

It was the second kidnapping of foreigners from their homes in a two-week period; the first was of two Italian women. My heart raced. I felt an urgent need to use the bathroom, but I could not feel my legs and therefore could not leave the seat on which I was sitting. Three colleagues of mine, I thought, had been taken from our office, and nothing but a delayed start to the day had saved me.

Then, after a few of the most terrifying moments of my life, I began to rethink this. The office (which like all Baghdad offices was a stand alone house that functioned as an office) did look like ours, but the reports placed this house in the neighborhood of Mansour, and our home was near Mansour but decidedly beyond its boundaries. That the Arab press repeated this was reassuring, because CNN did not seem to know Mansour from Mosul as their correspondents never left Army bases, but the Arabs tended to be better. Moreover, though the house looked similar, I remembered our balcony extending from the house from its left side, not its right. I tried to concentrate. Had I remembered incorrectly or was this a different house? And weren't any other expatriates associated with this project in Suleymania? Or was I imagining this?

Five minutes later, my heart still racing but my cognitive functions returning, I called the guard at our office on his mobile phone. He asked where I was and why I had not yet arrived at the office. I asked him if anything had happened, and he said that something had. Three foreigners had been kidnapped in Mansour somewhere. It was then that I allowed myself for the first time to believe that the house was unharmed and my colleagues were safe.

But I also knew I had to get to the office and evacuate from what had become a nightmare of a city. I went to the office and in less than an hour I cleared out everything I needed. I brought it home, called Zuhair, and told him I absolutely had to be on a plane to Kurdistan the next day. Strings were pulled, someone living in the Green Zone had their journey delayed a day, and I got my reservation. I packed that same evening. In the morning I kissed my ninety-one-year-old grandmother goodbye and departed. I thought I might never see her again. I might never eat at the Reef again. I might never have fish on the Tigris again or drive my car to the pool at the Babylon. I might never have another evening at the Hunting Club or jog another afternoon near Celebration Square. I was leaving Baghdad, my home for the past year and the city of my ancestors, and I didn't know if it would ever be safe to return. And I never had a chance to say goodbye.

I took the dreaded airport road for the final time, and felt a heavy depression weighing upon me. *This was it*, I told myself as we sped down the road. I'd go to Kurdistan and finish my contract, but only because I had committed myself to it. My desire to remain in Iraq had been all but extinguished. I was only counting days.

CHAPTER 46

A New Development

NOT TWO WEEKS AFTER I arrived in Suleymania in flight from Baghdad, I was certain that my time in Iraq was about to end—a foolish prediction, one I should have known not to make, as the world can change in a day, sometimes for the worse, sometimes the better. But with me at rock bottom less than two weeks after my evacuation out of Baghdad, I didn't think a dramatic turn for the worse was possible and found myself in somewhat desperate need of a miracle. I got one that week when I met Sara. The timing could not have been better.

I had hoped something like this might happen soon after my arrival in Baghdad, but the circumstances never seemed particularly fortuitous, the conditions hardly right for a romantic adventure. In the early, hectic, heady days following the removal of the former regime, I had a business to develop, connections to make, clients to attract, and a house to rent. Added to this was the complication that in Iraq, I simply could not invite a woman for lunch or coffee. Such interactions were entirely forbidden from a social standpoint. I had to use more subtle techniques—a visit to her brother's house, a casual meeting with her father while she was accompanying him, and when he ventured off to use the restroom, a quick conversation and a request for a phone number. These matters take time, effort, and persistence. I could afford none of these in those early days.

Then as Iraq continued to deteriorate, and as the turn toward disaster became unmistakably clear by April of the previous year, my feelings of despondency and despair were hardly consonant with the more hopeful and optimistic sentiments that were an inherent part of budding romances. I could not very well spend my days wondering whether I would be kidnapped or killed (and whether the country would drift into slowly increasing chaos from which it would take decades to emerge), and my nights dreaming of a wonderful life with a woman I loved.

Thus it came as an unexpected but pleasant surprise that I met the lovely Sara Burhan Abdullah, a Kurdish attorney working as a research assistant at the Suleymania University College of Law where she was completing her Fulbright application for study in the United States. Our first conversation began awkwardly.

"I am sorry, remind me of your name one more time?" I asked.

She looked confused, but replied, "Sara."

"Sara, Professor Saman said you were interested in applying for a Fulbright, and I would like to help you. Have you completed the application?"

Sara gave an uncomprehending stare and looked entirely confused.

"The application, did you finish it?"

Continuing look of confusion, combined with an intense concentration on something.

"Did you not actually apply for the Fulbright? Do I have the wrong person?"

She shook her head from side to side and stared at me, unsure of what I was saying. I decided to find Professor Saman. The problem with the younger Kurds was that they had a harder time with Arabic. I turned to the door. Suddenly, I heard a lovely voice.

"O thou Professor, dost thou refer to the application whose pages must be completed in full along with the most favorable recommendations sent by professors that doth hold me in the highest regard?"

I stopped, and this time, I was not sure I understood. So I said, "Huh?"

She looked confused again.

I tried another approach. "What dost thou say?"

With this, the most beautiful smile I had ever seen appeared on Sara's face. "I understandeth thy latest utterance thou professor of wisdom!"

"Dost thou understand only classical Arabic?" I was feeling rather stupid speaking this way but had no alternative.

"Indeed, I hath studied it many a year in school. The law is written thus, yes?"

"Indeed it doth. But regular people don't, I mean doth not, talk, I mean speaketh, this way, Sara."

"I speaketh with Arabs little, and so understandeth not the spoken dialect."

"Okay, I mean, great, no, I mean splendid."

"I hath heard you moved from Baghdad nigh. Is it so fraught with peril thou Professor?"

"Indeed I doth, and indeed it is so fraught with peril."

"Dost thou stay long?"

"Perchance."

| CHAPTER 47 |

Halabja

THROUGHOUT THE SUMMER AND fall of 2004, as the country continued to deteriorate, kidnappings continued to multiply, and the political situation grew bleaker, the very idea of considering the past was a luxury that could scarcely be afforded. Even Saddam Hussein, the man who had once occupied so many of my thoughts, whose forced removal brought me to this land after such a lengthy departure, and whose face once haunted my dreams and consumed my nightmares, became for me, indeed for many Iraqis, an afterthought, a footnote, as far removed from our daily existences as Pol Pot. All of which made my first trip to Halabja particularly valuable.

I went with numerous Arab professors who had also never been and who had come to nearby Suleymania for an academic conference we had planned. A few Kurds from the university faculty joined us as well, as did some Americans who had helped prepare and fund the conference. The conference was on the reestablishment of the rule of law in Iraq, and the trip to Halabja was, therefore, quite appropriate. We had planned and organized the whole event on a free afternoon when no lectures or seminars related to the conference were being held.

Halabja was the site of Saddam's well-publicized chemical attack on the Kurds in 1988. It is nestled among mountains on the Iraqi border with Iran, and throughout the war with Iran was never entirely controlled by the Iraqi army. The Kurdish militia, the *pesh merga*, was in the mountains nearby, frequently harassing the Iraqi positions. The militia finally took control of the city around 1988, toward the end of the war. Many residents, fearing the worst from Saddam, took to the hills, forsaking the city that was to earn its place alongside Guernica and Srebernica as a memorial to the cruelty that an unconstrained army can unleash upon a luckless village. The decision on the part of many to flee turned out to be a wise one, and Saddam, exceeded expectations, if such a thing were possible. Iraqi military aircraft dropped mustard gas and nerve gas over the entire city, killing thousands of men, women, and children; some combatants, but mostly peasants without the foresight to leave with the others.

Halabja itself was a nondescript town, and the memorial to the massacre was mediocre to poor. The pictures were not labeled, descriptions of what had actually happened were nowhere to be found, and even the layout, circular in shape, was baffling because it was difficult to make the slightest sense of the sequence as we traversed the circle. But really, none of this was the point. The point was that we remembered once again the deep roots of this nation's current agony and the darkness that had blighted this land for the greater part of four decades. We had to see this again now, and in Halabja, where it happened. For me and for all the Iraqis attending, this was a more meaningful experience than could ever be expressed in words. Not a dry eye could be found in our company, not among the Kurds, who had been here several times before, nor the Americans, nor the Arabs who were visiting for the first time.

The visit lasted just over an hour, and by the time we were midway through our ninety-minute return by bus, Iraqi jokes were again being told, and the conversation turned to more timely topics, such as the upcoming election, security, and the inherently dangerous return of the Arab professors to Baghdad. But it was an hour that I, and I daresay the others on the bus with me, desperately needed and would never forget.

CHAPTER 48

Sara

"I DO NOT UNDERSTAND, how long can it take to finish a Fulbright application? Zuhair asked as we were walking to the hotel from the university.

"We are taking time to get it right. There's a language problem that we have to work through."

"There's no language problem. Her Arabic is fluent, just funny," he said. Then, attempting to imitate her, he said something like, "'Zounds, doth thou entreat my presence at the respite locale to toil on the computer?' I personally think you should answer, 'I draw my sword for thee, and sweareth upon it my eternal allegiance.'"

I smiled.

"Also, you do go to her office quite a bit," he added.

"Yes, I guess I do."

"What do you talk about?"

"The application."

"Do you think I'm stupid? Did you say to yourself, 'let me see if I can find the stupidest man on earth to be the office manager' and then you found me?" Zuhair replied, gesturing wildly to mimic the thought.

"Zuhair, you know I don't think that."

"Then what do you talk about?"

"Nothing really. I mean if I related a conversation it would seem so boring to you. But it feels so comfortable, and so natural to me. I never want to leave her office, though I do have to after about ten minutes, given your stupid social rules."

"I think you want to marry her."

"I just met her, Zuhair."

"Well, this isn't America. We don't have sex and live together for seven years and have three kids and then decide to marry. She's an Iraqi, you know."

"I know."

"If you want to move, you have to move fast," he said.

"I know."

"In America, maybe you can be thirty-four and decide what you want to do with your career and if you want a baby, but for us at thirty-four you have a career and a family. You decide, and wham, it's decided, then you move on to the next decision. No treading water."

"I *know*, Zuhair."

"I never understood that anyway. How do Americans get places treading water? Do they just move faster once they do decide to marry and have a career?"

"I don't know, Zuhair." I was starting to lose interest in the conversation, and he noticed.

"Anyway, you have to move fast. Are you ready for that?"

"I am."

CHAPTER 49

Conversations with Sara

I WAS IN SARA'S office in late September, having another conversation with her about her Fulbright application, when suddenly she asked me her first personal question. "So what do you think of the invasion?" I was taken by surprisse.

Before I had a chance to answer, she nervously added, speaking very quickly, "Most Kurds like the Americans actually. It was Saddam we had a problem with. America kept Saddam away for thirteen years, and that is why we have our own autonomy and things go so well here."

"The Americans were here for a while," Sara went on, "and some people were a little upset because of the weapons they carried onto campus. But they left so quickly hardly anyone remembers that. What is your favorite color?"

I felt like a high school suitor with a nervous prom date. This entire affair was delightful in its innocence even if it felt a little silly for a man in his thirties. After thinking about her two questions and which would be safer to answer, I chose the latter.

"My favorite color is black, I guess."

She frowned. "Spoken like a true Shi'i, mourning for the dead Imam Hussein."

I had thought I was avoiding potential political controversy by talking about colors, but now it seemed I had waded into a religious dispute.

Fortunately, just then a professor came into the office. As it would be unthinkable for Sara to be having a personal conversation with a man not her relative or coworker without a legitimate reason, she quickly steered the conversation into a safer direction. "Now, what about this question on the application, I don't understand it . . . " she asked loudly.

I had several more conversations like this with Sara over the next couple of weeks. They would begin innocently enough and soon delve into personal details. The pace at which our relationship was developing was very fast, just as Zuhair had suggested. With each meeting, Sara was more open, and when nobody was looking, more visibly smitten. I felt much the same way toward her, having never been so taken with a woman so quickly. I made an effort to see her nearly every single day if I could.

Finally, two weeks after we had begun talking about our respective lives, I convinced her to meet me outside of the law school, where we could talk more privately for a longer period of time. By which I meant, of course, not a private room, as this would be unthinkable for an Iraqi woman, but a café. She wouldn't have agreed to do even this, because of the potential for rumor, but I had told her I was going to the United States for a visit and wanted to tell my parents about her, and she wanted us to have a longer talk before I did this. She met me for coffee on an afternoon in early October.

"You know this is rather difficult for me," she said almost immediately after walking into the café. "Meetings like this, people talk here."

"They need jobs, or something to keep them busy so they stop spreading rumors," I said.

"They have jobs, but they spend most of their time talking about other people. Like me, right now."

"I'm leaving for America soon, they'll forget."

"No they won't, unless someone else does something they can talk about. You are sure you are coming back?" Tears were welling in her eyes.

"Sara, you're being ridiculous."

Her glasses started to fall further down her nose, and her jaw set. I loved that look. I had seen it twice before, once when I told her she needed to finish something for her application in a day or so, and once when I said she needed to take English classes to have a chance at the Fulbright. The look meant she was determined to do something, and nothing on earth would deter her.

"What do you think of Moqtada Al-Sadr?" she asked.

"The cleric?"

"Yes."

"Good friend."

A look of concern crossed her face.

"I am joking," I added.

"Oh sorry, finish the joke."

American humor, particularly of the ironic sort, never seemed to catch on with Iraqis.

"The joke is over," I said. "Anyway, how can you ask that? I told you what I thought of extremists like him. He's a dumb ignorant thug."

"I meant his views on women."

"What did he say about women?"

"He doesn't have to say anything. Have you ever seen a woman near him, around him, talking to him, whatever? No, for all these guys, women are sex objects, not human beings. All we are is a tool for sex."

"Okay. I guess I've never heard him refer to or talk about women, but unfortunately that doesn't make him precisely unique among Islamic scholars."

"I know. Will your family be angry if you tell them I am a Kurd?"

"Furious. Really, really mad," I said.

There was a pause as she contemplated my plainly ironic tone and expression.

"Is that another joke?"

"Yes, you are catching on to American humor already."

"No, I'm not. I could tell you weren't serious but I am not sure why it's funny just to say the opposite of what you mean. What's the real answer to my question anyway?"

"Sara, we live in America. *America*. I am not saying that they raised us American, but their expectations are a little more realistic than to be mad about an Iraqi Muslim Kurd."

"Shi'i Arab is better, though."

"I guess, maybe, I don't know. Look, we don't think this way, and we weren't brought up to think this way. This matters to your family more than mine."

"No, my father, I think, might not agree, but because you live in America. It's far from him. I'm the last daughter here. I think I told you that my sister is in Germany. But my father lived amongst Arabs for many years, and he doesn't care about such things. If he did care, and forbade me to marry an Arab, I would cut off our relationship immediately."

"Just like that?" I asked incredulously. Sara and I were genuinely in love, I had no doubt, but she was telling me, at the request of her father, she would abandon our affair. Devotion to family, for Iraqis, always comes before romantic love. It was not until the matter began to affect me that I recognized the chasm of difference with similarly situated Americans.

"Just like that," she said confidently.

"What about love?" I asked.

"Any boy I could love, but only one set of parents raised me."

"*Any* boy?" I said.

"That was my joke. Was it funny?" she asked.

"I told you, you are catching on!"

"Okay," then she whispered, "I have to go, the dean just walked by the café. Be careful on your trip home. Please."

CHAPTER 50

Suleymania Departure

IT WAS OCTOBER 2004 and once again I was leaving Iraq, though I was fairly certain that this time the trip would be short. I had obtained some home leave and was desperate for some relief from the stultifying monotony of life in Suleymania. Because I could not speak to Sara for more than thirty minutes a day without "people talking," there was not adequate leisure activity to prevent me from going nearly insane. I found the customs as regards speaking with women annoying to deal with and difficult to accept. I could understand restrictions on premarital sex; dating was strictly forbidden in our household as a high school student. However, the idea that talking in a café for an hour or two or going to dinner with me, even if accompanied by my brother, suggested promiscuity struck me as extreme.

The restrictions, along with the monotony, meant that in Suleymania, an upcoming weekend or holiday brought with it a sense of dread, a feeling that I had to find a way to fill up the time. Thus, when I had an opportunity to take my home leave, I did, intending both to attend a friend's wedding in Germany and to inform my parents about Sara. I looked forward to the opportunity to do both, and to enjoy those many aspects of life that were necessarily on hold in Iraq, whether they be an afternoon at the gym, a gingerbread latte at Starbucks, or a game of American football.

The night before my departure, I took a walk in the cool evening air to get a glimpse of this city that was temporarily my home. I sauntered by Suleymania's main park, named Azadi (Freedom), once the headquarters of Saddam's dreaded security services and now a reasonably well-tended park with a playground, grass fields where young men play soccer, a small amusement park, and even a Speaker's Corner where anyone could go to the podium and say anything they wish. Nobody was at the Speaker's Corner (nobody was ever there), and the park was mostly empty. Only the playground was full. Children were shrieking and sliding down slides and crying at the unfairness of the larger children who didn't give them an opportunity to use the swings, as mothers attempted to chat with their friends and administer whatever quick justice they could among competing screaming, crying, laughing, and jumping children. Remove a few veils and it could have been a playground in New York City.

I walked on toward the Palace Hotel where dignitaries and United States military personnel stayed. Blast walls protected the hotel, the only such hotel so protected in Suleymania, but entry would be relatively simple after a brief body search. However, I did not enter, but slid past to Mawlawi Street, one of the main roads through the Suleymania souq. By the time I arrived it was dusk and most vendors were closing up shop. The enormous canvas bags of dates, nuts, apricots, spices, and other sundries that were laid out on the street for purchase throughout the day were being dragged into the tiny one-room stores, mostly by children working for their fathers. From time to time, the sound of iron gates closing and the clacking of padlocks being secured could be heard. Customers were loaded with bags, making their way home. There were no supermarkets in the area, no Wal-Marts, no locations even selling more than one general type of food or material, just a series of sole proprietors making small profits and serving the community. On many days, this was exacerbating and frustrating, as items cost too much and were too hard to find. But today, there was romance to it, a nostalgia for an era that seemed to have passed from our nation, when each man owned his business, where the business was a central part of the community with responsibilities and obligations to the community, and where business ethics meant something more than profit maximization at all costs within the bounds of the law. It might not be sustainable, but that is in many ways a tragedy.

After Mawlawi Street I began to make my way to the hotel and reached it by 9 p.m. Were I not leaving, my spirits might not have been quite as light, but as I was, I rather enjoyed the last evening for a while, in this temporary home of mine. I would miss Sara, I knew, but perhaps after my trip to the United States we would be spending more time and maybe even an entire life together. Just the thought of that made me happy.

CHAPTER 51

Final Descent into Baghdad

ONLY A MONTH AFTER I forswore Baghdad, I had thought forever, I returned for the last time, though only for a day, on my way to Germany, the United States, and beyond. Airplanes leaving Iraq always stopped in Baghdad, and I could not justify in my heart or my head avoiding a one day layover to see my grandmother and my brother to give them a proper goodbye, call up family members and friends, and walk the streets of this city once again, if only for an afternoon.

Being in Baghdad in October of 2004 was an entirely different experience from what it once had been. Even when compared to the previous summer, danger felt as if it were everywhere, not for me alone but for all those with whom I came into contact. The streets were deserted at night, the Internet cafés largely empty, and while foodstuffs and other items continued to fill shelves, the business of most people seemed to be to finish up their public affairs as early as possible and return to the relative, and I stress the word relative, safety of their homes. There was a palpable fear in the eyes of most Iraqis, and though they ostensibly carried on with their business, they kept their children a little bit closer, avoided eye contact a little bit more, finished their conversations a little more quickly, and generally seemed uneasy. In the Baghdad I remembered, sitting in the pool for more than ten minutes would inevitably result in a conversation, a tea stall for more than five would lead to a heated discussion. Yet on this trip I was able to consume two full teas at a tea stall and not a single person spoke to me, not even the proprietor himself. As for the pool, it was far beyond consideration at this point. I could not even visit my aunt Zahra. She strictly forbade it, as her home was in an unacceptably dangerous part of town.

"Aunt Zahra," I protested, "I am ten minutes away by car. How can it be that dangerous?"

"Car? You want to drive here? *Here?* What if the car gets stolen? If they shoot you to take it?" she asked.

"Aunt Zahra, if someone takes the car by force, I'll give it to them, no need to shoot me."

"This isn't Scotland, they aren't shooting you for the car. Maybe they'll hear your accent, think you are a Kurd and just shoot you for that. They kill now here, for any reason. We are leaving this house, someone will take it, and we'll take whatever belongings we can. If we can ever get it back is Allah's Will."

"You are leaving the house? Will you get compensation?"

"Still thinking like an American. If we have our lives in a year's time, we will thank Allah. Stay safe, and don't leave the house until your plane tomorrow. Not even to visit your cousin Ali."

"I'm going to visit Ali, Aunt Zahra, he's two houses away," I protested, finding this particular precaution silly.

"No! Ask Ali, see what he says, and if he says you can visit him then go. Or if your brother says it's okay."

"Fine." Then I said goodbye and hung up the phone. That was the last time I spoke to my aunt Zahra; she has since moved to a safer location where she is much harder to reach by telephone, and since then her children have fled to Kurdistan.

After I hung up, I expected my brother and my cousin to be less worried about my walking two houses down in broad daylight. They were not; both forbade me to leave the home, and suggested I could perhaps go out in the yard, but only before dark. I could not bear this. My new romantic adventure in Suleymania, along with the general security to which I had become accustomed, were lightening my spirits to some degree. I could not intellectually justify hope in the slightest, at least for the nation, but at least I had begun to feel better. The visit to Baghdad, however, reminded me of the madness, of the chaos, of the sheer failure that Iraq had become. Human beings could not live here.

And so I left with a heavy heart, with a great deal of regret, with a fair amount of pain and disappointment that was not likely to fade very soon. It was no longer a city I could visit, only a city for which to weep.

CHAPTER 52

Stranded

ON MY RETURN TO Suleymania from my three week trip to Germany and the U.S., I found myself stranded in Amman, waiting to get to Iraq but unable to do so for a number of days. This was because of a security operation designed to permit the Allawi Government to take control of Falluja, which required that all of Iraq's borders be sealed. I had enjoyed my time at a five star Amman hotel, but after these several weeks I was missing Sara terribly and therefore quite eager to return to Iraq at the first available opportunity. We were able to speak over the phone on occasion and from our talks I knew she felt the same.

"I can't stand this, I want them to open the border again so you can come. How much longer do you think it will be?" she asked, her voice quivering as she held back tears.

"Not long. Hachem Alhassani is staying in this hotel. I just saw him, and he's one of the top Sunnis in the government. They can't close the border for that long and leave all of these people outside of Iraq."

"Did you tell your parents about me?"

"Yes, they were fine, as I said."

"Just fine?"

"They were very happy, Sara. They will be happier if things iron out on your end. Just relax, my parents are fine, talk to your father."

"After you come, not before."

"Okay then, I am coming soon."

"I miss you very much, Haider."

"I do too, Sara. I even got you a present."

"Thanks, but I cannot accept it. It would be inappropriate for me to take presents from a man to whom I am not related."

"It's a woman's sweater, what would I do with it?"

Pause. "Is it a friendship present or a romantic present?"

I responded quickly. "A friendship present of course. I would never buy you a romantic present, and you can tell this to all of your friends."

This was a common refrain among Iraqi women. The idea of romantic involvement prior to engagement was strictly taboo, even when it was perfectly obvious that the couple were in love, as we were. Therefore, the ninety-dollar cashmere sweater had to be given purportedly out of friendship, and not as a romantic gesture, as if I were in the custom of giving such things to my friends for no reason. But of all of the fictions I was required to maintain for the sake of this relationship—the clandestine meetings in cafés and the pretense in her office that we were working on her Fulbright application, for example—this was relatively harmless.

"Haider?" she asked, as I was preparing to hang up the telephone.

"Yes, Sara?"

"I want to teach you a new Kurdish word before you go."

"Okay."

"In case one day you want to tell your mother, or maybe your aunt, 'I love you' in Kurdish, this is how you say it—Khoshem Ewet."

"Got it, I am sure my Arab mother and aunt will like that."

"Goodbye again, then, Haider."

"Khoshem Ewet, Sara Khan."

A pause, then, in English, a language she did not know well, "I love you too."

My trip had taken place during Ramadan, which is the Muslim holy month and involves a great deal of prayer, fasting, and other acts of piety. Eid al-Fitr, the celebration of the end of Ramadan and a holiday akin to Christmas, was to take place the following day. I was depressed that on Eid I would be neither with family in the U.S. nor with Sara. After that phone call, and our exchange of expressions of love in three different languages, I no longer felt quite so alone. I went to bed happy, enthralled by the advent of a day and a life of seemingly limitless possibility.

The next day, to commemorate Eid, I joined a second cousin living in Amman with whom I had been close during my college years. He, his family, and I feasted at a posh Amman restaurant to mark the end of the fast. But though the food was lovely and probably on balance better than anything I would have eaten in Iraq, though the conversation was delightful (mostly we talked about how our mutual friends and acquaintances were doing, a common topic in any society), and though it was a joy to see my second cousin once again, the day did not feel complete without Sara or my family.

I was accustomed to celebrating holidays with my immediate family. My parents, eager to ensure that I looked forward to the day of Eid more than any other, would spoil us especially on that day, letting us take the day off from school. As a family, we would shop for presents, go to a favorite restaurant, and drive to the amusement park. These were days of childhood bliss, as fondly remembered by me as many school friends remember their childhood Christmases. Since then, Eid meant something, and with each recurring Eid as an adult I strive, no doubt in vain, to relive those days of wonder, to feel once again as I did then, as a six-year-old boy lying in his bed the night before Eid in eager anticipation of the day that lay before me.

I had spent my last Eid in Baghdad, amid bombs and explosions, in a city known now for only death and mayhem, yet I was as happy as I could have been on Eid, excluding my childhood years. I was in my grandmother's house, relatives from everywhere came and went throughout the holiday, and I belonged comfortably, for at least that day, among them. An Amman five-star restaurant, while enjoyable, simply could not compare, particularly when I was so certain that darker days lay ahead for Iraq. My place was not here, and I was getting more and more anxious to leave.

CHAPTER 53

Nuptial Preparations

WITHIN A DAY OF my arrival in Suleymania, Sara and I arranged to meet in the same café where we had spoken just before my trip. This time, she carried no books, made no pretense of trying to hide from meeting me, and her face was, from the moment she entered, beaming with happiness and with relief at not having to conceal her joy. She came straight to me. As a result, I was sure she had good news to report.

"He agreed!" Sara told me, even before she sat down. "I can marry you because my father said it was okay!"

"I told you he would," I said.

"It did not take even a day for my father to agrec. I was so scared to ask, I could not believe it happened so quickly."

"I told you."

"He asked my mother about you, and she told him about you based on what she knew, and it didn't take much more. He agreed right away."

"I told you months ago it would work out."

"How did you know?"

"Sara, he is your father. He wouldn't deny you permission to marry someone for stupid reasons."

"This isn't Hollywood or *Titanic,* if he doesn't want it, that ends the story, you know."

"I know, we discussed this before, and I knew it before then, too."

While I had been distressed by Sara's previous quick expression of readiness to end our relationship if her father didn't agree to our match, I knew that this was a deep and longstanding Iraqi custom, and it was not uncommon for budding relationships to end for this reason. I felt it wasn't such a terrible thing either, as it didn't seem to me that the uncontrollable and fundamentally irrational passions of youth, were accurate indicators of a lifelong union. Cooler parental heads it seemed to me could very well act as a sensible gauge, so long as they truly had their children's best interests in mind. I had seen Iraqi parents refuse permission, however, for the silliest of reasons, among them the fact that the parents preferred another suitor due to a close family connection or that the person in question lived in another city. On balance, however, at least among the educated classes with whom I commonly associated, this was rare. More often, so long as the couple was in agreement, unless something was deeply amiss, the parents did not object.

There were other customs relating to parental permission that disturbed me more. I didn't understand why it was that a daughter would secure her mother's permission months before speaking to her father, so that a married couple of a daughter seeking engagement had a secret of this magnitude hanging between them. I couldn't see how a culture that took such pride in strong familial ties could possibly justify something like this.

I did not tell my friends outside of Iraq about the importance of my relationship with Sara until days before our actual engagement. I had no ready explanation for my delinquency. I was happy, I loved Sara, and I was sure my decision was the right one, but somehow I could not help but feel just a little sense of embarrassment about how the engagement had proceeded to this point. As open and accepting as my American upbringing was, as tolerant and kind as most of my Americans friends were, there was a tinge of cultural bigotry in American society that time had not erased. There was a sense that those of us from the Arab and Muslim world were in some unexpressed way inferior and silly, the kind of people who traded women at camel auctions, and the kind that engaged in antiquated wedding traditions such as these, where matches were made in weeks rather than years.

Nobody would dare express that; it would be deemed highly inappropriate. Yet I never could dispel the thought that most, if not all, Americans felt this way and just chose not to say anything. This gave rise to insecurity and some level of self-loathing on my part.

So when I thought of telling my American friends about Sara, I could only think of the questions they would ask, not to me, maybe not even among themselves, but within their hearts. I did tell them ultimately, and most seemed happy, though quite surprised. Not so much because I hadn't told them, but more because my faith, my upbringing, and my own deep cultural identity were not aspects of my life that were well-known to them. They saw me as I chose to present myself to them, as an American (as they themselves were), certainly of differing ethnic origin and religion, but as a jetsetter, and a well-heeled child of the Ivy League, living in New York or Hong Kong with weekends in the Hamptons or Saigon. They assumed I had gone to Iraq to contribute and would return soon enough, or perhaps take a job in London and spend my weekends in Paris or Madrid. That Iraq had the power to change me so profoundly, that in Iraq's social fabric I would find a place I could in many ways call home, and that Iraq was much more than a passing fancy made slightly more significant to me by mere circumstances of birth was never something that had occurred to any of them. Perhaps I should have been more forthcoming and honest with the people I considered close friends, but I found this difficult to do. At the end of the day, I don't think there is any way any of them could really understand. Nobody really does.

CHAPTER 54

Kandakher

IN DECEMBER, I DECIDED to take a trip to the mountains with Professor Saman and a few Kurdish attorneys. I was not entirely enthused about the trip, given my previous experience, but Saman assured me that this would be different, as our fellow travelers would be in our age group. I had politely declined previous invitations out of fear that I was being misled, but guilt over constant refusals of Kurdish hospitality, particularly Saman's brand of earnest and willing hospitality, overcame my reluctance and so I went.

The trip was quite different. We took only two cars, incredibly loud music was played in neither. We went to a single location at the mouth of a largely deserted yet stunningly beautiful mountain valley called Kandakher. Unlike my last trip, there was no folk dancing, or litter. We left the cars on a dirt road and descended to the valley's mouth. Rising steeply before us were two mountains split by the valley and dotted with brush. An odd deciduous tree still shedding leaves stood before us, and two or three scattered herds of goats skittered about searching for whatever fruits and seeds remained. In front of us was a gently sweeping downward plain with much the same vegetation two to three groups of people were sitting further down, about half a mile away. Other than this, nobody was here. Beyond the plain several miles away were other ragged mountain peaks.

We created a fire, and the Kurds started drinking.

I began the conversation. "Iraqis are very masculine it seems to me,

Professor Saman. Look at all your drinks—whiskey and beer. Men tend to prefer those I think."

"Even in America?" asked one of the Kurds.

"Oh yes, Irish even more. Most Irish, I think, drink only whiskey and beer. Professor Hama over there with the port, though, that is a bit more feminine compared to the rest of you."

Silence. "Doctor Haider, port has alcohol," one finally said.

"Of course."

"So why is it feminine, it has alcohol."

"Women prefer it in the West."

"Really? Only women drink this alcohol? And they are regular women, not prostitutes?"

"No, they are not prostitutes, and men drink port, too. I just meant whiskey is a little more traditionally masculine, I think."

"This is all very confusing; it is simpler here. Alcohol is for men and whores. No confusion."

"In America, we would call that 'politically incorrect.'"

"What does that mean?"

"It means you have to show respect for all genders and ethnic groups and races. You can't categorize any of them."

Howls of objection arose.

"Westerners feel that stereotypes are wrong," I added.

"They aren't wrong, they are usually true," said another.

Saman, who always tried to defuse cultural tensions whenever he could identify them, interjected, "Come on, who cares about this nonsense. Professor Haider, you talk about this exercise the Americans always do, and you like it too, it seems. Let's do some. What mountain should we climb?"

We found one, and judging by his facial expressions, I am not convinced Professor Saman came to any epiphanies on the subject of the benefits of exercise, but he did enjoy the views along the way and his heart may be stronger from the experience.

We returned from our climb and enjoyed a proper Iraqi barbecue, similar to an American barbecue except that the fire is an open one, rocks serve as the grill, salt as the barbecue sauce, and the staple is shish kebab. The Kurds began singing in Kurdish and carrying on, until they noticed that I, who didn't speak Kurdish, was not participating. Ever hospitable, in this case more than I would have preferred, Saman pressed me to provide my own contribution in English. I kindly demurred, more than once, but realizing this would not succeed, I sang a few bars of *American Pie,* and to my surprise they actually enjoyed the chorus. Minutes later there were seven Kurds with heavy accents and one American in a lovely valley near Suleymania, singing to the goats about Chevys and levies, whiskey and rye, and the day the music died.

After the meal and before the fire had gone out (my suggestion that we douse it with water was met with confused facial expressions, and we had no water in any event), we began to walk in the valley. It was still mid afternoon, but the valley was already growing dark, the steep rocky surfaces of the mountains blocking out some of the sunlight. On and on we walked, perhaps for twenty minutes, over rocks, through caves, across streams, and all the while I was wondering to myself when we would turn around to the sun and the fire, and perhaps some tea.

And then I saw what we had come for. Carved into the side of one of the mountains, about forty to fifty feet tall, was a depiction of an Assyrian king, majestic and proud, seemingly stepping on bodies below, who I thought were enemies but my companions assured me were slaves. The Kurds told me that this carving was completed in 3000 B.C., which must have been roughly accurate because that is when the Assyrians controlled this region in Iraq. It had stood here peacefully in this valley since that time, though clearly the past two decades had taken their toll. Bullet marks could be seen on the carving, parts of it had been chipped away, perhaps sold on the black market. Yet it remained clear enough to awe an accidental tourist in this ancient spot I had never heard anything about.

It occurred to me then that this was the first Iraqi antiquity I had seen since entering Iraq as an adult. The ruins of Nineveh, the hanging gardens of Babylon, the world's first city of Ur, all lie here, near the modern cities of Mosul, Hillah and Nasiriya, respectively, but I had not seen them since 1978, or in the case of Babylon, 1990. They were a part of my heritage, a heritage of which I was constantly reminded as a child, and of which I, like all Iraqis, was deeply proud. As a school child, when schoolmates would taunt me to the point of tears about how my parents were filthy boat people who would soon be sent back on another boat to where they belonged, I remembered the calm and regal manner in which my mother reacted to my childish weeping: a firm grasp of the hand, a stiff neck, and a stare straight ahead.

"Tell them," she said, her voice trembling, "tell them your ancestors were building the world's first cities when theirs were hanging like monkeys from European trees."

I never forgot that moment. I did as she said, and earned a bloody nose for my troubles, but it mattered little. What I remembered best was that for the first time I felt like I had nothing to apologize for. (I later learned this nugget of information had not actually come from my mother but from an Egyptian family friend who had given her son the same advice, substituting the word "pyramids" for "world's first city." Not that this is of great significance, but credit must be given where it is due.)

Then in 1990, when I returned to Iraq, I saw what Saddam had done to Babylon, one of the empires in which we had taken so much pride. Saddam had built over it, destroying it in the process, in order to "reconstruct" it and appropriate the earlier imperial glory that the city represented for himself. He was the despot casting himself in the role of emperor. Walls and walls of new brick were everywhere, in some cases built over the original ruins, in some cases bearing no resemblance to them. He expanded the palace of Nebuchadnezzar, the emperor's palace, to nearly twice its original size. But more monstrous, more horrible than this was what he had written on the bricks, one in every twenty by my count: "The city of Babylon, built by Hammurabi, rebuilt by Nebuchadnezzar, and rebuilt again by Saddam Hussein, the third builder of Babylon." This delusional maniac, apparently unconcerned with the fact that Babylon had ceased to exist as an empire for thousands of years, had destroyed the country, killed its people, and now was robbing it of its history, all to feed that same vainglorious and insatiable appetite that had caused so much misery to Iraq. Even our Babylon had become nothing but a paean to a madman.

The madman had fallen, but the ruins were inaccessible. They were unsafe and whatever valuables survived Saddam had largely been looted. Even the Iraqi museum had not reopened. If it had, it would have had precious little to show because it had been looted as well. I feared that one of the chief sources of our pride, among Arabs and Kurds alike, this central and essential part of our identity, was steadily eroding. My mother could take me to Iraq's museum when I was a child, I could explore the ruins of Babylon then, and Mosul's children could take school trips to what remained of Nineveh. These places were real, the artifacts physical objects before our young and formative eyes. What Iraq's children have today, memories and pictures in textbooks, cannot compare. I hope that I am mistaken or exaggerating the extent of the damage. Only time will tell. From my own selfish perspective, there is little to fear; my children will see the British Museum and the Metropolitan Museum of Art, whose collections of Mesopotamian artifacts are extensive. But I cannot help but fear that when an Iraqi father talks to his own child of Iraq's glorious history, he will be able to show him nothing more than a ten-meter stone carving in a little-known valley in Kurdistan.

CHAPTER 55

New Year's Day

As 2005 BEGAN TO approach, life in Iraq had become increasingly difficult for me. I was committed to my project, for the time being, and of
course I was not intending to leave without Sara, but my patience was
growing increasingly thin. I had spent more than eighteen months living
in Iraq without the basic amenities to which most Americans were accustomed and without a plan for the future. I began to realize that I needed
to organize myself, to establish plans and ideas and goals for a post-Iraq
existence, if I was truly going to leave. It was therefore a time of some
excitement given my upcoming marriage, return to the U.S., and reor-
ganization of my professional aspirations, as well as for apprehension,
given the uncertainty of the future. It was during one of my many
periods of rumination about such matters that Professor Saman
approached me with an invitation.

"Doctor Haider, you must come to my house on New Year's Eve!" Professor Saman urged.

"Okay, Professor Saman, I will do that. I missed last New Year's in
Baghdad. Only madmen are out at that hour in Baghdad these days."

"I hear from friends it used to be so wonderful in Baghdad, almost like
America," the other professor privy to the conversation added. "Better
than America. Our parties are better than America now, I bet."

I tried not to let my skepticism show, and changed the subject. "In
America, they pray at Christmas and then they drink at New Year's," I said.

"Christmas? That's the 25th of December, right?" Saman asked.

"Yes, as big a holiday as Eid is for us," I said.

"You mean they get a day off and everything?" Saman asked.

I smiled. Iraqis had no conception of how important Christmas was in the rest of the world. It meant nothing to them.

As it turned out I had to walk five miles to Saman's house on New Year's Eve because the police had closed the main thoroughfares to vehicle traffic in order to prevent any random act of terrorism. I hoped taxis would be back on duty before I needed to get home.

I enjoyed the walk; the streets were eerily quiet. During almost every other celebratory event in Suleymania, when cars were not banished from the roads, the primary means of celebration was all-male cruising accompanied by a liberal honking of horns in whatever pattern struck a driver's fancy. The din could be unbearable. This time, without the cars, residents were at a loss as to how to celebrate. Mainly they stood or walked along and looked about hoping, I supposed, that someone else would give them an idea of what to do. Every so often a storekeeper would start playing loud Kurdish music, and several youths would begin dancing in front of his establishment.

Eventually I arrived at the professor's tiny apartment, which turned out to be more or less a hovel. It was located in a two-floor, grimy, dark building with a few simple businesses on the first floor. The professor's room was no more than one hundred square feet, with a single bed, a television, an inexpensive, worn rug that could not have been less than ten years old or have cost more than twelve dollars when purchased, and a shared bathroom so dirty I hesitated to use it more than once and even then under dire emergency. This party was not quite Truman Capote's Black and White Ball. I couldn't imagine living in such quarters, but Saman seemed perfectly content with his accommodations.

"I am happy in this place, Doctor Haider. I have a bed, a television, a bathroom. The biggest problem is I cannot marry and bring a woman here. A woman needs a home, you see, and I must provide that for her, of course," he said.

"I hope you get what you want and always remain happy," I told him.

"Doctor Haider, what is better, our parties or American parties? American parties for sure, I think. You have pretty women at your parties; we are all men," Saman said loudly, hoping to start a conversation on the subject of beautiful women.

"But such handsome men!" added Sayyid Lutfi, a judge who was not very happily married and whose mannerisms made me question his affinity for women. "Look how young and attractive Saman and Haider are. Don't you like looking at them, isn't that enough?" he asked. Questions like this only raised my suspicions.

Saman answered, "Professor Haider yes, but me, I am too short and need to lose weight. I will get married soon, however, and then I can forget all of that."

"Saman, don't you have a tape recorder, let's hear some music!" shouted Sayyid Lutfi. "I need a beer, too, I had a miserable day. My wife was nagging me about taking the kids to see Santa on the street so they could take a picture. It took me an hour to find that idiot in the red suit, and he turned out to be pretty ugly."

"But the kids enjoyed it?" asked another professor.

"Yeah, they were so happy it almost made me forget that hell of a womb they came from," he said, I think jokingly.

They then started to play music from a cheap tape recorder that looked like it had been manufactured in the 1950s. Here we were—a professor, three doctoral students, a judge, and me sitting in a room that would compare poorly with the simplest dormitory room in the United States, and a bathroom that resembled, if anything, the lavatory of a truck stop. Some were drinking Diet Pepsis, the Kurds had cheap beer, and we were having as good a time as any I have had in much more affluent surroundings. I paid $350 once for two tickets to a New Year's Eve celebration in New York, and it turned out to be a miserable experience. This I found much more fun. We spent hours on the floor discussing almost anything we could think of.

"You know," I said, later into the evening, "in America we have a tradition of creating New Year's resolutions at the end of the year, and then trying to meet them by the end of the following year."

A silence ensued. The guests looked at one another in bewilderment. Finally, Sayyid Lutfi spoke. "Then I wish that my wife disappears and

Rose takes her place!" (This was a reference to Kate Winslet's character in *Titanic*. It was common in Iraq not to refer to actors by their real names, but by their memorable characters' names. Not a soul I knew could identify the name Sylvester Stallone, but everyone knew who Rambo was.)

"No, no, Sayyid Lutfi, it's not a genie in a bottle, it's a resolution you will actually try to make happen. For example, I can resolve to learn Kurdish. Then I learn Kurdish for the rest of the year."

One of the postdoctoral students interrupted, "But what if you have to move back to America?"

"Then I would buy a book and learn Kurdish."

"What if you have to get married because your parents say it is time, and then you have children and you are in America and cannot find many people to speak Kurdish to?" asked another.

"If I prefer, I can make the resolution marriage instead of learning Kurdish. Or I could lose weight," I answered. I noticed the confusion that remained on their faces, except for Sayyid Lutfi, who still seemed distracted by the thought of being wed to Kate Winslet. Perhaps he was not gay, I thought.

"This makes no sense, it is like resolving to change the flow of the Tigris River, or Sayyid Lutfi marrying Rose," another added.

"I've got a better chance than you, you ugly donkey," Sayyid Lutfi quickly replied.

"Well, I will make some resolutions, I think," Professor Saman said. I was not sure whether he had said this out of graciousness to me or because he really wanted to make a New Year's resolution.

"Think about them, Saman, I am going home," said Sayyid Lutfi who by now had firmly established himself as the life of the party. "It is late, and my wife will nag me when I get there for being drunk."

"It's not midnight, is it?" I asked.

"It's eleven fifteen. What are we going to do at midnight, kiss each other? We're all men," Sayyid Lutfi said.

The party soon broke up. The roads had cleared, most residents had gone home, and Sayyid Lutfi was kind enough to drop me off at home.

"Good luck on those resolutions, Doctor Haider. I resolve for peace and stability in Iraq!" He smiled. "Is that a good resolution?"

"*In sha'Allah*," I answered. "When the Tigris reverses its flow and you marry Rose."

I went inside, smoked a cigar to welcome in the New Year, and called Sara. She was at home with her parents, and given our imminent engagement, it was not difficult for her to arrange to speak to me at midnight. We talked about our respective evenings; I mentioned Sayyid Lutfi and indicated that I thought he might be gay.

"There are no gays in Iraq," Sara said confidently and entirely without judgment, as if she were only describing the reality of the situation, much like one would say that it never rains in Iraq in the summer.

I smiled, knowing she had a bit to learn about this when we moved to the United States.

"The guy who cleans our offices is gay," I told her.

"Salah? How do you know?"

The man wore a pink apron and affected the mannerisms. It was funny to imagine anyone not at least suspecting within seconds of meeting him what his sexual orientation was. This was impossible to explain to Sara, so I simply said, "Trust me."

"I wish we could celebrate New Year's together at a proper party," she said, changing the subject. "I'm watching a movie and they are all wearing tuxedos and fancy dresses and it seems lovely. I'm wearing sweatpants and listening to my father snore."

"Next year, we'll try something like that, I promise."

"I will hold you to that!" she exclaimed. Then we wished each other a Happy New Year and hung up, right around midnight.

The following year, we were invited to a friend's apartment on the Hudson River in Greenwich Village, and we decided to go. Even though the occasion did not call for it, we dressed formally, at Sara's request.

CHAPTER 56

Engagement

MY PARENTS CAME TO Suleymania from the United States in early January in order to initiate my engagement to Sara. This was our custom: no diamond rings and no suitors on bended knee; instead my father would ask her father for permission for me to wed his daughter and, permission granted, a ceremony would be scheduled the following day, then a celebration after that. Given the importance of this series of events, they had come specifically for this purpose, leaving on New Year's Eve in order to attend, and they were planning on leaving a few days after that, following a short trip to Baghdad to visit relatives. Unfortunately, the first of these events did not go entirely as planned.

We were all sitting around a coffee table in Sara's living room, which could hold about ten to fifteen people comfortably but now had something like twenty-five people in it. Most were from Sara's family, and some had traveled from hours away to hear my father ask for Sara's hand. Instead what they were treated to was a series of jokes from my father, for well over an hour.

"Dad!" I whispered, urgently, just as he was beginning yet another joke, this one involving a Kurd, an Arab, and a donkey. "Are you clear on what you are supposed to be doing?" I was speaking English, so that others could not understand.

"Yes, I am. Remember, I am the Iraqi here, son," he replied.

"Well, these people are waiting for you to ask for Sara's hand. Her uncles and aunts came from miles and miles away, and you're telling jokes."

"I am waiting for a hint."

"A *what?*" I asked, incredulous.

My mother interjected, also in English, "Haider, can I tell the funny story about the parents who went to the house of the woman and they were all waiting and they never proposed?"

At this point, to my relief, my brother almost exploded. His intervening made it clear to my parents that it was not just me who was being unreasonable. "Mom, you are doing the same thing!" he said. "You're the groom's parents, you are in the house of the bride, ask the damn question already! We've been here two hours."

"I know, can we go soon?" my mother asked. "We have to meet my second cousin, she lives here with her husband. How much longer do we have to stay?"

"You can go when you propose," I replied in English, nearly shouting.

Sara asked me, in Arabic, in a whisper, "Is something wrong?"

"No, everything's fine, just hold on for one minute," was all that I could say.

"I still think we need a hint," my dad said.

"For the love of Allah and his Apostle Muhammad, and the people of his house, Ali, and Fatima, and the Leaders of the Youths of Heaven, Hassan and Hussein, there are no more hints. They let you in their house, that's your hint. Jesus, is this simpler in America. At least I could do it there!"

"Enough with this Jesus talk! Let me think about giving them a hint to give me a hint."

Finally my mother mercifully intervened. She mentioned why we had come, and my father said something like "ditto." By the time they had gotten around to this, half of Sara's relatives had already left, but this was of little consequence. They would be back the next day for a party we had planned to celebrate the engagement.

CHAPTER 57

Work

Shortly after my engagement, a USAID officer with whom we had been working, Ann, came to Suleymania to visit. I had found her to be among the best of the staff with whom we worked. Ann was genuinely interested in the success of our project and this made me eager to meet her whenever she contacted us. She had come to the university to check in and monitor our progress.

I met her just outside of a conference hall as a meeting was taking place inside, and we exchanged pleasantries and general information about our lives for a few minutes. She then asked us about our work and I eagerly began to explain everything that we were doing.

"Well, we have been arranging a number of conferences for the faculty at the various Iraqi law schools to interact with one another, just like this conference," I said.

"I know about that, it's great!" she exclaimed.

"Right, and we are instituting practice-based programs in the law schools. We have built moot courts for the students and they are using the courts to show how law is practiced. We've had judges come into these courtrooms and show the students what happens, and students in some cases have been doing a little bit of this as well."

"Great!"

"We also are revamping the libraries, though my colleague Kim is much more involved in that than I am. From what I know, the library is being totally overhauled and books are being purchased, electronic resources procured, it is all very impressive."

"It sounds like it."

"It really is. Things are moving more slowly than I would have liked, and security in the south is a big issue, as you know. Sometimes I have to kick some people in the butt to get them to take any initiative or do anything . . ."

"I hear that!" Ann said, clearly sympathetic to these problems, given that she suffered similar ones during her time in Baghdad.

"Because of that, we did not do everything we wanted, but we did most, I think. Or we did most of what we had set out to do. The longer term goals will take much more time, I think. You should really come see all three law schools," I said. "It is very good work and it is your money, after all."

"I really wish I could, but we have these rules for travel regulations imposed on us these days because of security, so it is almost impossible to get anywhere. And the Basra dean won't allow us to come anymore because he does not like our personal security detail with all of its weaponry. I can't say I blame him. But I will try, I really will."

"And funding?"

"I am trying so hard to get money for these projects, but we're fighting an uphill battle, they really want most of the money to go to security. These types of soft projects they are not interested in."

"So more personal security details, and more weaponry, and less education."

"I guess you could put it that way."

"And hearts and minds?" I asked.

She shrugged her shoulders and smiled. As immensely frustrating as this was to hear, I couldn't blame her. It was obvious that this was neither her policy nor did she even seem to support it, but it was swiftly becoming a reality. Programs like ours were becoming irrelevant. The money that had been committed would be spent, but with minimal supervision and certainly nothing more would be forthcoming. This was all that remained of my once grand ambitions in Iraq, working on a dying project of dwindling importance to anyone save the few who happened to be involved in it.

Final Extension

IN JANUARY I AGREED officially to extend my contract with DePaul a final time, through the end of May 2005. While I remained as pessimistic as ever over Iraq's future, I ultimately decided that it was in my best interest to stay for a combination of reasons ranging from the logistical to the oddly patriotic.

Most important, DePaul and the International Law Society in the U.S. both asked me to coach the first team that Iraq would field in the Jessup International Law Moot Court Competition, the largest and most well-known of international legal competitions available to law students. The team would be from Suleymania University, and I was certain that this experience would prove to be extremely valuable to them. It was also likely to be my most significant professional achievement in a year that had been filled with obstacles and frustrations.

The Jessup competition involved selecting four students to act as a team and represent a nation at a simulated International Court of Justice (ICJ) proceeding against another team, representing the other nation involved in the proceeding. The facts of the case and the nations involved were prepared weeks in advance by volunteers. Each team had to take the role of both nations twice, and had to file written briefs, called Memorials in ICJ parlance, as well.

This was not something that any Iraqi law student or faculty member was likely to understand very well. The faculty I knew would more than

FINAL EXTENSION

likely to ask a number of questions like, *Why students and not faculty? How could students be qualified to act as attorneys in simulated proceedings? How does anyone benefit from watching children ruin an international proceeding?* That said, I carried with me the reward of a trip to the United States for four students and perhaps one or two professors as assistant coaches—a dream for most Iraqis, particularly here in Suleymania, and therefore, I knew I would have the support of the administration.

I did have other reasons for agreeing to extend my contract, Sara's visa among the more prominent. While we anticipated no difficulties in obtaining this visa because she was the fiancée of an American citizen, we had come to accept that time is necessary in the post-9/11 world to get a visa to the U.S. In addition, my life was not quite as miserable once Sara and I were engaged. We could now go to restaurants, take walks in the park, and watch pirated movies on DVD together.

While these were the same restaurants I had already been to many times, and while the DVDs were bad copies of movies I had already seen, the events felt new because they were new to Sara. As far as restaurants were concerned, her preference seemed to be for Chinese food, which she had never eaten before meeting me. She watched in amazement the first time I used chopsticks in front of her, and asked me to teach her how to use them. I started to explain that it wasn't necessary, but when I saw the jaw set and the glasses slide down her nose, I knew there was no use in arguing. Three trips to the Chinese restaurant later, Sara was about as adept with chopsticks as I was.

Despite the fact that Iraq had become bearable because of Sara, my extension at DePaul was truly final, as I could not remain happy in Iraq. I had already accepted a position as a fellow at Columbia Law School, where I expected to teach and undertake legal research on the land and religion I loved, and knew was desperately in need of change. I told everyone I knew that this was the better course, that my research could influence policy and that only by leaving could I really expect my work to be valuable. Sometimes I even believed this. But in my heart I knew better. Nobody would leave Iraq and the Islamic world to go to America to make a positive contribution to Iraq and the Islamic world. I'd given up. I did hope and expect that my future work would prove to be useful, but that had nothing to do with my decision to leave. I just wanted to be happy, and productive. I needed work that was important, not a tangential position on a project in which few showed interest. The personal needs were no less significant. I needed an opera quartet at the Met, nights at the Philharmonic, a Sunday on a golf course, an outing at the museum, Vietnamese food, espresso with an old friend, movie matinees, all of those things that I had deprived myself of for so long, those tiny daily events that together contribute to a full and well-lived life. I was too emotionally exhausted; I could spare nothing more for this country. I had done what I could, for as long as I could, and could bear no more duty, no more despair, no more unhappiness. I had to leave. I had to live.

CHAPTER 59

A Trip to Kirkuk

THOUGH I HAD DRIVEN through Kirkuk several times, in late January I needed to make my first trip into the heart of the city to the U.S. Embassy's regional office in order to hand over some visa applications related to our project. The United States Embassy in Baghdad was now able to process visa applications for the most part, though American entry rules still required an interview in Amman. The process appeared to be considerably better than the fiasco that had transpired the summer before, and the embassy more cooperative in assisting us in visa procurement.

I left Suleymania in the middle of a snowstorm with a fair amount of trepidation. A professor at the university, Muhammad, drove me. As a Baghdad-born Arab, Muhammad had no idea how to negotiate a car in a snowstorm, or indeed even how to start it in unusually cold weather, nor did he believe that I might be able to offer any assistance. After flooding the engine several times and nearly killing the battery, he did manage to get the car moving finally, though he immediately attempted to put the car into gear, and of course it stalled.

"Professor Muhammad, you are flooding the engine, please just give me the keys, let me show you," I said.

"No, you have to flood the engine, I know, trust me."

"I come from the land of snowstorms. Trust *me*, flooding the engine is not right," I insisted.

"It is, ask anyone. My friend Abu Mazen knows many mechanics, and his wife is from the north," replied Muhammad.

"Who is Abu Mazen?"

"My friend at the Ministry of Foreign Affairs."

"A foreign affairs official told you? Just hand me the keys, please!"

Muhammad reluctantly handed the keys to me and seemed nonplussed when the car began working in relatively short order. He attributed it to the fact that he had warmed the car himself with his engine-flooding battery-taxing technique.

This is a problem to which I have become accustomed in Iraq. For example, the previous summer I found myself in the midst of a debate concerning what Iraqis refer to as a "whelf" in a car and whether it needed to be removed. I had no idea what a whelf actually was, all that I knew was that Iraqis had wildly differing notions about when it should be removed. I remembered vividly the conversation in Baghdad.

"Professor Haider, you must remove the whelf in the summer, it heats up the car, just ask my friend Abu Abbas," Abu Ahmed stated, rather matter-of-factly.

"Who is Abu Abbas?

Professor Haider, don't listen to him. It's Abu Mustafa who knows everything about cars, he used to live in Europe! The whelf does not come off in winter, trust me, I know this," Ra'ad countered.

"No, no, you are both wrong, the whelf cools the car down, it does not heat it up, my second cousin's husband is a mechanic, I heard him with my own ears. I know," a third said.

Similar reasoning pervaded on the issue of road safety, I found. "If you go on Road X through Kirkuk, it is quite dangerous. My third cousin had an uncle robbed there just the other day," Professor Anwer once told me.

"No, but it is safer than Road Y. I read a report that ten people died o Road Y yesterday," Saman immediately replied.

"That is why Road Z is the best, nothing happens on Road Z," the dean then said.

"No actually it does, Dean. I had this friend whose car was hijacked there," Professor Anwer said in response.

"Really? Never mind then."

In Iraq, rumor was information.

Having finally started the car, Muhammad and I began what is always the next step in Iraq before taking a long trip, a search for gasoline. Despite having the world's second largest oil reserves, and despite having been free of the regime of Saddam Hussein for nearly two years, Iraq remained a gas starved country. Subsidies that encouraged smuggling did not help. Fortunately for us, I had a few 20-liter containers of gasoline in our home to be used as storage for our generator, and after about an hour of fruitless searching, we decided to use those, hoping that more could be found before our generator required more fuel. We began our trip around 11:30 a.m., about two and a half hours after we had originally planned. In Iraq, this is a roughly on-time departure.

When we finally reached the Kirkuk highway, the conditions of travel were less than ideal. Though Kurdistan had a reasonable number of vehicles available to move snow in winter, the notion of using salt had apparently not gained acceptance in the area, or perhaps a rumor had been spread that salt in fact increases the ice level. In any event, snowplows moved the snow off of the road, and a sheet of ice remained packed below. Despite this danger, the cars traveled in tight lanes (effectively three lanes on a two-lane road) and at alarmingly high speeds. All around us we saw huge trucks blaring their horns, pickups loaded with young Kurdish laborers dressed in their traditional attire and cold weather headgear, and cars full of families apparently out enjoying the cold weather, all packed into lanes of ice, moving along at over thirty-five miles per hour. Never had I traveled this speed in blinding snow on a pack of ice, much less attempted this with a car on either side of me moving at the same speed. But Muhammad and the other drivers on the road were perfectly at ease. I found the increasing number of checkpoints and stalled cars on the road to Kirkuk a relief, as they forced a winnowing of the lanes, and a slowing down of the cars to about twenty miles per hour. This did cause a delay, however, in our arrival to Kirkuk by another seventy minutes, so that by about 1 o'clock, we were running about three and a half hours behind schedule. This was considered late in Iraq, though not an unusual one.

Two-thirds of the way to Kirkuk, the snow stopped, suddenly. We were no longer in the middle of a snowstorm, but instead, a rain shower. One to two feet of snow were replaced with water and gravel. I was rather surprised by the change in weather, but Muhammad was not. He told me that it never snowed in Kirkuk, that the change in altitude from Suleymania to Kirkuk accounted for this sudden difference, and that it was therefore entirely expected.

We made considerably better headway when the snow was finally behind us. We quite easily passed the Kirkuk checkpoint and were once more beyond the limits of Kurdistan Iraq. While Kirkuk was not Iraq's most dangerous city, it was by no means safe. Assassinations, murders, car bombs, improvised explosive devices, and kidnappings were common in Kirkuk. My heart began to race as we made our way through the streets. I was back.

Moreover, Kirkuk had an added danger in that it was also a city boiling over with ethnic tension, a legacy in large part of the rule of Saddam Hussein. Historically, it was a prosperous city, located near a series of rich oil fields and populated by Iraq's three ethnic groups: Arabs, Kurds, and Turkomen, all of whom more or less managed to live peacefully for decades alongside one another. This changed under the rule of Saddam Hussein, when an Arabization policy cruelly and forcibly uprooted tens of thousands of Kurds and replaced them with Arabs from the south that were given free, confiscated homes and other financial inducements. As a result, when I sought to marry a Kurd, Sara's friends reminded her that Arabs removed her, forcibly, from her home (though that removal was for reasons relating to her father's refusal to join the Ba'ath party and not part of any Arabization policy in the area of Kurdistan in which she resided). How could she betray her people, they would ask, by seeking to marry one of *them*? Of course, neither my father nor I, nor anyone in my family, had participated in the atrocities in Kurdistan, and we as Shi'is in the south were victims of similar atrocities, but blind hatred was often seductive and could not compete with colder, more measured reason and logic.

In any event, the horror of Kirkuk and Arabization occurred during Saddam's rule, and the Kurds seemed determined, contrary to every single historical lesson that could be learned from other parts of the world, to turn back the clock to the way things were before Saddam Hussein defiled the nation. They wanted to remove the Arabs, or those Arabs that came to Kirkuk in the time of Saddam Hussein (the so-called new Arabs) and return the Kurds to their original homes, sometimes to the detriment of those Kurds.

I had a colleague and good friend, Dr. Maruf, who was expelled from Kirkuk as part of the Arabization policy. Rather than sit idly in a refugee camp and wail about the unfairness done to him, he fled the nation, obtained a doctorate in law abroad, returned to become a professor at Suleymania University, and is now a dean at Koya University, about two hours outside of Suleymania. A man with a home, a wife, and a successful career, all of which he had managed in spite of the grievous injustices done to him. And for a while it seemed as if the injustices done to him were about to be repeated, by the Kurdish authorities themselves. Eager to repopulate Kirkuk, they ordered him to return there and leave everything he had built behind. Dr. Maruf managed to gain a reprieve from the demands to return, and it did not appear as if any are interested in renewing the matter of his return, but the matter is telling, and indicative of the absurdity and potential harm done to Kurds and Arabs alike when the attempt is made to turn a clock back by decades.

Nevertheless, with the Kurds determined to gain back Kirkuk, the Arabs determined to stay their ground, and the Turkomen concerned about their own positions, tensions in the city ran very, very high. This was a potential flashpoint, and a dangerous one at that. That said, the tensions were not at such a point that a Kurd would not help give directions to two Arabs obviously not from Kirkuk. I began to relax, as the fact that I was only going to be in Kirkuk for two hours and told nobody I was going lessened the possibility that I could be targeted. To those on the street, we were lost Arabs, not agents of the American occupation or sympathizers of Saddam Hussein. As I relaxed, I began to pay closer attention to my surroundings and began to wonder what everyone was fighting about.

Kirkuk was a devastated city. Most the streets in which we traveled were not paved, and the paved streets were riddled with potholes. Houses were dilapidated, stores were often hovels held up by aluminum siding and offering the simplest of goods, from the smell and the overflowing drains the sewage system appeared to be entirely nonfunctional, at least on a rainy day. Cars everywhere slowed at random potholes in streets overflowing with water and raw sewage, some unable to continue, others pressing forward, seeking to find a means around the hesitating cars, honking as they passed, gesturing with their hands, and receiving hand gestures in return. Cars refusing to drive through the sewage and cars stalled in the sewage because of the water level eventually made the street impassable. Left to right, back and forth, we moved along the unpaved potholed roads, trying to negotiate a way through a city with roads seemingly older than Babylon's, and a sewage system more primitive. We pressed forward slowly, avoiding sewage-laden areas when we could, forcing our way through them when we could not.

In a troubled country, this was the poorest, least developed, and most desperately lacking city I had seen, Basra included. I could not imagine anyone fighting over the right to live here. Even relatively nice homes lay on potted, muddy roads adjacent to empty dirt fields that functioned as garbage dumps or sewage pits. Calcutta was the only city I had seen in comparably poor condition. Quite simply, the city did not seem worth the trouble. *If the Kurds wanted Kirkuk,* I thought, *let the Kurds have Kirkuk.*

The symbols seemed more important than the reality, important enough to light a flame that could spread through the entire country. It simply made no sense.

We made our way through the streets, eventually dropped off our documents, attended our belated meetings, and made it back to Suleymania by six o'clock, about five and a half hours behind schedule. A bit late, but not by much, Muhammad noted.

CHAPTER 60

Pre-Election

I KNEW THAT BY mid-January, in some parts of Iraq, mostly Sunni-dominated, there was a great deal of fear concerning the elections, and that as a result significant sections of the electorate might not vote. The Shi'a looked at things differently. Two days before the election, I was speaking with Sayyid Hussein, a cousin from Baghdad and one of the nearly hundred that I seem to have, who has always been ardently sectarian in his views. His lack of fear respecting the upcoming election was surprising, even among a fatalistic people such as the Iraqis.

"Of course they will strike, the terrorists. They don't want to see the Shi'a take control. Haider, we are on the verge of something special, the first state controlled by us in this land where we are the majority since Imam Ali died 1400 years ago. This is going to be something. How can you not take part in this history of Shi'i assertion of control because of some silly fear of death?"

"I will vote here," I said, "but you in the south, be careful."

"I will be as careful as I can, but if I die, then I die a martyr. This is my *jihad*," he said with certainty. "Sunni *jihad* is cutting off people's heads like they were sheep, this is our *jihad*. If we don't vote, we deserve the shackles of the tyrants. If we don't vote, then we are no partisans of the Leader of the Martyrs, Hussein the son of Ali."

I wondered after all of this if he was running for office himself.

In Suleymania, the sense of duty was no less pronounced. The Kurds knew that they would have a voice, also for the first time, and a significant one. They aspired to no less than the presidency of Iraq. Moreover, the mood here was in no way tempered by fear; it was safe enough to make considerations of martyrdom unnecessary. In fact it was almost a party. On every single night during the week preceding the election, cars, trucks, pickups, and tractors cruised up and down Salim Street, Suleymania's central thoroughfare. The vehicles were almost all decorated in green (the color of the dominant Patriotic Union of Kurdistan, or PUK) and layered with posters of Jalal Talabani, the PUK's unrivalled leader. They honked their horns in rhythmic fashion, played patriotic Kurdish music, sat on the sills of the car windows, and shouted slogans. On the streets, many walked up and down, all dressed in green, carrying their own placards and doing their own shouting.

Once, walking down the street with Sara en route to her home and entirely unable to hear myself think from the din, I complained to Sara about the noise levels.

"You think you are the only one bored here?" Sara asked me.

"What?" I was confused by the question. "I'm not bored, I'm annoyed by the damn horns!" I shouted, to make myself heard.

"You always say no movies, no tennis courts, no this, no that. Just you suffer?"

"I'm not sure I know what you are talking about," I said. "Who is talking about movies?"

"There are no movies is my point. This horn thing is all they have by way of recreation, so this is what they do. It seems annoying to you, but it's either this or television, and they already watch too much television."

After that conversation, I was more sympathetic to the revelers.

There did seem to be some level of freedom of speech here, the PUK's absolute dominance on the streets notwithstanding. Posters of other parties could be seen, including the poster of the dominant Shi'i alliance, List 169, its placards in Suleymania calling for a federal Iraq to attract a Kurdish vote. (Parties and ethnic groups had coalesced by and large into larger alliances, and had registered with the election commission as such. The population referred to these alliances largely by the number that the commission had assigned to them. The Shi'i alliance was List 169, and the Kurdish alliance was List 130.)

The Kurdish posters contained a picture of the entire nation of Iraq and promoted themselves as a national party—no small irony for an organization that sought maximum autonomy for the Kurdish region. Each party, it seemed, was advertising a position almost diametrically opposed to its ideological convictions in order to attract votes. The only exception was the Communist Party, which had been around for too long in too many nations to be able to affect much of a change in their image here and now.

Even with the Communists, however, ethnicity trumped ideology. There was a Communist slate in Iraq, but the Kurdish Communist party would not be on that slate. Rather, they had joined forces with the unified Kurdish slate, List 130. Also on the list were the Kurdish Islamic parties and a few Christian groups. Nothing other than ethnicity unified these elements, just as nothing other than sect and some at least slight element of religiosity unified the Shi'i groups.

So the posters, while entertaining, were ultimately pointless. The vote throughout the country would divide entirely along ethnic and sectarian lines, the Shi'a for 169, the Kurds for 130, and the secular Sunnis and a few secular Shi'a for Ayad Allawi's list. As for the regional parliamentary vote, at least here in Kurdistan, the entire affair was almost ridiculous. The only two large parties in the region had joined forces and agreed to divide the Kurdish regional parliament between them. Given their relative size and existing control over Kurdish affairs presently, the unification effectively stripped the voters of a choice; it would be as if the Democratic and Republican parties agreed to run on a single ticket and divide Congress on the basis of some deal they had struck between themselves.

Welcome to democracy, Iraqi style.

CHAPTER 61

Election Day

ELECTION DAY, JANUARY 30, 2005, was a beautiful day, but I just couldn't seem to enjoy it. The weather was lovely, the streets unusually peaceful, and, of course, Iraq was holding its first free election in my lifetime. Millions heroically braved the mortars and the bullets and the threats and the intimidation to face down, nonviolently, those elements of our society, and of Arab and Islamic society more broadly, who seem to support nothing but nihilism, seek nothing but death and destruction, want nothing other than some primitive form of chaos to rule the earth. They took a beating on this day, the first after what had been almost two years of unrelenting success. Yet I greeted it all rather nonchalantly.

The scenes did move me, of course. Elderly men who could barely walk braving their way to the polling station, elderly black-clad women weeping about the sons they had lost to the previous regime, praying aloud that this will change things forever, younger men and women dancing and singing and reveling in unqualified joy at the birth of something many of us never thought we would see—a democratic Iraq. I suppose I should have been dancing along with them, celebrating as freedom rang from the northern mountains to the southern swamplands, from the western deserts to the eastern plains. Finally, after decades and decades, it was here. Walking the streets of Suleymania, I should have felt proud to be part of this country and the remarkable transition in which it found itself. It was the same road I had walked several days before, the central thoroughfare of Salim Street, but this time there were no cars, only men, women, and children walking up and down the road, dressed elegantly in traditional Kurdish garb or business suits, more solemn than they had been the days previous, but also happier, overjoyed that the day had arrived, and that they had done their duty.

Everyone but me was absolutely euphoric. Sara was overjoyed at first, but my melancholy mood disturbed her. When I phoned her, and she noticed my mood, she asked about it immediately. I tried to explain.

"Sara, doesn't it bother you that no Sunni Arabs voted in this election? They all stayed home."

"That's their fault," said Sara. "We Kurds won't give up the presidency because they chose not to vote."

"Well, that sentiment explains my problem with this election. The 'Kurds' are not an electoral bloc. There are communist Kurds, Islamist Kurds, nationalist Kurds, the idea that you throw all of this into one 'we the Kurds' party already shows that this didn't work."

"It takes time to develop these ideas. We aren't there yet, this is step one, and a great step. You can't expect America in a day."

"This is not the first step to democracy, but the first step to war. There are no parties; there are ethnicities. A politician can't attract the other side with better ideas when the political groups are ethnicities. The Shi'i groups can't win Kurdish votes, and vice versa. It's just permanent division establishing itself, and all anyone in government is going to do is look out for their own."

"You're being very grumpy. Even the CNN guys are jumping with joy, practically. I think you're just a pessimist all the time," Sara said wearily. "The whole world is celebrating, and you are moping."

"Fine," I responded. "I am happy the election took place, mainly because I do not think there was an alternative. That so many turned out to vote is highly encouraging. However, if the election made anything clear it is that the divisions of sect and ethnicity are very serious, and they are going to get worse with the Sunnis out of government now. Given that, it's a little hard to celebrate."

"Iraq won, democracy won. Stop reading a speech and come out and celebrate!"

CHAPTER 62

Request

My uncle Hummam, with whom I had traveled to Kadhmiya many months earlier, came to Suleymania shortly after the election. We spent an evening together, and then as he was leaving he called me to his car.

"It is time to return to Baghdad, Haider. This is the opportunity to write the Constitution. We will be forming the government soon, and we will need legal expertise to help. You should come," he said.

The request came as a surprise, and not an entirely pleasant one. When I had first come to Iraq, this was precisely the kind of work I had been intending to do. It was as if my prayers were being answered, but much too late. So much had changed since my arrival. I had become deeply disillusioned with everything that had transpired in this country particularly at the political and legal levels. I was very pessimistic about its future, while on a personal level my relationship with Sara and my appointment to Columbia Law School had made me much more optimistic for my own future. I was just starting to become happy again, and I was not about to risk life and limb to return to Baghdad to work on a constitution for a country heading in precisely the wrong direction. I replied to my uncle carefully.

"The last time, when we went to Kadhmiya, I listened to you, Uncle Hummam. I left private practice, and you were right about it. It was not time to make money. But I cannot do this, I am terrified of Baghdad."

That was certainly part of the reason. I left undisclosed the other part:

Iraq as a nation had failed, it had been carved up into fiefs, each controlled by a combination of chiefs, clerics, militias, and tribal elders. A constitution reflects the will of an entire people, and here there was no such collective will, at least among the elites who would do the negotiating. No legal compact could create a social compact that did not exist. This would not be a constitution; it would be a treaty among warlords.

"You could live in the Green Zone for a short time until things get better. I thought the Constitution and law was what you had talked about as your contribution?"

"Not like this, I did not imagine this," I said, my eyes staring at the car floor as my uncle looked directly at me. I could not bring myself to raise my head to speak to him directly.

"Think about this, talk with your father. It is a great opportunity to participate in Iraq's future."

"I am tired, Ammu, I am tired of living like this, I am exhausted from almost two years of this. I need something else. Aren't you tired? Isn't your life with your family in Iran better?"

"Yes, but we have duties to our people," he said, though his call to duty no longer had the same resonance with me that it once had. "Come to Baghdad for a wedding party. Speak to your father."

"I will, and if he tells me to come, I will, if Allah wills it," I told him. "But I am scared of Baghdad right now, and I do not want to be killed." Then I paused. "I will speak to my father and we will see."

"*In sha Allah*" my uncle said.

"*In sha Allah*" I replied.

I had turned him down, in the only way that an Iraqi nephew could turn his uncle down, indirectly, and he knew it. He never urged me to return to Baghdad again, even after he was named, only two months later, head of the Iraqi Constitutional Committee.

CHAPTER 63

Ho-Hum

AFTER THE TREMENDOUS EXCITEMENT of January with the elections, my engagement, my extension, and my decisions regarding career changes, the month of February proved to be fairly quiet. Some took heart in the fact that the insurgency seemed to have quieted down, but I did not. They had geared up for the election, the election was now over, they had failed to disrupt it, and I thought they would sit quietly for a bit, and wait. This turned out to be largely what happened. It was too late for hope; the insurgency was too deeply rooted, too multi-headed, and too maddeningly diffuse to be defeated for years to come.

In addition, ethnic tension was rising, though not dramatically. After the Sunni election boycott and months of steadily rising tensions, I began to view as inevitable a civil war with the Sunnis on one side, the Shi'a and Kurds on the other. Matters could be contained for the time being because nobody's rhetoric had risen to the level of war and the 150,000 U.S. troops on Iraqi soil would deter any militia from openly engaging in sectarian warfare. However, the trend toward war seemed irreversible.

Work continued steadily, and I had begun to focus virtually all of my efforts on the Jessup team. The first two to three weeks with the team was, as I expected, extraordinarily difficult. None of them could read English sufficiently to make use of the volumes of English language source material available on the subject in question, and what little Arabic material did exist appeared to be unattainable in Suleymania. When added to the fact that the students did not know how to use word processors or type, so that they handwrote their drafts, I was impressed that we were making any progress at all.

The administration had a higher opinion of the students, the university, and themselves, than was warranted. Zuhair and I met with the dean in his large, well-appointed office about a month before our trip to the United States for the Jessup competition. I had thought the meeting was about the competition, but it turned out to be concerning another matter entirely.

"Professor Haider, we need an English seminar here," the dean told me. I was taken aback by his request. We had just planned a trip for two of his professors and four of his students to the United States. We had already sent him and two of his professors abroad for conferences elsewhere, and he wanted more.

"I understand, Dean, but it is hard to teach legal English when the regular English level is not that high. Can anyone here read a newspaper article in English?" I asked. The dean's request was silly but I was making every effort to deal with it respectfully.

"Well, we don't want grammar and all that 'has, have' nonsense again, we know that already, we learned it in school for eight years. We need something where we can learn the language," he replied curtly.

"Okay, so what do you mean exactly?" I asked.

"A tutorial where we speak English and have an instructor that helps teach it, and then we learn. Maybe two hours each week," he replied wearily, as if I should have realized this already.

"I think it takes more effort than just going to a tutorial to learn a language," I told him.

"No, it doesn't, you just need to teach us properly. You have let us down not doing this for us, Professor Haider."

I was not sure what surprised me more, his seemingly sincere belief that two hours of instruction a week for eight weeks would make his faculty masters of English, or his suggestion that I had some sort of obligation to provide him with anything at all, let alone a full English training program.

"Dean, it's not my money," I said, restraining a strong impulse to add, *or yours,* to the end of the sentence. "It's U.S. government money, I can't make them spend it any way that you or I might think important."

He ignored my response, continuing with his criticism. "You never did this, I told you it was important. I also asked for the moot court to have robes for the judges, and you never got us those."

"Have you used the moot court, Dean?" I asked.

"Not yet, we will, but it is disappointing that we don't have robes. It might affect the students at the Jessup," he said.

I was starting to lose patience. "So you haven't used the court, the students are handwriting Arabic drafts to me based on the three books your library has, you have no access to electronic resources, none of your top students can read a newspaper article in English, much less a legal source, but you are disappointed about robes?"

"Well, the English, as I said, is your fault really. The rest is Saddam's."

Apparently now my sin respecting the omission of the English program was akin to the crimes of the former dictator. "Anything else?" I said, trying very hard to keep my voice from rising.

"The money you give to faculty to help you, $500 a month, it isn't enough. They all complain, sometimes they have to work an extra four hours a day with you, and they spend nights sometimes working until as late as 6 p.m. For $500 a month. Is that what you make?"

"I wonder, Dean, rather than what I get paid, what do you pay them?" I asked.

"I don't pay anything, it is government wages. But you are the Americans, they pay you so much, and you pay them $500? Why is that fair?"

"Because it more than doubles their salary, Dean," I explained. The requests had by this time gone from offensive to so ridiculous as to be amusing. A man whose staff earned $200 a month was complaining about our paying them an additional $500.

"Sorry, Dean, this is the way it is," I said firmly. Noticing the tone in my voice, he dropped this line of conversation, and Zuhair and I left his office.

CHAPTER 64

University Invasion

A FEW MONTHS AFTER ANN'S VISIT, I received an e-mail from a member of USAID, our sponsor for the legal education project, indicating that they wished to visit Suleymania's law school to monitor our progress. We were immediately concerned, not so much about their presence, which we welcomed, but about the security that would come with them. Worried about rising casualties and determined to limit these at any cost possible, the United States Embassy and USAID at this time required a "personal security detail" (commonly referred to as a PSD) to accompany their personnel everywhere, whether or not it was requested. Thus the PSD and USAID personnel traveled as one.

The PSD acted effectively as a private military unit. Though PSD personnel detested the appellation "mercenary," they talked, smelled, and conducted themselves like that very species of duck. They traveled with heavy weaponry, paid no attention to local laws or regulations, did not seem accountable to anyone other than their clients, consisted almost without exception of former military personnel, and, much more than their military counterparts, had notoriously twitchy fingers. We went to meet the USAID personnel and their PSD at their hotel in the morning before their visit to the law school, nervous about what might happen and aware that in Basra the dean of the law school had banned the PSD (and thus USAID) from coming to campus, risking a cutoff in funding from USAID rather than endure the mistreatment at the hands of their PSD a second time.

Trouble began almost immediately upon our arrival at the university, when the USAID SUVs, driven by the PSD personnel, arrived at the university gate and refused to stop for the local guards, nearly running over a student in the process. Rather than apologize, the mercenaries pointed a semi-automatic weapon at the student and any others unfortunate enough to be nearby and barked at them to back away. The SUVs then approached the College of Law and several of the mercenaries burst out, weapons pointed everywhere. Eventually the USAID employees (as well as myself and an equally reluctant colleague) came out to the same campus where we went on a daily basis, unarmed and without protection. I slipped on the icy pavement and an elderly professor who knew me rushed toward me to help me up. A mercenary thrust a forearm into the professor's neck and he fell to the ground, out of breath. Another aimed his gun at him and threatened to shoot him. I managed to get myself up and assist the professor, staring as roughly as I knew how at the mercenaries. We then made our way up the stairs of the College of Law to the dean's office where two of the mercenaries stood guard outside with weapons drawn, pointed downwards, but fingers on triggers and eyes twitching nervously about, threateningly gesturing to anyone that drew too near.

I saw Sara on the way up to the dean's office, in the law school's central staircase. I was about to say hello when she interrupted me with a hostile question.

"And your project is about the Rule of Law," she asked me. "Is this the Rule of Law, or the Rule of Klashinkovs? They could have really hurt Professor Anwer, he is quite upset by what they did to him." Apparently she had seen the entire incident from a window.

"He should be," I said, "I do not like to deal with these people either, but USAID funds us, and the USAID people need the pseudo-military folks around."

"A petition is going around already about these men with their big guns. The dean will have a problem if they come back, I know our university will lose money, but they need to understand, they can't treat people like this. This is wrong."

"Now you know how the Iraqi Arabs feel about the occupation," I said.

"Now I do."

Our USAID supervisors were on campus for less than two hours, with the behavior of their security personnel, the PSD, more or less remaining constant. By the time they left, an impromptu student demonstration had begun, the petition Sara mentioned had been circulated, and several of the faculty informed the dean that if they saw this again they would promptly resign their posts. This took place in, let me stress, a relatively peaceful city that consisted almost entirely of Kurds, by far the most pro-American population that exists in Iraq.

Two hours later, the dean called me in to his office and said only four words, in English, before letting me leave for that day. "They can't come back."

I informed him of the consequence of banning the PSD, that it was equivalent to banning their USAID supervisors from campus, and that this might well mean a potential cut in USAID funding.

He only repeated, again, "They can't come back," before asking me to leave the office, because he had other work to get done.

CHAPTER 65

Nawruz

Nawruz was probably among the most pleasant days I had spent in Kurdistan, at least until the evening. It falls on March 21 each year, the day of the equinox, and is the Kurdish and Iranian New Year. No holiday compared in size or scope—not even the Islamic holidays imposed on these conquered peoples over thirteen centuries ago and long since an inherent part of their culture.

Sara, Zuhair, and I, along with a few close friends, spent the evening before Nawruz dressed in Kurdish attire and wandering the main streets of Suleymania with hundreds of other pedestrians in a similarly festive mood. Everywhere, men, women, and children of every conceivable age were gaily dressed in traditional Kurdish outfits—baggy pants and a tight cloth belt for the men and flowing layers of gold, red, and silver for the women. After some walking, we dropped in on a lovely antique store not 1,500 feet from where I lived and whose existence I knew nothing about until today.

"Why am I finding about this great place now? Sara? Zuhair?"

"What's so great? It's not the supermarket. It's just a bunch of old stuff," Sara said.

"Antiques from the time of the monarchy! Phonograph machines! Brass tea makers! Iraq, before the Shadow!"

"True, Professor, though the tea maker is not that special. There's a guy in Karrada not far from your grandfather's house, he makes it there,"

Zuhair said.

"With this?"

"Yes, Professor."

"Zuhair, you never took me?"

"There is better tea in Baghdad, Professor."

"As punishment, you both have to stay here with me for at least an hour," I teased. "I love these things."

Surprisingly, nobody protested. I think they enjoyed the dip into history slightly more than they admitted, even if it was not as interesting to them as it was to me. After we left the store, we walked back onto Salim Street. As the open fires that were a Nawruz tradition burned more brightly in the creeping darkness, as young men began to dance, and older ones to sing, and as the festivity of the Kurdish occasion began to be felt in my own thoroughly Arab blood, I felt something I hadn't felt for quite some time here in Iraq—pure, unmistakable pleasure. For the first time in months I was unconditionally happy. I was in Iraq, and I didn't want to be anywhere else.

Shortly after our browsing through the antiques the fireworks began. I remembered the Fourth of July as a child, when I used to look forward to the evening fireworks with relish. But not this time. Now the sounds disturbed me greatly. They reminded me of mortar fire, car bombs, rocket propelled grenades. When the earth shook, I wished to seek cover, when the smoke hit the air, I wondered whether it was coming from the direction where a family might live, and when the sounds grew ever faster, I thought of where a television might be, so I might understand what was happening. Throughout the display, my sweat poured profusely, my heartbeat quickened, my eyes started to tear, and I felt an almost irrepressible urge to use the restroom. I had seen too much to enjoy this in Iraq, even on Nawruz.

CHAPTER 66

Two-Year Anniversary

I RETURNED TO IRAQ from the Jessup competition in Washington, D.C., two days after the second anniversary of Saddam's fall and in considerably better spirits than I was one year earlier, for a variety of reasons. First, the second year had proved more successful, or at least less of a catastrophic failure, than the previous year. The security situation had continued to deteriorate until fall, but the worst of all scenarios, civil war, had thankfully not occurred as yet. An election had been held and key government positions finally announced just days before the anniversary. Inclusion of the Sunni minority, a festering issue, had not been solved but the new government had at least taken some steps to address the matter. I would not describe much of this as progress, but less deterioration than might have been possible.

The second reason for my generally higher spirits was that those past few weeks did prove to be about as successful as I could have imagined from a professional perspective. The students had gone to Washington, competed with schools far better equipped and trained than they, and more than held their own. The students' performance was nothing short of incredible, the team's ability to develop and hone the legal skills necessary not only to perform respectably, but indeed to win two of their four matches against schools historically strong in legal education and in Jessup performance was amazing, and I was proud to have been a part of it. If I could say nothing else of my actual work in Iraq, I was the coach and organizer of the first

Iraqi team to participate in this pinnacle of international legal competitions, and I would carry this pride with me forever. The hours I worked for this were comparable to if not exceeding those I used to expend at the end of a corporate deal (sixteen to eighteen hours a day, seven days a week), but the rewards made the effort worth it. For the first time in my life I was exhausted, physically and mentally, for a cause, a small cause but a noble one, and I would not have changed places with anyone.

This is to say nothing of the tremendous personal benefit each of the students had received by just being able to travel to the United States. There would have been no other opportunity for them, at least in the near future, and in many ways for them it was a dream come true. We had changed their lives for the better. Virtually everything they saw, from the tours of the Senate floor to the halls of the Supreme Court to the dinosaurs at the Museum of Natural History to the rockets at the Air and Space Museum, was incomparable to any prior experience of theirs. Even if I could not fix Iraq, there were at least a few Iraqi lives within it that I did help make just a little bit better, and for this I felt a deep and lasting pride.

And finally, of course, there was Sara. Nothing had occurred that gave me an ounce of hesitation about my decision to marry Sara, and the more I became acquainted with her, the more certain I was that my decision was the right one.

Upon my return to Iraq from the Jessup competition, it was my task as the groom-to-be to begin the marriage preparations. Fully three weeks before the wedding, we had rented a hall and done little else. However, by Iraqi standards we had ample time as Iraqis did not seem able to engage in advance planning of any kind. The fact that I could arrange a decent wedding in Iraq in three weeks' time caused me to reflect to some degree on whether or not the six months of hair-pulling, nerve-wracking hard to bear anxiety to plan a wedding in the United States was truly necessary. It was after all just a party.

In theory, and as is the custom, I had authority over the matter of wedding arrangements (and sole financial responsibility as well), but in practice Sara very much wished to be a part of this, and I could not imagine a more miserable three weeks if I were to plan this on my own and try to please everyone concerned. So while Sara of course could not contribute financially (her $100 monthly salary not being sufficient to allow that), she was an equal partner in all our wedding arrangements. As a result, many Iraqis mocked me incessantly and told me I was whipped by my spouse prior to my own wedding. Given the alternative of planning a wedding on my own, I could live with the jibes.

Regardless, two years after Saddam's fall, I neared my own wedding and the end of my time here in Iraq with generally high spirits. All things considered, things were okay, at least for me.

CHAPTER 67

Ahmedawa

A WEEK BEFORE MY wedding, I was inundated with the multiple tasks of distributing invitations (because there is no mail), ensuring that relatives would arrive safely into Suleymania, and generally troubleshooting. Sara and I therefore decided to take a break from all the madness and accompany the faculty and staff of the College of Law to their annual outing in Ahmedawa, located high in the Kurdish mountains near the Iranian border.

Until the American invasion, Ahmedawa was a stronghold of the Saddam funded Islamic extremist group known as Ansar al-Islam, which once claimed as a member Abu Musab Al-Zarqawi, Iraq's most well-known terrorist, until his death in June of 2006. The Ansar did not last long after the American arrival. Between U.S. firepower and Kurdish *pesh merga* ground support, they lost their strongholds days after the war began, and those left alive quickly scattered and regrouped in the south (Abu Musab among them) while chaos enveloped the land. What the Ansar left behind was land, mountains, and clear streams of stunning beauty, dwarfing in their majesty the trash pits that Ali Beg, Jundiyan, and many of Kurdistan's other natural wonders had become. Why Ahmedawa was clean while Ali Beg had deteriorated into a waterfall running through a mass of untreated sewage I did not know, but I was happy to finally see something in Kurdistan that fully justified the pride that the Kurds had about the region's natural beauty.

The place where we picnicked was a large, pleasant grove of trees, shielding us from the heat of the sun, already starting to pound us by this late April date. A fast-moving clear stream ran through the grove and we could see other similar streams to our left and right. Upstream and up the mountains was the source of all of this water, a mountain stream that develops into a waterfall before branching into various directions as it moves downhill. Or so we were told when we arrived; none of this was visible from our picnic location.

As was typical of events of this kind in Iraq, and particularly Kurdistan, the picnic instantly developed into a folk dancing session with a great deal of food. Sara and I placed ourselves at a respectable distance from the main group, meaning essentially close enough to be seen and far enough away to talk about whatever we wanted. Anything else would have been deemed improper, and even the most minor display of public affection would have been heavily criticized. So we sat and talked, an activity we never ceased to enjoy, while others sang and danced and barbecued shish kebabs.

After a short while, having eaten shish kebab and grown tired of the continued sitting, Sara and I decided to take a walk. Unfortunately it was not a very long one, because the Ansar had heavily mined the entire Ahmedawa region, and neither Sara nor I wanted to be among their last victims. So we decided to extend our walk by finding the source of the streams in the mountains, where we were told there were not likely to be mines. Others who had come before had told us that this was the premier attraction in the region. Passersby had told us that reaching the source required a jeep, of which there were many all along the main road. Having walked about 1,200 feet, we soon spotted and flagged down an appropriate vehicle, already loaded with six young Arab Iraqi men, two quite heavy, all tourists. Given their generally friendly demeanor, this would have been pleasant enough, except for the fact that the unpaved mountain road on which we found ourselves was filled with rocks and potholes and our jeep was particularly unsuited to deal with them. We bumped along and swayed in every direction, as our companions shouted excitedly at each large bump and attempted to realign themselves by weight at each particularly unnatural swaying.

Fortunately the ride was not long, and after ten minutes and 2,000 Iraqi dinars, Sara and I had arrived at the car park. The others in the jeep jumped ahead and we stayed behind to gather our bearings, drink some water, and start our walk up to the source. The walk to the source from the car park took about forty-five minutes and was stunning at various points throughout. The streams were clear, fast and cold, and in numerous places small falls and areas of rapids could be seen. We made our way up, stopping frequently for pictures. The ascent finally brought us to the final section before the source, a high, wide, and lovely waterfall. It was no Niagara or Victoria, but quite a sight to behold nonetheless. We caught our breath and admired the scene and then, with Sara in the lead, slowly began our ascent to the top.

Sara's desire to see as much as she could was particularly admirable for a woman raised in a culture that did not prize athleticism among women. I had expected to be the one leading the trail, coaxing her one way or another slowly up the mountain. As it turned out, perhaps inspired by the beauty of it and perhaps bolstered by my presence, which in turn legitimated hers, she showed not a hint of fatigue or timidity and in fact reached the top well before I did and, seemingly, with less effort.

Upon my arrival, I promptly plunged myself into the caves in the side of the mountain that were the source of the water, out of which the water flowed to create the waterfall. Sara watched silently, happy to be where she was, but clearly disappointed that in Iraq, she could not join me in the swim. She vowed to participate next time, in America.

Several hours later we made our way back to our fellow picnickers who predictably had not moved an inch. If there were any people on earth more content than Iraqis to sit in a single place for hours on end and do absolutely nothing, I would like to meet them. Having spent almost two years in Iraq, I had become convinced that most of the insurgency could have been nipped in its bud if the Americans had left the army intact and required it to sit in air-conditioned barracks far from the cities for hours on end each day, for a stated salary, doing absolutely nothing. In air conditioning, on salary, and drinking tea while doing little else was for most Iraqis a form of paradise.

Some in our group eventually found their way to the water source for a brief stay, though not a single woman other than Sara made the climb.

"Aren't your friends into nature, sweetheart," I asked.

"Well, I don't think they like working out quite like I do, actually," Sara said. "But even if they did, what would they do, climb by themselves, just women?"

"Yes."

"And how many women have you seen do that here?"

"You just climbed."

"With my fiancé, and they probably could with their brother or father, but by themselves, just women, on their own? People would talk."

"What's wrong with climbing a mountain?" I asked.

"To me, nothing, to them, nothing, to everyone else, a lot. People would say they were trying to attract attention. I told you, people here look at women as sexual objects. So if there were seven single women climbing a mountain, it would attract attention. Half the people would leer, the other half would tell them to stop making men leer. What woman wants to be a part of that?"

CHAPTER 68

Wedding

ON THE DAY OF our wedding in Suleymania, Sara's visa was still pending. And therefore a legal marriage ceremony remained impossible because then Sara would be my wife and no longer my fiancée. However, given my approaching departure from Iraq, and the inability of nearly all of Sara's friends and family to attend a wedding held elsewhere, we decided to have a large (non-wedding) party as scheduled without any religious ceremony, civil ceremony, or actually anything else, other than a party.

I considered this party a farewell of sorts as well as a celebration of union. It was, after all, only days until my departure from Iraq. Given this, Sara and I went through extraordinary efforts to be sure that it would be remembered fondly. I had lofty expectations for the event, and they were amply exceeded. Other than my many Iraqi friends and relatives, five of my loyal friends from abroad, none Arabs or Muslims, attended the ceremonies. Sara and I thought it sufficiently safe in Kurdistan for them to come and their presence meant a great deal to both of us. Hundreds of others also attended, roughly the number we expected, but bearing only a rough correlation to our invitation list. We had hand delivered invitations, but could not very well ask for RSVPs given the absence of a mail system, so we were unsure of who the final attendees would be until the party began. Some came, others didn't, and quite a few ended up bringing their families with them. The more polite ones advised us in advance of the additional people they intended to bring. Sometimes it was a lone sister, sometimes a set of parents, and often several others, including a house-keeper, a friend of a cousin and his family, and the father and sister of a fiancée. Soon the wedding hall had a fair number of people whom neither Sara nor I nor anyone in our families had ever seen. Apparently our non-wedding wedding had become the social event of the season.

Our entrance was grand enough. We drove to the hall in a black, rented convertible amid ululations of women and loud traditional Arabic music. Small sparklers and candles lit our way to the dance floor, where amid a smoke machine and a Lionel Richie CD, we began our dance ("Endless Love"). I was in a suit and Sara had on a white gown. Should this sound rather Western in form, it was. The music and dance (other than Lionel Richie) was largely Iraqi, and the food certainly was, but all Islamic tradi-tion was intertwined with the non-legal ceremony that came at a different time. The actual, legal wedding (which was how this event was planned, until it became impossible for visa related reasons to have an actual wed-ding, religious or legal) was a later addition, perhaps no more than a cen-tury old, and was with slight variations essentially Western in concept.

After the dance, we sat upon our very Arab dais decked with flowers, silk brocades, and two very large chairs, dubbed thrones by our American guests, as others took the dance floor. We would participate, of course, to a great extent, but at first it was our task to sit on our "thrones" as everyone observed us. All were clapping, the younger men began to dance and hoot, and the girls all smiled and whispered to each other, hiding their mouths with their palms should anyone attempt to read their lips. All of my friends and co-workers with whom I had toiled so long—Professor Saman, Professor Anwer, Professors Muhammad and Ma'ruf, the Dean, several Judges, Sayyid Lutfi, Zuhair, and my friends from abroad stood and cheered us on our thrones. My grandmother had come with Sa'diya, and my uncle Nawfal, with his wife and one daughter, had made the trip as well. Zahra's son had arrived the day before, and Ali was in attendance. Nearly everyone who had made my life in Iraq so intensely rich and mean-ingful had come, partly for the wedding, but mostly, I knew, because they thought it might be the last time we would see each other. Iraq had become a disaster, they realized I was leaving, and they didn't know when circumstances would allow me to return. Sara's many friends and relatives had come to honor her wedding, but everyone I knew had come to bid farewell, possibly forever.

I looked at my ninety-year-old grandmother, old, frail and yet doing what she could to show how happy she was, and I began to cry. Nothing in Iraq had moved me to tears like this. The idea that this beloved woman who had kept me in her home for eighteen long months had come to Suleymania from Baghdad, knowing, as I did, that it was possibly the last time I would see her, was too much for me to bear.

I did not have the chance to talk to my grandmother for very long at the party (I was too busy speaking to everyone else) and to this day I regret it. As I think she knew, I was never to see her again. She passed away in August of 2006. I will never forget her.

Naturally, the wedding was filled with more joyous events for the most part. We left our seats at the dais shortly after we had sat down and joined all of Sara's friends and relatives in the folk dancing. The music, both Kurdish and Arabic, was immensely enjoyable, and I had not danced so much, nor been so happy, in my life. Sara was slightly irritable at first, as her hairdresser had delayed her for some time, and we had entered an hour and a half late. Nevertheless, soon the sheer merriment of the occasion overcame her annoyance at the hairdresser, and she danced as merrily as I did.

There was the usual amount of food, but it was rather unremarkable, and in any event I barely ate. I was pulled out onto the dance floor too often to eat too much. In keeping with Muslim practice, there was no alcohol, but if there was something I had learned about Iraqis long before, it was that rowdiness and merriment did not require those kinds of spirits. Mostly, there was singing and dancing and a very long period of time spent in the middle of the party placing inordinate amounts of jewelry on Sara—presents from the many guests who attended. It was absolutely the best time of my life, tinged as it was with the sadness of my imminent departure.

Finally, we did toss a bouquet at the end, but, in admirable Iraqi style—we did it together.

Epilogue

ON JUNE 5, 2005, I left the nation I loved so dearly, bound for America and for an academic job in New York. Yet even though I spent only two years in Iraq, in some ways, I felt like I had spent an entire lifetime there. So much has changed for me, for Iraq, and for the world as I once knew it. I reconnected with a culture I once knew, had largely discarded, and once again grew to admire. I am no longer an international commercial lawyer whose interest in the land of my parents' birth is almost incidental. Iraq, the Middle East and Islamic law now form a central part of my research agenda, and it is inconceivable to me that this will ever change.

And so I remember with some sadness the life that I lived for twenty-three long months, and why it had to end. I wanted to stay, but between air conditioning failures, power cuts, limited grocery options, appallingly slow internet connections, a near entire lack of recreation, and, of course, a constant fear of annihilation, life was becoming unbearable, my ability to write limited, and my efforts to teach Iraqi students psychologically exhausting. I felt myself wasting away.

Indeed, all of Iraq was wasting away, civil society was crumbling, and part of my sadness certainly related to the abject and unending horror that had emerged from all of our once fondly-held hopes and dreams. Just ten days before I left, I caught a neighbor stealing our electricity by splicing a wire and putting it in his home to power his air conditioner. My office mate was indignant, my driver offered to send a group of thugs to deal with the offender, but I had no stomach to do anything other than cut the wire. The land in which the world's first legal code was drafted, proud of its traditions and its communitarian ideals, had been reduced to senseless petty thievery among neighbors and physical reprisals. As it played out on a grander scale in the political arena, everyone was out for themselves and their clan exclusively.

In thinking of Iraq's failure, I am always forced to confront my own decision to leave while the nation was in this state. From the time I was a child growing up in America, coaches and teachers, not to mention Hollywood movies, taught me that to give up, to surrender is a sign of weakness, and that with persistence and fortitude I could achieve anything I wanted. I fully adopted this outlook and found it, overall, a useful way to lead my life. But right now, I wish I had a touch of the Eastern fatalism. I want Iraq to work; I have wanted it to work for the past four years, and I can not help but feel responsible even if I am not. Leaving Iraq, I felt I had failed: for the first time in my life, I had sought to achieve something but could not, and that feeling of failure continues to haunt me.

Lest my epilogue be cast too thickly with black gloom, I should note that on many fronts, my life has taken an extraordinary turn for the better. Sara and I are living a wonderfully blissful life, my legal experiences in Iraq made me entirely bi-jural and bi-cultural, a large advantage in my career, and I began a teaching fellowship position at one of America's most prestigious law schools which landed me a professorship at the University of Pittsburgh that is extraordinarily difficult to obtain. It is hard to imagine how things could have turned out much better.

Still, I left, and my thoughts return often to that heady day when I first arrived, my thoughts back then racing in every conceivable direction, the hope, the dreams, the ambitions, the worries about what would become of me and the nation. I wanted to stay, possibly forever, I wanted to help create a new nation, I wanted to be one of many expatriates who returned, for lack of a better word, home. When I think of that, and when I think of where we are now, it is hard to extinguish the gloom, and the realization that I failed.

I love Iraq, and I cannot and will not justify, explain, or change that. I hoped, and continued to hope for this country. Even when I was leaving the land, the land did not leave me. Still, on pleasant, cool, dry nights, when I sit by the banks of the Monongahela with a cigar in my hand, I think of my nights on the Tigris with a similar cigar and allow myself to dream that one fine morning, we will see a miracle.

We Shi'a believe in an Imam, or Leader, a direct descendant of the Prophet Muhammad through his daughter Fatima and her son Hussein, the Lord of the Martyrs, who has been living in hiding among all of humanity for centuries. He is known to us as the Companion of the Times, and we believe one day he will emerge from obscurity, and he will guide the earth once again to righteousness and justice. Some say he will reappear from the place where he disappeared, in the city of Najaf, in the Valley of Peace, in the country of Iraq. Perhaps the readers of this memoir will indulge me in what might seem to them like belief in the fantastic mythologies of children, but like all Shi'a, when I think of all that has happened to Iraq, I cannot help uttering the words recited by us: *quickly, quickly, Companion of the Times. Quickly. Quickly.*